A Sourcebook for Families Coping with Mental Illness

A Guide for Preventing the Other Shoe from Dropping

Edited by Michael R. Berren, Ph.D.

"An inspiring, informing and a must-read resource for families who live with serious mental illness. It's chocked full of suggestions and facts that will provide not only clear direction but also hope and confidence in navigating the confusing and frustrating mental health systems. Perhaps the greatest gift to readers is the comfort in learning you are not to blame and you are not alone. Help is available and people care. Congratulations to the authors and those who made this sensitive book possible."

Cheryl Collier
Executive Director
Mental Health Association of Arizona

"This is the Bible for any family or individual who is facing one of the most frightening and most misunderstood diagnoses known to the human species. It not only offers the step-by-step, nuts-and-bolts blueprint for understanding and coping with all stages of mental illness, it also delivers much-needed nuggets of inspiration and actual human experience with the mysteries of these diseases. What a kind and readable resource for families!"

Carla McClain
Arizona Daily Star
Medical Reporter

"A Sourcebook for Families Coping with Mental Illness is must reading for all families experiencing mental illnesses, especially those families who have a newly diagnosed family member."

Jack Harvey
Executive Director
Mental Health Advocates of Arizona

"Thanks for the comprehensive resource book for families who have an adult member with a serious mental illness. Families now have one book that contains answers and information that help their loved ones and themselves. Thanks for including short stories of success, courage and love. My hope is for every family to have this valuable resource."

Herschella Horton, RN
Arizona State Representative,1991-2001

Some of the awards received by Representative Horton include:
Legislative Award, Mental Health Association of Arizona, 1999
Mental Health Leadership Award, Arizona State Hospital, 1999
Distinguished Legislator Award, National Alliance for the Mentally Ill, 1998
Family Empowerment Award, Alliance for the Mentally Ill of Southern Arizona, 1998

"This book will certainly be on the 'most helpful' list of those who have an adult family member recently diagnosed with mental illness. I found the up-to-date information on all aspects of the illness, the system of care, and most especially, the motivational chapter on recovery to be of benefit to all of us, no matter how long we've been struggling."

Elly Anderson
Family Member, NAMISA Board Member, Community Activist

"This book is a timely and practical tool for consumers and their families. It combines the best of science with the wisdom of family members."

Leslie Schwalbe
Deputy Director
Arizona Department of Health

"Dr. Berren has added another bright facet to his already productive career. This psychologist, author, artist and researcher, now has created a much needed guide for families of a person with mental illness. A Source Book is an up-to-date text that thoughtfully and intelligently addresses the concepts of rehabilitation and recovery. Its' well referenced information and meaningful insights make it a ideal resource for families as well as practitioners working with people having serious and persistent mental illness."

Glenn Lippman, M.D.
Chair, Department of Psychiatry, Maricopa Integrated Health Systems

"Sourcebook for Families Coping with Mental Illness, edited by Mike Berren, is a welcome addition to the support and advocacy literature. This book provides very practical information regarding all significant aspects of mental illness and treatment, presented in a cogent and sensitive way. It combines this essential information, geared towards family members and other non-professional caregivers, with inspiring anecdotes and examples from the lives of real clients and their families. I know that the community-based mental health programs and family advocacy groups…will find this an invaluable resource."

David A. Pollack, M.D.
Associate Professor of Psychiatry, Oregon Health and Science University and Board Member for the American Association of Community Psychiatrists

"The Sourcebook gives readers easy-to-digest information about mental illness, treatments and services. It provides useful tools for navigating Arizona's mental health and legal systems. More importantly, it offers positive messages and inspiration about recovery. The Sourcebook is a valuable resource for consumers and families coping with mental illness."

Michael Faenza
President and CEO of NMHA

"Here are many answers that have been much needed by our family and supportive friends. How fortunate we are that it is all now together in this book."

Dorothy Inglee Gallagher
Family Member

"Arizona families who have a loved one with a serious mental illness will find a number of chapters in this book useful as an additional source of information. Several of the book's contributors strongly advise families who are searching for information, support, and advocacy to join their local affiliate of the National Alliance for the Mentally Ill (NAMI)."

Sue F. Davis, Executive Director
Arizona Alliance for the Mentally Ill (AAMI)-NAMI Arizona
NAMI National Board of Directors, emeritus

Published By McMurry Publishing, Inc.
Phoenix, Arizona (602) 395-5850
ISBN:0-9646238-1-1
Manufactured in the United States of America, First Edition

For more information, contact Mike Berren at shoestopm@yahoo.com

Funding for this sourcebook provided by St. Luke's Health Initiatives.

To The Families

A Sourcebook for Families Coping with Mental Illness

A Guide for preventing the other shoe from dropping

Preface

For decades families of individuals with a serious mental illness were treated unfairly. They were perceived variously as people to pity, people whose bad parenting caused mental illness or later as individuals who should be quiet and thankful that a mental health system was there to help. It is only recently that systems of care have begun to recognize that not only do families not cause mental illness, families are one of the greatest sources of strength in the rehabilitation and recovery process. The participation of families should be not only welcomed, but also encouraged.

In our system of care in southern Arizona we recognize families as allies. We know the strengths that a family brings to the table can serve to make the life of their loved one with a mental illness better. We also know that family participation makes the system of care stronger. The purpose of this book is to help provide families with tools and knowledge that can enhance their strength. The chapters are all written by individuals whose careers have been devoted to providing services to individuals with a serious mental illness or working to improve systems of care for individuals with a serious mental illness. They have prepared a book that is informative and at the same time easy to read. It is written as though the authors are sitting down with you in your living room for an informal discussion. But most importantly it is written by authors who have the utmost respect for the importance of collaborating with families.

Neal Cash, M.S. Chief Executive Officer
Community Partnership of Southern Arizona

Acknowledgements

There are more people to thank than I can possibly name individually. First there are the family members who met with me in focus groups in the early stages of this project. Your comments and insights helped shape this book.

There are the authors, without whom we would not have a book. Each did a fantastic job of taking volumes of complex information and distilling it to create informative, readable chapters. To one of the authors, Eric Schindler, I am deeply indebted. Dr. Schindler was the first person with whom I discussed this project, and had he said at lunch that afternoon, "Don't even think about it," this book would likely not have been written.

To all those who read chapter drafts, I shudder to think about the errors of omission, commission and sensitivity that would have been missed without your careful and thoughtful comments.

A special thanks to Cheryl Collier and the Mental Health Association of Arizona for loaning me the only remaining copy of a manuscript that had been worked on ten years earlier, but was never quite completed. The work on the manuscript, *Shoved Under the Rug*, was coordinated by Nancy Eaton-Sher, and hopefully I have been able to resurrect some of their wonderful project.

Without St Luke's Health Initiative and Roger Hughes this project would have never gotten off the ground. Good ideas can die without resources, and Roger provided the leap-of-faith funding to make sure that this book would become a reality. Elizabeth McNamee of SLHI has also been supportive at times when support was needed.

The goal for this book is to provide families with some of the tools they need to deal with mental illness and its myriad consequences. One particular family, a family that has played a significant role in improving the system of care in Arizona, is the model for what we want this book to accomplish. To the Schorr family, thank you for what you have done for families in Arizona. Your legacy is that your actions will forever have a ripple effect.

I am very fortunate to work in a system of care where everyone, including case mangers, psychiatrists, psychologists, nurses, administrators and members of boards of directors, recognize and support family involvement. To the staff and board of the Community Partnership of Southern Arizona and the providers in our system of care, thank you for allowing me to observe and learn from a system of care that has its heart in the right place.

The final thank-you goes to Dr. Alan Beigel and Dr. Jose Santiago. While others played an important role in helping me put this book together, had I not worked with the two of you and learned from you, I would have never even have thought of undertaking this project. Dr. Beigel, you are still sorely missed.

—*Mike Berren*

Contributors

Charles L. Arnold, J.D.
Charles Arnold is a specialist in estate and trust law. In addition to having a private practice, he serves as a judge pro-tempore. He was formerly the Maricopa County Public Fiduciary, and in that role served as the named plaintiff in the class-action suit of Arnold v. Sarn. He currently serves as counsel to the court monitor in that long-standing case. In addition, Mr. Arnold serves on various boards of directors, and has otherwise distinguished himself in areas dealing with mental health law, incapacity and disability.

Rhonda Baldwin, MSW, CISW
Rhonda Baldwin has worked in the mental health field for almost 20 years in both clinical and administrative positions, including directing the statewide mental health system in Arizona. Currently, Ms. Baldwin consults on a national level, and pursues volunteer activities with several organizations, including the Mental Health Association of Arizona.

Michael R. Berren, Ph.D.
Dr. Berren is the director of system development and evaluation for the Community Partnership of Southern Arizona. Dr. Berren has been involved in the public mental health system for more than 25 years and has published numerous articles and book chapters dealing with mental health issues.

Mario Cruz, M.D.
Dr. Cruz is an assistant professor of psychiatry in the department of psychiatry at the University of Arizona Health Sciences Center. He is also a board member of the American Association of Community Psychiatrists. His current research activities include the evaluation of the effectiveness of tele–mental health services, and the influence of psychiatrist communicative behaviors on treatment outcome.

Christina A. Dye
Christina Dye is chief of the Bureau for Substance Abuse Treatment and Prevention Services at the Arizona Department of Health Services, Division of Behavioral Health. For her work in developing unique methodologies for assessing substance abuse prevalence and treatment need she was appointed Visiting Scientist to Harvard University's National Technical Center for Substance Abuse Needs Assessment. She has also been elected to the board of directors of the National Association of State Alcohol and Drug Abuse Directors.

Martha P. Fankhauser, M.S. Pharm.

Martha (Marti) Fankhauser is a clinical associate professor with the department of pharmacy practice and science at the University of Arizona in Tucson. She received the college's Clinical Pharmacy Educator of the Year award for 1987–88, 1992–93, 1996–97 and 1998–99, and is the program director for the ASHP-accredited specialty residency program in psychiatric pharmacy practice. She is a Fellow of the American Society of Health-System Pharmacists and is board certified in psychiatric pharmacy practice.

Michael Franczak, Ph.D.

Dr. Franczak serves as chief of clinical services for the Arizona Department of Health Services, Division of Behavioral Health. Dr. Franczak received his Ph.D. in psychology in 1976, and for the past 25 years he has been involved in mental health, substance abuse and developmental disability services in Pennsylvania, North Carolina and Arizona. Dr. Franczak's current interests include housing for persons with a serious mental illness, jail diversion programs and integrated substance abuse/mental health treatment models.

Edward M. Gentile, D.O., MBA

Dr. Gentile is the medical director of the Community Partnership of Southern Arizona. He is certified in general psychiatry by the American Board of Psychiatry and Neurology. He has held positions in public, private and academic settings and has recently earned a master's in business administration from the University of Arizona's Eller College

Suzanne Baldwin Hodges, J.D.

Suzanne Hodges serves as in-house legal counsel for the Community Partnership of Southern Arizona. She has worked providing legal counsel to behavioral health entities for the past nine years. Previously, she spent six years in the Pima County Attorney's Office, where she represented petitioners in involuntary treatment procedures.

Barbara Montrose, BSBA

Ms. Montrose decided 15 years ago to translate her business degree and experience to the nonprofit sector and become an advocate for housing for homeless and low-income individuals. Her experience includes housing program grant writing, development, site rehabilitation and administration. Ms. Montrose is currently the housing specialist at the Community Partnership of Southern Arizona.

Kathleen A. Oldfather, MSN, ANP, GNP
Kathleen Oldfather has spent 26 years in nursing, the past ten of which have focused on mental health quality management. She has a master of science in nursing, and adult and geriatric nurse practitioner certificates. Her graduate work focused on the integration of primary and behavioral health care with a focus on prevention and early intervention for medical care needs of the mental health populations.

Eric E. Schindler, Ph.D.
Dr. Schindler is a clinical psychologist with more than 20 years of experience in community behavioral health. He is currently the director of clinical services for La Frontera Center, Inc., a large nonprofit behavioral health care organization. He is responsible for overseeing a broad continuum of mental health and substance abuse treatment services. In addition, he is an adjunct faculty member at the University of Arizona, where he teaches in the department of family and consumer sciences.

Michael S. Shafer, Ph.D.
Dr. Shafer is the director of the Community Rehabilitation Division at the School of Public Administration and Policy at the University of Arizona. He oversees a variety of behavioral health services research and educational initiatives regarding persons with serious mental illness, substance abuse and homelessness issues. Dr. Shafer received his Ph.D. in education in 1988 from Virginia Commonwealth University.

Beth C. Stoneking, Ph.D.
Dr. Stoneking is the director of a recovery and empowerment program (Project RISE) at the University of Arizona. She has spent her career in community mental health and psychosocial rehabilitation in various roles, including faculty, teacher, trainer, researcher, manager and service provider. She has been instrumental in several SAMHSA-funded grants employing consumers as case managers, crisis residential providers and employment providers.

CHAPTER 1

Introduction

"You can stop the waves but you can't stop the surf."
– Unknown

Michael R. Berren, Ph.D.

I've been carrying this stuff around much too long!

We've all heard the saying, "Waiting for the other shoe to drop." But what does it really mean? *What does it feel like* to spend your days and nights waiting for that other shoe to drop? If you are a family member of a person who has a serious mental illness, *you know* what it feels like to wait for the other shoe to drop. You know about the long sleepless nights. You know the feeling of waiting for a phone call from your family member telling you that they are alone, they have no money and no place to stay. They tell you they are frightened and need help.

Perhaps your awareness of that other shoe dropping is waiting for an angry or belligerent call from your family member. Because of your worries and concerns you probably find that occasionally you yourself have difficulty concentrating on your job or household responsibilities. You might even have a difficult time concentrating enough to be able to read a book or enjoy watching television. It is possible that the anticipation of the other shoe falling prevents you from enjoying hobbies, other members of your family or your friends. You rarely sleep soundly because you are not sure if your family member is safe. When you lay down at night questions run through your mind, "This time how long will he remain in the apartment that I helped find?", "How many more changes of case manager is she going to have to endure?", "Is someone going to take advantage of her because of her illness?", "What will the next few years be like?", "Is he taking his medication?", "What's going to happen to him when we are gone?"

Some evenings you feel like you are sleeping with one eye open, waiting for a call that might be from the police, informing you that your family member has been arrested for some minor offense — or worse — they have been arrested for a more serious crime. In the back of your mind there is always the anticipation that the call might be from a hospital emergency room to inform you that your loved one has been injured and that you need to come to the hospital immediately.

Luckily, on most nights a call never comes, but that does not mean that the next night your sleep will be any more restful. It doesn't mean that the same fears and anticipations will not be there to greet you as you lay yourself down in the evening or awake in the morning. Yes, families of those with a mental illness are all too familiar with what it is like to wait for the other shoe to drop.

My goal for this book is that it can be used as a resource to help families *prevent* the other shoe from dropping. In order to achieve that goal, the book is grounded on two assumptions: *families need to be empowered to take an active role in the rehabilitation and recovery of their loved one and that there are two complementary components to family empowerment, **Information** and **Inspiration**.*

- **Information:** Families need information across a variety of areas if they are going to be helpful to both their family member and themselves. This book has in common with other "How To" books (ranging from buying real estate to losing weight), the assumption that specific and strategic information is a fundamental ingredient of being able to take appropriate action.

- **Inspiration:** While information is a necessary ingredient of empowerment, it is not sufficient. Inspiration, although intangible, also plays an important role. Thus, portions of the book are devoted to stories of success, courage and love. The stories have been included to let other families know that they are not alone. We have also included a number of stories and parables that have been handed down over time and can serve as lessons in living.

Much of the concept and focus of this book came from a number of focus group meetings I held, where families talked about their sons and daughters and the course of their illness. I also heard from brothers and sisters about their siblings and even from spouses about their husband or wife. While the stories that they told were always unique, there were a number of themes that emerged. One of the themes was of anticipation — anticipation that something awful was going to happen. Whether it was imminent or in the distant future, something awful would happen. At one particular focus group where families were invited to come tell stories about how mental illness has impacted their lives, the parents of a young man with schizophrenia articulated their situation quite well.

They were a middle class couple and ran a family-owned retail business. The lives of three of their children, who did not have a mental illness, rarely gave their parents cause for concern. The son with a mental illness began having problems in his middle teenage years. Initially, his odd behavior and the inappropriate manner in which he interacted with others were blamed on *teenagehood*. For most of high school he was somewhat withdrawn, but did have a few friends. He did not seem to have any major problems and did average work in his classes. Nothing in particular suggested a serious mental illness, but slowly he seemed to fit in with his peers less and less. By his senior year there could be no denying the fact that this young man was having serious symptoms— but the family was in denial. Reasons and justifications for his isolation, moodiness, and odd behaviors were offered. "He's just shy", "A friend moved away and that is why he's so isolated", "He's very sensitive", "He's a nonconformist". Throughout his high school years no one in the family was willing to discuss the possibility that he might have the beginning indications of a mental illness.

Following graduation from high school, with average grades, he enrolled in junior college. He was unable, however, to remain in school past the first month of his first semester. The summer between high school and Junior College was quite unsettling. His isolation was becoming more exaggerated and no longer did he appear to be just a sensitive, shy, non-conforming young adult.

He began eating most of his meals in his room rather than with the rest of the family. He spent the majority of the day in his room, leaving it for only short periods of time. At one point he did not leave the house for two entire weeks. It was over the course of that two-week period that he drafted grandiose plans describing how a subculture was going to take over control of all world governments. The writings contained odd religious references and "evidence" of the existence of beings from another planet. There were also drawings with complex symbols. He slept for only about three hours a night, and when he communicated with the family, it was with great impatience. He became angry when his parents and siblings did not understand how his actions would lead to world peace and prosperity for third world countries.

His personal hygiene deteriorated and contacts with friends became rarer and rarer. His parents indicated that he would pace in his room and appeared to be mumbling to himself. He often seemed to be almost totally unaware of anyone else who might be in the house. The only change in mood occurred when he had an occasional outburst of anger. In order to avoid conflicts, the rest of the family treated him with "kid gloves."

His family's sleepless nights began with an apprehension about what was happening to their son. By the end of that summer between high school and junior college, the concerns increased. He went out one evening and did not return until well after 2:00 a.m. This was totally out of character given the fact that for months he had not ventured from the house. He became angry when questioned about his whereabouts. Over the next few weeks the late nights continued, as did the family's lack of knowledge about where he was going. His poor hygiene and secretiveness continued. The parents described themselves as being concerned whenever he left the house and not being able to relax until he returned. He was, however, 19 years old and they indicated that it was difficult to put a curfew on a 19-year-old. They described their relationship with their son as feeling like there was a sheet of cellophane between him and the rest of the family. He was there, but just not touchable, physically or emotionally. Little by little their lives began to revolve around waiting for a phone call like the ones described at the beginning of this chapter.

After the couple finished sharing their story other families in the room gave approving nods indicating that they could identify with the situation. One woman shared that her family's story was very similar. She suggested that I ought to have a subtitle for the book, and it should be ***Waiting for the Other Shoe to Drop.*** The group of families that was assembled that evening all seemed to like the subtitle. They agreed that it captured the essence of being a family member of an individual who has a mental illness.

A somewhat elderly woman talked about her nearly 50-year-old son's thirty-year struggle with schizophrenia. She told of activities that she participated in to avoid having to just sit around and wait for that other shoe to drop. She had hobbies, participated in support groups, had a close circle of friends, and did volunteer work. She got involved so that she would not have to dwell on the inevitable "dropping shoe." When she finished talking, someone else in the group indicated that perhaps a better subtitle for the book would be ***While You're Waiting for the Other Shoe to Drop.*** Such a subtitle would communicate that you do not just sit around. You need to get on with your life. As more family stories were shared another woman who had been fairly quiet said that she had another idea for a subtitle. She said that her idea was based on the belief that rather than just spending time with distracting activities, it is also important to get involved in things that might help *prevent* the other shoe from dropping. Thus, rather than ***While You're Waiting*** she suggested that a subtitle should emphasize ***Prevention.*** By the end of the evening, there seemed to be consensus for the subtitle that was ultimately selected for the book. ***A Guide for Preventing the Other Shoe from Dropping.*** This final version of the subtitle clearly makes the point that I wanted the book to convey: there are things that families can do to help reduce the negative consequences of mental illness. There are things that families can do to help ensure that a loved one with a mental illness has every advantage possible, and that those advantages can make an important difference in their recovery.

The remainder of this book is designed to provide you with tools and information that you can use to help ensure that your family member has every advantage possible.

- Chapter 2 provides an overview of mental illness; *what it is and what it is not.* The chapter is based on the belief that if families are going to be supportive and helpful to their family member, they should understand some of the major underpinnings of the illness, from biological as well as historical and social perspectives.

- Chapter 3 addresses specific things that families need to think about after learning that a family member has a serious mental illness. We also emphasize that a diagnosis of a serious mental illness is *not a death sentence*, either for the individual with the diagnosis or for the family.

• Chapter 4 focuses on the symptoms associated with mental illness. The chapter has been prepared to provide family members with an understanding of the symptoms of mental illness, and relationship between those symptoms and the behaviors of an individual with a mental illness.

• Chapter 5 is a chapter that you might want to reread on a regular basis. The point is made early in the chapter, that *families do not cause mental illness*. It is pointed out, however, that the approach that families take to communication and problem solving can either help to alleviate or make symptoms of mental illness worse.

• The past decade has witnessed dramatic improvements in the effectiveness of the medications used to treat serious mental illness. In Chapter 6 we discuss the medications used in the treatment of mental illnesses, how they work and possible side effects.

• While medication is certainly important in the treatment of serious mental illness, it is still only part of the rehabilitation picture. The other components of systems of care are addressed in Chapter 7. In this chapter families will learn how they can participate in their loved one's recovery.

• Many individuals with a mental illness also abuse alcohol and/or drugs. In Chapter 8 we discuss the co-occurring disorders and the best approaches to treatment.

• Homelessness and substandard housing seem to go hand in hand with serious mental illness. Chapter 9 focuses on housing issues and options.

• In Chapter 10, the relationship between mental illness and physical health status is addressed. The chapter also contains information that can be used to help ensure good physical health for your family member.

• Mental illness can have a significant financial impact on a family. Chapter 11 provides specific information families need to lessen that burden. The chapter includes information about entitlement for both income and health care insurance.

- There are a variety of legal tools that can be used by the family to enhance care and protect the quality of life of their family member. This is particularly true if and when your family member is incapable of making good decisions about treatment. Chapter 12 has three sections, family law, the civil commitment process, and the criminal justice system.

- The Arizona system of care is described in Chapter 13. The chapter addresses topics such as how the system is organized and funded, where to go for services and what to do if you are dissatisfied with the services that your family member is receiving.

- Individuals with mental illnesses *can and do* lead productive lives. In Chapter 14, we address the concept of *Recovery*. We have made it the final narrative chapter because it is the going home concept that we want to leave you with — individuals with mental illnesses can recover. Even though we have included it as the last chapter, it might be the first chapter you want to read.

- In Chapter 15, we provide information about Internet resources that can be helpful to you and your family member.

REFERENCES AND HOW WE USED THEM

In preparing the chapters, each author was reminded that the book was being written for families, not academicians. We wanted chapters that were focused and to the point. Recognizing that the chapters would not be long enough to share everything that families want to know about a topic, the authors were instructed to identify resources for where families could go for additional information. To that end we have included, at the end of the book, a listing of recommended readings. The listed readings are either primary sources the authors used, or readings that the authors believe contain important information.

You Are Not Alone

As a parent with a 43-year-old son with schizophrenia my heart goes out to anyone who has just been informed that his or her loved one has a mental illness of any type. You are absolutely devastated, you already knew something was wrong, but just didn't understand what and where to turn to find out the answers and why.

Twenty years ago I felt I was all alone and was so ashamed because I felt that by being a single parent it was all my fault and it was something I had done wrong. I didn't speak of it much to my friends and my other three children. I kept the fear and hurt mostly to myself. Twenty years ago there just weren't support groups for families or education classes to help us understand the illness.

After attending several programs in Phoenix, Tucson families started their own support groups here and I began to feel it was not my fault and I was not alone. Everyone felt the same way and we were all searching for the answers and some type of help. We haven't found all the answers yet but there are many places to turn to in the community and keep remembering —

"You are not alone."

Contributed by ME

Never Give Up

Sir Winston Churchill took three years getting through eighth grade. It seems ironic that years later Oxford University asked him to address its commencement exercises. He arrived with his usual props. A cigar, a cane, and a top hat accompanied him wherever he went. As Churchill approached the podium, the crowd rose in appreciative applause. With unmatched dignity, he settled the crowd and stood confident before his admirers. Removing the cigar and carefully placing the top hat on the podium, Churchill gazed at his waiting audience. Authority rang in Churchill's voice, as he shouted, "Never give up!" Several seconds passed before he rose to his toes and repeated, "Never give up!" His words thundered in their ears. There was a deafening silence as Churchill reached for his hat and cigar, steadied himself with his cane and left the platform. His commencement address was finished.

Reprinted with permission of Afterhours Inspirational Stories.

Psychologist with Paranoid Schizophrenia Recovers

Frederick Frese has an astonishing story. In 1973, he was placed in a locked psychiatric facility in Ohio. He was dazed, delusional, and suffering from paranoid schizophrenia. Twelve years later, he was the Chief Psychologist within the very hospital system that had confined him. Along the way, despite ten other hospitalizations, he married, had four children, and earned a Master's Degree and a Doctorate.

Dr. Frese is smart, impassioned, and dedicated. After hundreds of public appearances as well as playing a major role in a national campaign to end discrimination against the mentally ill, Dr. Frese gained prominence as a person who lives successfully with schizophrenia. Dr. Frese's accomplishments are remarkable by anyone's standards, especially given the often devastating nature of schizophrenia. Afraid, withdrawn, and tortured by inner thoughts and voices, people with schizophrenia often lead unfulfilling lives, estranged from family and society. Individuals with mental illnesses make up a significant portion of the homeless population while many others are in jail.

Dr. Frese, of Hudson, Ohio, contends that he is not all that unusual. He believes that many individuals with schizophrenia can and do lead fulfilling lives. In community after community where he speaks, Dr. Frese receives standing ovations from families, individuals with mental illness, and others that are inspired by his presentations of hope. Dr. Frese is living proof that schizophrenia need not be the end of life.

The Executive Director of the National Alliance for the Mentally Ill, says, "Fred embodies the hope we all have for the recovery of our family members." "His talent, intellect, complete openness and humor have made it possible for a lot of people to believe that it's possible to follow in his footsteps."

When Dr. Frese had his first psychotic episode, he was a young college graduate and a Marine Corps Captain guarding atomic weapons in Jacksonville, Florida. He developed the paranoid belief that enemy nations, in a plot to take over the U.S. atomic weapons supply, had hypnotized American leaders. The marine base's psychiatrist took Frese to the Bethesda Maryland Naval Hospital. He was discharged five months later without knowing what he really had or whether he should take any medication.

Dr. Frese had several classic symptoms, notably the inability to separate fantasy from reality and hearing inner voices.

His second psychotic episode came about one year later in a Milwaukee church. He pictured himself changing from man to monkey, then dog, snake, fish, and finally, an atom. He saw himself inside an atom bomb being loaded for use. He believed that he was the instrument to usher in Armageddon. He was hospitalized for a few weeks, then released. He wandered the streets for the next year.

In the summer of 1973, when he was 27, he was apprehended, jailed, and taken to court where the State of Ohio declared him insane. He spent three days in a cell in a maximum-security mental hospital. The story he tells of the stay depicts him at rock bottom, screaming for water, trapped in a room with no toilet, guarded by attendants who wouldn't let him out to go to the bathroom.

From there he was transferred to a Veteran's Administration hospital. He was put on a medication that began to control his delusions. Over time, though he was in and out of the hospital ten times, he was able to hold jobs, including a management position with a major corporation. He earned a degree in International Business Management from the American Graduate School of International Management, in Phoenix, Arizona, and a Doctorate of Psychology from Ohio University. For a number of years, he served as Director of Psychology for the Western Reserve Psychiatric Hospital, in Sagamore Hills, Ohio, the same hospital where he once was a patient.

Throughout the early days of his illness, as difficult as it was, Dr. Frese benefited from good fortune. First, he seemed to recover quickly once on medications. Secondly, he was hired into a management position at a major corporation without being asked for his health history. And thirdly, an administrator recommended him for a job over the objections of several people who questioned whether someone with psychiatric problems should work in the mental health system.

At Ohio University, Frese met his wife, Penny, a former nun, while they were both graduate students. *In A Love Story: Living with Someone with Schizophrenia*, the last half of a two-part video Penny Frese produced with her husband, she describes how her husband confided in her about his mental illness only after they had been friends for quite a while. Curious about the disease, she devoured books on the subject and spent hours talking to Frese about his illness. He opened up his life to her. What she saw was a man who was not only charming, but also funny and intelligent.

They married and had three children (Dr. Frese also has a fourth child from a previous brief marriage.) All four children, now adults, have been diagnosed with depression. Dr. Frese also has a cousin who has schizo-phrenia.

"They are all doing wonderfully," Penny Frese says of their children.

A son, so painfully shy in the middle school that he sat in the Principal's office to avoid gym, graduated seventh in a class of 400 and enrolled in college.

A daughter produced her own video, entitled My Story, to describe her last five years of coping with depression.

Thirty plus years of living with schizophrenia have taught Frese and his family to cope. "As you get older, you are better able to spot the symptoms and to cut them off," says Frese. He was hospitalized in 1974 and a few years ago, he suffered a severe enough relapse that he was almost hospitalized again. First, Frese says, a person with a serious mental illness must acknowledge his or her disability and take medication. Denial is common, particularly at first, because "you don't think it through very carefully," he says. "You just hope it goes away."

Employers, friends, and neighbors usually attach such strong stigmas to mental illness that many people pay a price if they tell others, Frese says. Frese describes the disease as an "inherited vulnerability to breakdown" exacerbated by stress, conflict, substance abuse, death, or other losses. When he feels his own symptoms worsening, he increases the dose of his medication. He also may take off time from work or remove himself from a stressful situation.

For particular sticky situations he can't avoid, Frese carries a wallet-size card that he hands to people if it becomes necessary. It asks them to rephrase criticism in a less threatening manner because he is a mentally ill person who doesn't handle conflict well. Criticism, even perceived criticism, can be paralyzing, he explains.

Frese's wife says that she has learned more about how to communicate with her husband. She no longer is bothered when he doesn't establish eye contact with her. She understands that people with schizophrenia have trouble picking up on social cues, so they have trouble ending a conversation appropriately or even sustaining one. She also avoids statements that might be interpreted as accusations.

Dr. Fred Frese became the Director of Summit County (Ohio) Recovery Project, a program that helps mentally ill people find jobs and fight discrimination. He is also active in the Campaign to End Discrimination, an effort by the National Alliance for the Mentally Ill. "As I often say," states Dr. Frese, "in all my years of living and dealing with schizophrenia, there's never been a better time than now to be a person with a serious mental illness. There's more hope now than ever before."

Reprinted with permission of the Treatment Advocacy Center

CHAPTER 2

Mental Illness: What It Isn't and What It Is

"There are some things you learn best in calm, and some in storm."
– Willa Cather

On a daily basis, families across the country are confronted with the reality that mental illness is something to which they are not immune. Sons and daughters, nieces and nephews, aunts and uncles, parents and grandparents may have a severe mental illness. A review of the numbers tells us something about how common mental illness is:

- Just over 1 percent of the population has schizophrenia (which translates to approximately 2.5 million Americans).
- Approximately 2.5 percent of the population has bipolar disorder.
- Approximately ten million American adults suffer from major depression.
- According to the World Health Organization, four of the 10 most disabling diseases are mental illnesses.

The intent of this brief chapter is to help you to understand both *what mental illness is not*, and *what it is*.

WHAT MENTAL ILLNESS IS NOT

As we entered the 21st century, we are aware that we still have quite a bit to learn about mental illness. But with all that we need to learn, we know a great deal about what mental illness is not.

- Mental illness is not a curse, it is not a function of demonic spirits, and it is not payback for sins, real or imagined.
- Mental illness is not anyone's fault, any more than other illnesses, such as diabetes, heart disease and muscular dystrophy, are anyone's fault.
- Mental illness is not a function of bad parenting.
- Mental illness is certainly not a reason for those affected by it and their families to give up on their dreams.
- Schizophrenia in particular is not a "split personality," as depicted in numerous offensive motion pictures such as Jim Carrey's *Me, Myself & Irene*.
- As indicated above, mental illness is definitely not uncommon.

WHAT MENTAL ILLNESS IS

While scientists continue to make refinements in their theories, we know that:

- Schizophrenia and other mental illnesses are brain diseases.
- Even though mental illness is a disease of the brain, risk factors and protective factors (both of which are discussed in detail later in this chapter) can impact the extent of an individual's disability.

- Mental illness can have a significant social and economic impact — not just on the individual, but on the entire family.
- Mental illness is something from which individuals can and do recover.

The Biology of Mental Illness

The umbrella term "mental illness" comprises a number of distinct illnesses (described in detail in Chapter 4). While each illness might have its own unique cause, one of the most common theories underlying mental illness has to do with *neurotransmitters*.

The brain can be likened to a giant switchboard. Billions of wires (neurons) pass information from one part of the brain to another. Each neuron has a front end (cell body), a middle (axon) and back end. As the messages pass from neuron to neuron they travel in a direction from the cell body, down the axon and then to the back end. Once reaching the back end the message is passed to the cell body of the next neuron via a neurotransmitter substance. The neurons do not touch. Instead there is a small distance (somewhat like a channel) between the back end of one neuron and the cell body of the next. This small distance is referred to as the synapse. As with a switchboard, the messages are passed at a speed equivalent to an electrical impulse.

In the normal brain, the neurotransmitter substance is passed from neuron to neuron with precision. Each preceding neuron releases just the right amount of neurotransmitter. The neurotransmitter crosses the synapse and stimulates the next neuron. This depiction of the normal process is presented in Figure 1A.

Mental illness is often a reflection of one of a variety of neurotransmitter problems. One specific problem is when not enough neurotransmitter is available to properly stimulate the succeeding neuron. One reason for too little neurotransmitter is that some of the neurotransmitter reenters the neuron from where it came. This is called a "reuptake" (and as you read Chapter 6 you will learn how medications can help correct the reuptake problem). The reuptake problem is depicted in Figure 1B.
Another neurotransmitter problem occurs when there is too much neurotransmitter at the synapse, and hence too much stimulation. Over-stimulation is depicted in Figure 1C.

As scientists learn more, they are finding very specific areas of the neuron where problems exist (and hence where medications can be effective). In addition to neurotransmitter problems, there is some evidence that the structure of the brain might be related to mental illness. Pictures taken with MRI (magnetic resonance imaging) demonstrate that individuals with schizophrenia have structures that are somewhat different from brains of individuals who do not have schizophrenia.

For example, the ventricles (hollow areas of the brain that carry cerebrospinal fluid) of individuals with schizophrenia show a tendency to be dilated, or enlarged.

While we do not know all the causes of mental illness, and have not yet confirmed a mental illness gene, we do have good evidence indicating that genetics plays a role. Just as some families have a greater likelihood of developing heart disease, some families are more predisposed to mental illness.[1] There are also other likely causes beyond genetics, and in the future we might be able to identify specific viruses and toxins that play a role in some mental illnesses.

gure 1

Figure 1A Normal Neurotransmitter at the Synapse

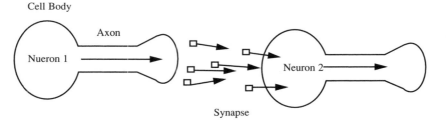

Figure 1B. Some of the Neurotransmitter Returns to the Preceding Neuron (Reuptake)

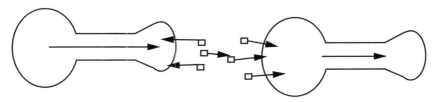

Figure 1C. Too Much Neurotransmitter at the Synapse (Overstimulation)

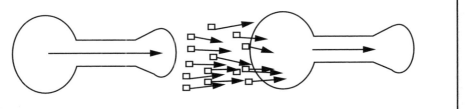

---

[1] If someone were to read this book in the 22nd century she would likely be amused at how little we currently know about mental illness. By the 22nd century, scientists will have identified specific subtypes of mental illness and genetic markers that may lead to genetic cures for many mental illnesses.

The Relationship Between Mental Illness, Risk and Protective Factors, Symptoms and Disability

Even though mental illness is clearly a brain disease, factors other than the disease impact both the severity of the symptoms and the extent to which the illness will lead to disability. These are generally referred to as *protective factors* and *risk factors*. Figure 2 describes the relationship between mental illness, protective factors, risk factors, symptoms and disability. As can be seen, protective factors, such as family support, medications and rehabilitation, serve to reduce the impact of illness. Risk factors, such as inadequate housing, poverty and lack of social support, tend to make the symptoms worse.

Built into the protective and risk factors model is the recognition that an individual's symptoms are more than a consequence. Symptoms can also play a role in actually increasing the stressor level. For example, the more symptomatic a person is, the greater the likelihood that he will isolate himself from others and in turn have a reduced support system.

As can be seen in the model, symptoms are not synonymous with disability. A person's level of disability is also dependent upon community supports. The greater the community support system, the less the disability, regardless of symptoms. Let's use another medical condition to make a point. An individual with a spinal cord injury will be much less disabled (that is, much better able to function) in a living environment that is wheelchair accessible and built with someone with a spinal cord injury in mind. A lower kitchen counter and other architectural modifications will vastly improve the maneuverability of an individual in a wheelchair. The more that can be done to accommodate the needs of an individual with a spinal cord injury, the less disabled the person will be. The same is true for an individual with a mental illness. The person with a mental illness will be much less disabled in an environment (and a community) that makes reasonable accommodations for his or her special needs.

The fact that protective factors and risk factors play a role in disability is not unique to mental illness. The same factors play a role in many illnesses. A simple example can be seen in diabetes. Someone with diabetes who eats starch and sugar and does not exercise or relax is likely to be impacted by the illness to a greater extent than the someone who maintains a proper diet, exercises and relaxes.

The important point to remember is that just because mental illness is a brain disease does not mean that other factors do not play a role in determining the extent to which the illness can lead to symptoms and disability. Thus, important roles for families and systems of care are a) to help the individual develop as many protective factors as possible, and b) to minimize risk factors. Minimizing risk includes both creating supportive environments and helping the person to learn how to cope, on their own, with life's inevitable stresses.

ure 2

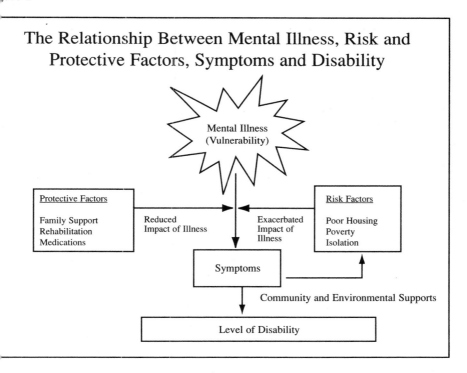

Mental Illness Affects the Entire Family

All severe and chronic illnesses affect families. Whether the illness is multiple sclerosis, cancer or AIDS, families worry about their ill family member. Some illnesses cause more worry than others do. Some illnesses cause a change in family routine more than others. Some illnesses can have a significant economic impact on the family. But the common element of severe illness is that families are impacted.

Mental illness carries the additional impact of stigma. While things certainly are better than they were, we still live in a society where the truth about mental illness is not understood by everyone. There are those who still believe that mental illness might be caused by families. Some people might still believe that mental illness is just a matter of lack of self-control. Something that you might want to consider is how active a role you should play in your community to help to destigmatize mental illness.

People Recover From Mental Illness

The final point to know about mental illness is that it is something from which people may recover. Chapter 14 is dedicated to recovery. Who knows, maybe you should read Chapter 14 before you go any further.

The purpose of this book is to give families the information they need to help ensure that the protective factors and risk factors are tilted in favor of their family member to reduce the disabling consequences of this brain disease illness.

The Letter

It has taken me many years to write this letter, but the time has finally come. I am writing to apologize for many things. I know that it is too late, but I need to tell you things that I never told you before. In our family mental illness was something that was not accepted. My parents were strict disciplinarians, and bad behavior was bad behavior. There were no excuses. I suppose I grew up believing that too. So when you became ill, I believed that it was *just* bad behavior and weakness. At the same time, at some level, I knew that it was not just bad behavior, but I couldn't help myself to help you. As a matter of fact, I guess I did everything *but* help you. I didn't support you in getting treatment because treatment isn't a cure for bad, weak behavior. Treatment would have been an admission that our family could not take care of its own problems. So instead of doing what might be best for you, I was only concerned with your bad behavior. I apologize.

I apologize also for being ashamed. I was ashamed to discuss your problems with the rest of the family. Instead we isolated you. I was ashamed to let the neighbors know that you were ill, because I was afraid of what they might think and how they might treat us. Even after the doctor told us that you were ill, I didn't want to share the news with anyone. I am not sure why I was embarrassed, but I was. So instead of supporting you and helping you get treatment like I would do for any other person with an illness, I "hid" you.

Because I "hid," you didn't get the help that you needed. And now you are no longer with me. But I want you to know that because of you I am now involved in helping others. I do volunteer work with a mental health program. I talk to other families and let them know what we went through and how wrong we were in our approach. I guess I serve a purpose as a model for what not to do. But I think that I am making a difference in the lives of others. I hope so anyway.

I miss you so much and I apologize.

Submitted by D.D.

My Mother

I was 16 and home from school for the summer. It had been four years since my mother had begun to act strangely now and then. Since then, no one had spoken to me about what my mother was suffering from. But it was plain to see that something deeply troubled her. That something took almost any memory I had of the strong, confident and beautiful woman she'd been. On that summer day, I was planning on going to the beach. Those plans were immediately dashed like so many others over the last four years when my mother came into my room. One second she was crying, the next yelling expletives at me followed by a litany of symptoms from chest pains to diarrhea to headaches. I decided I'd drive her to her therapist and get some answers. While on the freeway, my mother began screaming, and crying, and laughing. I had such trouble calming her down and driving that I was pulled over by a highway patrol officer. I got out of the car so my mother would not have to see the officer. I tried to tell him that my mother was sick and I was driving her to her therapist, but the words would not come forth. I accepted the reckless driving ticket reluctantly and resumed driving. I remember thinking how much I hated my mother for putting me in these spots so often, yet how much I loved her and wanted no shame to come to her. I felt that the worst shame I could never allow would be someone outside of her closest family and friends knowing that my mother had a mental illness.

Personal account of the author

CHAPTER 3

Your Family Member Has Been Diagnosed With A Mental Illness – Now What?

"Learn by experience – preferably that of others."
– Unknown

Eric E. Schindler, Ph.D.
Michael R. Berren, Ph.D.

Parents have hopes and dreams for their children. While the specifics might vary from family to family, depending on culture and individual background, they all have something in common. Parents want their children to grow up to lead happy, fulfilled lives. Parents hope that their children will have rewarding careers, raise families of their own and make a positive contribution to their community. Siblings want to have that special person with whom they can share memories and see the future in the eyes of nieces and nephews. Given this vision, the news that one's son or daughter, or brother or sister, has a serious mental illness is one of the last things that a family member would ever want to hear.

The diagnosis of a serious mental illness occurs daily, in countless hospitals, clinics and private practitioner offices across the country. For some families, the diagnosis of a mental illness is experienced as nothing less than a death sentence. It is the death of the dreams and aspirations that they have for their son or daughter. When family members first learn that their loved one has a mental illness, a flood of questions, fears and doubts will likely arise: Will she ever get better? How badly will schizophrenia affect him? What can we do to help? These are just a few of the countless, but normal, questions that families deal with when confronting a serious mental illness. For some families, "What do we tell the neighbors?" is another question they will ask themselves.

Serious mental illness affects each person and family differently. As with other chronic illnesses such as rheumatoid arthritis, diabetes or multiple sclerosis, the severity of symptoms and impairment can vary from person to person. And for each person the impact of the illness can vary from day to day and year to year. Some individuals will experience significant impairments and will struggle daily to cope with debilitating symptoms. Others will be lucky enough to be less seriously affected or will learn ways to adjust to their illness and live fulfilled, productive lives.

In later chapters of this book we will review very specific information that should be helpful to family members in assisting their loved one to live as fulfilling a life as possible. In this chapter we would like to address two areas that are important upon learning that a loved one has a serious mental illness: what to expect, and things to do.

WHAT TO EXPECT

The most common questions that families ask about any illness (not just mental illness) include: Now what? What can we expect? When will she recover? When will he go back to work? Will she suffer?

We wish that for mental illness there were a simple answer for those questions. Unfortunately, there is no easy answer. The course of the illness and treatment will be different for each individual with a mental illness. The answer to "What can we expect?" will be different for every family. Support systems, economics, the system of care in the local community and family cohesiveness will all play a role in determining the impact of the illness on the family member with it and on the rest of the family. One thing that you should accept from the beginning is that in many arenas you can have an impact on your family member's quality of life. There are, however, other aspects of the illness and systems of care that are likely out of your control. Hopefully, this book can play some role in helping you have a positive impact on those things that are within your control.

Before we get started we want to tell you about an individual whose story makes it clear that mental illness is not a "death sentence."

Patricia Deegan was diagnosed with schizophrenia when she was a young adult. The psychiatrist who gave her the diagnosis told her about her serious illness and informed her of the consequences of the illness. He told her that she was going to need to accept the fact that she would never really have a career or a productive life. He told her that she would likely have many admissions to psychiatric hospitals and was essentially doomed.

Despite having the diagnosis of schizophrenia, Patricia went on to get a Ph.D. in clinical psychology. She now lectures across the country on the topic of how to live with and recover from mental illness. Her talks are both informational and inspirational. She tells her audiences about the time she was making one of her presentations about hope and recovery. At the conclusion of that particular presentation, as with most presentations, people came up to her to ask her questions or tell her something that they wanted to share. On that occasion a gentleman told her that he wanted to apologize. He wanted to apologize for the manner in which he had treated her years earlier. He was the psychiatrist who had given her the diagnosis of schizophrenia and told her there was essentially no hope of her leading a normal life.

Not all individuals will be as successful as Dr. Deegan in recovering from mental illness. Some individuals will struggle with the persistent, painful effects of their illness and grow discouraged or angry at their situation. One of your roles, as a loving family member, is to help your family member achieve the greatest level of functioning and highest quality of life possible.

THINGS TO DO

We believe there are eight action steps you can take to help ensure the best possible outcome for the family member who has a mental illness, for you and for other members of your family. They are:

- Learn all you can about mental illness and the specific diagnosis of your family member.
- Take care of yourself.
- Learn about approaches to treatment and recovery.
- Learn about local systems of care.
- Be involved in the care of your family member.
- Learn about financial and legal issues.
- Consider joining support and advocacy groups.
- Give yourself permission to grieve your loss.

Learn About Mental Illness and the Specific Diagnosis

The knowledge base concerning mental illness is growing exponentially. Behavioral scientists are coming closer and closer to understanding the mechanisms of mental illness. In learning about mental illness, you don't need to become a "mini psychiatrist." You should become as familiar as possible with the whys and ways of the illness, the impact of medication, and approaches to rehabilitation. You also want to understand the social aspects of the illness. You obviously will want to become knowledgeable about the services and treatments that are available locally for your loved one. Finally, many families find it important to learn about systems of care, and how to become an advocate for better care for individuals with mental illnesses.

Take Care of Yourself

I was on an airplane traveling between Dallas and Tucson when I had a revelation of sorts. The concept for this family handbook had been developed, and I was clear about the chapters that needed to be written. The selection of authors who might write various chapters was nearly complete. I had met with more than 15 focus groups to help me clarify important topics and a format for the book. I knew from the beginning that while the book was going to be a "how-to" guide, it would be different from other books written for families dealing with serious mental illness.

The difference would be in the combination of "how to" with "inspiration." The book would also be written in such a way that it would inform families that not only was it okay for them to take care of themselves, but that it was *important* for them to take care of themselves. The reason for the self-care of the family seemed pretty clear to me. If families were going to put forth effort to ensure good care for their sons, daughters, brothers and sisters, they needed to have the physical and emotional energy to do so.

But as I said, it was during the flight from Dallas to Tucson that the importance of self-care for the family became crystal clear. During the usual pre-flight speech to which most of us rarely pay attention, I *was actually listening* as the flight attendant spoke to us.

> "Ladies and gentlemen, welcome aboard flight 35, nonstop service from Dallas to Tucson. While we never expect to lose cabin pressure, if at any time during the flight we should experience a sudden reduction in cabin pressure, yellow oxygen masks will drop from the area just above your head."

The flight attendant went on to indicate that the masks have an elastic band and that they should be securely fastened. Once securely fastened, we were to continue to breathe in a normal manner. The final words were the ones that really hit home in terms of this book.

> "If you are traveling with a small child, make sure you secure your mask before you secure your child's mask."

On a couple of occasions, I have recognized that it made sense to secure your own oxygen before assisting your child. On this particular occasion, however, it was an insight. It was as if that flight attendant was helping me draft an important section of this chapter. I imagined that she was standing before a group of families who had a member with a mental illness. The families had just been informed that their sons or daughters had a serious mental illness. The diagnosis was schizophrenia or bipolar disorder. The sons or daughters were in their early twenties and had just been admitted to the county hospital. The admission to the hospital was through the emergency room, where the police had taken them. In my imagination, the flight attendant was preparing family members for possible turbulent times ahead. She was letting them know that not only was it acceptable to take care of themselves, it was *important* to take care of themselves. If they were going to be of any help to their sons and daughters, they needed to be healthy and energized. They needed to take care of themselves if they were going to be of assistance to anyone else.

There is no need to feel guilty about taking care of yourself. There

25

might be times when things are not going well for your son or daughter. There will be other times when things are going very well. And there will certainly be times when your family member needs your assistance more than others. As a consequence, there will be times when you will need to make yourself more available or be more involved. Regardless, it is all right to recognize that you have needs that are independent of your family member and his or her illness. If you do not take care of yourself, your ability to care for your family member will be diminished.

Learn About Approaches to Treatment and Recovery

There are two main aspects to the treatment of mental illness, medication and a wide variety of approaches to therapy, including psychosocial and vocational rehabilitation. Different systems of care emphasize different approaches. Some psychiatrists are more comfortable with particular medications than others. Some communities have long histories of providing particular types of treatment. Given the fact that there are a variety of approaches to treatment, it is important that you are familiar enough with them to be a knowledgeable member of the team when you attend treatment planning meetings. After all, you know your family member better than any of the staff do. You probably have a good idea of what approaches might be most effective with your loved one.

Learn About the Local Systems of Care

Health care in this country, for both physical health and mental health, is in flux. Not only are treatments becoming more focused and much more effective, systems of care are changing. We are in an era where understanding the structure of health care corporations and public health care legislation can be just as important as understanding issues around the biology of mental illness. You will need to learn all you can about the way behavioral health care is organized, delivered and funded in your state and local community. We believe that it is absolutely true that the more you understand about the system of care in your community, the more likely it is that you will be able to take advantage of it for your loved one. One of the best approaches to learning about local systems of care is to talk to other family members and become actively involved in your local mental health association or the local affiliate of NAMI (formerly the National Alliance for the Mentally Ill).[1]

---

[1] If you are not familiar with NAMI, it is a national self-help, support and advocacy organization of consumers, families and friends of people with a sever mental illness. Many communities have local affiliates. You can phone NAMI at 800-950-6264. The Web site address is www.nami.org

"I sell real estate for a living, commercial real estate to be more specific. In the field of commercial real estate there is an axiom that is so true it has become common terminology for everyone, not just those involved in real estate. It is: "The three most important aspects of property are location, location, location." In living with my daughter, who suffers from mental illness, I have found a similar axiom. It is: "The three most important things a family can do when they are living with and/or dealing with a loved one with mental illness is Join NAMI, Join NAMI, Join NAMI."

Be Involved in the Care of Your Family Member

Mental health professionals are, for the most part, caring individuals. They have chosen their profession because of a sincere desire to help others. They are also, by and large, an overworked group. A common characteristic of the public mental health system in most communities is that case managers, psychiatrists and therapists all have high caseloads. Because of those high caseloads, they might not always give the ideal amount of individualized, personal care that you might want and expect. The mental health professionals need family members to be active partners in the ongoing treatment of the person with a mental illness. Your involvement can include participating in treatment planning, helping to ensure that your family member complies with treatment, monitoring medication side effects and providing staff with information about successes and setbacks that occur in your family member's life.

Learn About Financial and Legal Issues

We make the point in chapters 11 and 12 that financial issues and legal issues are areas where families can have a very specific impact. In Chapter 11, we provide a comprehensive review of the entitlement programs currently available and direct you to additional resources if you want to learn more.

In Chapter 12, we address the issue of guardianship, conservatorship and protecting assets that you might want to provide for your family member. It is also very important, however, for you to work closely with your family member's case manager or primary clinician concerning financial and legal issues. It is also appropriate, depending upon your situation, to consult an attorney and/or a financial planner.

Consider Joining Support and Advocacy Groups

There are so many reasons to get involved in support and advocacy groups that I cannot even begin to mention all of them. I do, however, want to mention the most important reason: *the comfort you will feel from knowing that you are not alone*. There is often nothing as helpful as knowing that other families are dealing with many of the same issues that your family might be dealing with. To know that you are not alone somehow makes the struggles more bearable. Being part of a "community of families" can also make the good times even sweeter.

The support that you receive through a group like NAMI will likely be of two types: unconditional acceptance and the wisdom that comes from experience. You will meet, among others, doctors, lawyers, plumbers, teachers, salespeople and homemakers. The bond that brings them together is the mental illness of a family member. They understand the impact of the illness and they understand stigma. They understand what you are feeling like no one else possibly can. They can give you strength when you feel as though you have nothing left. NAMI chapters also have a collective wisdom that you can tap into if you ever find yourself confused as to what to do next. There is a good chance that through NAMI you will find a family that has had to deal with issues very similar to just about anything that you might be dealing with.

> While we hope that this book is useful and of some comfort, it is not intended to take the place of the support and wisdom that occur through local and national support and advocacy groups. We urge you to consider getting involved in such groups.

Give Yourself Permission to Grieve Your Loss

A teenage child is suddenly killed late one night, struck by a drunk driver. When we hear about such tragedies in the news, we naturally imagine what life will be like for the surviving family members. It is human nature to feel sad for the parents and siblings of the victim (and maybe some relief that our family members are safe). The grief and loss that parents must endure after a child has died has been identified as one of the worst possible traumas to affect a family. A family never really gets over this loss; but, in time, people adjust and are able to move on with their lives, even though they are permanently changed as a result of the tragedy.

Do the parents of a child diagnosed with a serious mental illness have anything in common with the parents of the murdered teen?

In one sense the answer is no—nothing can compare with the death of your treasured child. Yet, from another perspective, parents struggling to cope with the diagnosis of a serious mental illness can identify with the pain and loss.

The person learning to live with a serious mental illness has to adjust and cope with his or her symptoms, while the family members need to accept the loss of dreams, hopes and desires for their child.

A diagnosis of mental illness is often made in late adolescence and generally alters career and education plans. A picture of a son or daughter getting a university degree and embarking on a successful career may need to be "repainted." Your child may not choose to marry and there might not be grandchildren. There might be hospitalizations, medication regimes, visits to case managers, and increased need for parental monitoring and supervision. At a time in life when many parents believe that their parental role is about to change in the direction of less involvement with the care of the children, the diagnosis of a serious mental illness could mean increased involvement. There are a whole host of other changes that require adjustment and time and can be viewed as a type of grief over the loss of one's image of a "normal" child.

It is important to understand that there is no one right way to grieve your loss, nor is there a universal period of time needed to "complete" this process. But, all parents and family members should give themselves permission to grieve in their own way. They should recognize that they will be spending weeks, months or even years, coping with the realities of caring for a family member with a long-term illness and adjusting to their losses.

Mental health professionals have identified a number of stages of grief that people can pass through. In essence, these stages are coping tools that we use to help us gradually come to accept loss and change. Both individuals newly diagnosed with mental illness and their family members are going through a grieving process, and thus a basic understanding of the grief process is important.

Elizabeth Kubler-Ross, a noted psychiatrist, identified five stages of grief that people *might, but do not need to, pass through*. The first is denial. In the denial stage, people cope with loss by simply refusing to believe that anything is different. They reinterpret reality or flat-out deny what has occurred. Consider, for example, the case of parents who try desperately to explain away their daughter's psychotic symptoms as simply the result of too much stress or perhaps a food allergy. It is of course much more comforting to believe that your child has a less-serious condition than a severe mental illness. Perhaps a consultation with a famous specialist or some special treatment will allow everything to get back to normal. Eventually, however, the weight of evidence accumulates and denial is no longer effective as an explanation or a coping technique.

A later phase of grieving is referred to as bargaining. In this stage, people attempt to negotiate with God or the world. "If I take up intensive prayer, I can cure this illness" is one form that bargaining can take. A parent of someone with a mental illness can make a private "deal" to contribute all their money to charity if their child can be cured. Or, bargaining can be smaller in scale. Sometimes family members will pray that their child be given only a mild form of illness and in response they promise to behave in certain ways. Bargaining can have some positive benefits. For example, a person who is ill and promises to exercise and stop smoking in exchange for better health might in fact experience better physical health.

Some people still grieve despite their efforts at negotiation and then they can become bitter or dejected. These stages are labeled anger and depression and are understandable reactions to loss. The newly diagnosed person and their family members have justifiable rage against the world. This grief stage is often characterized by a belief that the world is not fair. "There is no good reason why my child should have been cursed with schizophrenia." Anger may cause family members to lash out against those who are trying to help and support them. At some point the anger will end and might be followed by a period of profound sadness and depression. This phase is the classic way grief is thought to be experienced. Tears, isolation, lack of energy, and profound feelings of loss or maybe guilt can characterize this stage. The family members are mourning.

Finally, grieving can end when the person and their family ultimately understand that a mental illness is a part of their lives and they must cope as best they can to make the most of it. And, unlike the parents of the murdered teen, there is plenty of room for hope and recovery. A life with mental illness is not a life that is over. It is a life that is changed. But it is also a life that can be rich and fulfilling. There are numerous books available at any bookstore on grief and loss. There are also professional services available. What is key is for you to understand that you will likely go through a grieving process. Having knowledge about how grief affects a person will assist you in moving through that process in your own time.

How Do You Do It?

Not long ago an acquaintance said to me, "Mary, you are amazing. You do so much." The compliment was followed by a request that I join her in working for the election of a particular candidate for statewide office. She wanted me to participate in the campaign because she knew that my involvement would attract a significant amount of energy and built-in support from potential supporters if they knew I was involved in the campaign.

I say this not so much to toot my own horn, but out of amazement that I am in this position. This is not what I anticipated at the time my son was diagnosed with schizophrenia. I was never a joiner or a doer. I was content to make a good home for my family. It might be somewhat like Ozzie and Harriet, but I actually never had the desire to do anything more than be a good homemaker. Although I went to college, I never considered a career. A part-time job to help pay for summer camp or a family vacation fit me fine. I had a close circle of friends, but our friendships revolved around social activities and our children, not community activism.

All of that changed when our son was diagnosed with schizophrenia. At first I was numb. I really didn't feel sorry for myself—I didn't feel anything. As time went on, I had resentments. I resented my son, and I resented my husband, who seemed to be leaving me with the burden of dealing with our son's illness. Also, I resented our friends who had children who did not have a mental illness. I resented the mental health center that didn't seem to have a qualified staff. At one point, my son was being treated by a young woman who looked like she was still in junior high school. His psychiatrists were generally medical residents who changed frequently. On a month-to-month basis we were never sure who his "primary case manager" was going to be. I resented the state and county government that didn't provide enough funding to ensure that a consistent, qualified staff would be available to treat my son.

I am not sure when it happened, but one day I woke up and decided that I wasn't going to resent anyone any longer. I was going to take things into my own hands. I had been too busy wanting and expecting others to take care of things for me. I didn't have a barrel full of issues that I was interested in. I was interested in only one thing—making sure my son received adequate and consistent high-quality services.

As I look back over the years, it is hard to remember when wanting better services for my son turned into wanting better services for others' sons. And when wanting better services turned into a passion for wanting better education for children. And then better education for children somehow led me to become involved in homelessness, particularly homeless children. I don't think that there was ever a conscious attempt to connect the issues to each other. They just sort of folded in on each other.

Now, here I am, someone who is sought out by others for support and consultation. My son is still a major focus of my life. At times he does quite well. And thankfully, due to newer medications, he is doing well more often than not. But my son is not my only concern. I am concerned about my community. I want it to be better place to live. I want it to be better for my son, for other people's children who have mental illnesses, and for other people's sons and daughters who are not ill.

Submitted by A.R.

Sorrow

In this sad world of ours, sorrow comes to all, and it often comes with bitter agony. Perfect relief is not possible, except with time. You cannot now believe that you will ever feel better. But this is not true. You are sure to be happy again. Knowing this, truly believing it, will make you less miserable now. I have had enough experience to make this statement.

—Abraham Lincoln

Bend But Don't Break

One of my fondest memories as a child is going by the river and sitting idly on the bank. There I would enjoy the peace and quiet, watch the water rush downstream, and listen to the chirps of birds and the rustling of leaves in the trees. I would also watch the bamboo trees bend under pressure from the wind and watch them return gracefully to their upright or original position after the wind had died down.

When I think about the bamboo tree's ability to bounce back or return to its original position, the word "resilience" comes to mind. When used in reference to a person, this word means the ability to readily recover from shock, depression or any other situation that stretches the limits of a person's emotions.

Have you ever felt like you are about to snap? Have you ever felt like you are at your breaking point? Thankfully, you have survived the experience to live to talk about it. During the experience you probably felt a mix of emotions that threatened your health. You felt emotionally drained, mentally exhausted and you most likely endured unpleasant physical symptoms.

Life is a mixture of good times and bad times, happy moments and unhappy moments. The next time you are experiencing one of those bad times or unhappy moments that take you close to your breaking point, bend but don't break. Try your best not to let the situation get the best of you. A measure of hope will take you through the unpleasant ordeal. With hope for a better tomorrow or a better situation, things may not be as bad as they seem to be. The unpleasant ordeal may be easier to deal with if the end result is worth having.

If the going gets tough and you are at your breaking point, show resilience. Like the bamboo tree, bend, but don't break!

Reprinted with permission of Afterhours Inspirational Stories

CHAPTER 4

The Symptoms and Behaviors Associated With Serious Mental Illness

"Start by doing what's necessary, then do what's possible, and suddenly you are doing the impossible." — Saint Francis of Assisi

Edward M. Gentile, D.O., M.B.A.
Michael R. Berren, Ph.D.

There are some illnesses and medical conditions where the onset is rather dramatic and the symptoms are clear-cut. An example might be a spinal cord injury. An individual with a spinal cord injury can go from being healthy and mobile one moment to being unable to walk the next. There are other illnesses where the onset is gradual and the symptoms less clear. Mental illness often falls into this second category. Mental illness is not something that ordinarily appears overnight. Awareness of the symptoms and acceptance of the fact that a family member has a mental illness might take months, or even years. When the family ultimately does become aware that something is wrong, it is likely for one of the two following reasons:

• Abnormal or Unusual Behaviors: The family member has some behaviors that are abnormal or unusual when compared to other people, or compared to how he or she used to be ("he just doesn't seem like himself"). Examples include strange verbalizations, expressing beliefs that seem odd or even absurd, moods that appear extreme and not related to things going on in the "here and now," staying awake all night, or what appears to be talking to him- or herself. The number and severity of these unusual behaviors can range from few and mild to numerous and so extreme that friends, relatives and neighbors (and even others such as store clerks) are aware that the behaviors are abnormal.

• Absence of Normal (Expected) Behaviors: In addition to behaviors that are unusual, there is also the likely absence of certain behaviors and roles that are ordinarily expected. There might be a lowered interest in school, work or hobbies, or significantly reduced participation and inter-action with friends and family. For many young adults the absent behaviors might be the opposite of what had been characteristic for the person. For example, a young woman who was previously very clean and well groomed begins to show signs of poor hygiene. A bright, articulate college freshman stops attending class and isolates himself in his dormitory. A previously outgoing young woman becomes withdrawn and avoids her friends. A young man in his mid-twenties spends all day "hanging out" in a local park. While there are many reasons other than a mental illness that may explain the example behaviors (i.e., drug use, social conflicts, sexual identity issues), a dramatic change in behavior could possibly indicate *prodromal* (the very early) signs of a mental illness.

Both the unusual and absent behaviors are similar to the concept of the "tip of the iceberg." That is, while behaviors are what we are able to observe, there is more to the illness that we cannot see. The unusual and absent behaviors are the consequence of not readily observable symptoms. In this chapter we will address both the behaviors associated with mental illness, as well as the less-observable symptoms.

The Mental Illness Iceberg

• Knowing what is "beneath the surface of mental illness" can be helpful in understanding *why an individual with a mental illness tends to behave in a particular way.*

And

• Understanding what is beneath the surface can help families with interventions that assist their family member to recover. For example, if you focus primarily on behavior (such as the person's current inability to be gainfully employed), interactions with your family member might be quite a bit different than if you understood that the current employment problems were a natural consequence of underlying symptoms.

Let us turn to a medical condition other than mental illness for comparison. It's easy to understand that an individual with a spinal cord injury is not going to just get up and walk because someone tells him to. His inability to walk is a consequence of an underlying neurological impairment. Although encouragement and a positive attitude may help him in rehabilitation, no amount of cajoling will cause the underlying neurological damage to repair itself and allow him to immediately get up and walk. It is just not physically possible.

The same is true for the individual with a mental illness. Families must understand the core underlying symptoms and the resultant behavior changes associated with mental illness. Otherwise, although well intentioned, efforts to be helpful may cause conflict and frustration for all involved. It is important for family members to be aware of the underlying symptoms of the illness so that they can know both what their family member is capable of, and what are the best approaches to facilitate rehabilitation and recovery.

This chapter is divided into six areas. The first addresses the basic question what is mental illness? The next five review the five diagnoses commonly considered as serious mental illnesses.

• What is a Serious Mental Illness?
• The Symptoms of Schizophrenia

- Schizoaffective Disorder: A Cousin of Schizophrenia
- Bipolar Disorder
- Major Depressive Disorder
- Personality Disorders (Particularly Borderline Personality Disorder)

As you read the rest of the chapter, remember what was pointed out in Chapter 2: *There is not always a direct relationship between mental illness, the symptoms and the resulting level of disability.* One person with a serious mental illness might be less symptomatic (or even able to mask his symptoms) and be much less disabled than another person with exactly the same illness.

WHAT IS A MENTAL ILLNESS?

A great deal of time went into deciding on the title for this book. It was not an accident that "mental illness" as opposed to "schizophrenia" was selected. Most books available for families of individuals with a mental illness, including some truly excellent books, focus on schizophrenia. The term schizophrenia is not included in the title because there are a number of individuals with a serious mental illness who have a diagnosis other than schizophrenia. Even though schizophrenia is often considered to be the most insidious of the mental illnesses, there are other serious mental illnesses, and families dealing with them need a guidebook with which they can identify.

Addressing both schizophrenia and other serious mental illnesses made the task of compiling this book somewhat complex, primarily because the term "serious mental illness" does not even appear in the official diagnostic manual used by psychiatrists. While "serious mental illness" (and the three-letter abbreviation, SMI) is a common term, it is not a psychiatric diagnosis. Instead, it is a term used to group a number of psychiatric diagnoses into a common category. A determination of serious mental illness is usually based on a combination of diagnosis, history and level of disability. It is a term that is often used by state mental health authorities to make decisions about eligibility for services. Different states might include different diagnoses and different levels of disability within their definition of serious mental illness.

> Serious Mental Illness (SMI) is a concept used by state mental health authorities and other funders to determine eligibility for services. It is not a psychiatric diagnosis.

Psychiatric Diagnosis

An accurate diagnosis is extremely important in the rehabilitation process. Treatment planning is based on identifying a person's diagnosis, and his or her protective factors and risk factors (Chapter 2 addresses protective and risk factors). Without an accurate diagnosis, the likelihood of prescribing the correct medications and implementing the best approaches to rehabilitation is significantly reduced.

Psychiatrists use the *Diagnostic and Statistical Manual of Mental Disorders* (DSM) as the official guide for diagnosing mental illness. DSM-IV (the fourth edition) provides standard criteria for applying the art and science of psychiatric diagnosing. Using DSM-IV results in diagnoses that are reliable (multiple psychiatrists should come up with the same diagnosis of an individual) and valid (the diagnosis is likely accurate).

While we do not believe that it is important for families to become familiar with everything that is in the manual, it is important to have a basic understanding of DSM-IV. You will be a more knowledgeable consumer and better understand some of the jargon used by the professionals.

The first thing that you should know about DSMI-IV is that a psychiatric diagnosis is defined through five "axes" or concepts.

Axis:	The Axis Identifies:
	Clinical disorders such as schizophrenia, bipolar disorder and major depression
	Personality disorders
	Medical Conditions
	Psychosocial and environmental concerns (i.e., economic problems, problems with the legal system, housing problems)[1]
	The individual's functioning level (based on a 1 to 100 scale ranging from *persistently dangerous to self or others to superior functioning*)

It is important that when you discuss your family member's diagnosis with the clinical team that you are given information about all five axes. This will provide you with a more comprehensive understanding of the illness than if all you are told only is that your family member has a particular illness such as schizophrenia. Asking the treatment team to review all five axes with you will also be a clear message that you are an informed consumer who will pay attention to the services received by your loved one.

---

[1] In the terminology that we have been using, Axis IV contains risk factors. It is unfortunate that DSM-IV does not have an axis to indicate protective factors, but perhaps that will be coming in a future DSM edition.

Before discussing the specific diagnoses that are generally considered to be serious mental illnesses, there is something else that you should know about DSM-IV diagnoses. There are three letters that you might hear, *N-O-S*, which stands for Not Otherwise Specified. It is the official way of indicating that, for example, the Axis I or Axis II diagnosis is unclear or uncertain either because of inconsistent information, the person's presentation is atypical or because there is lack of clarity as to whether all of symptoms required for the diagnosis are present. There is nothing inherently wrong with a diagnostician giving a diagnosis that includes NOS. It is better to indicate NOS than to make an incorrect diagnosis.

THE SYMPTOMS OF SCHIZOPHRENIA

Persons with schizophrenia may experience symptoms across four areas:

- Cognitive Deficits
- Mood Symptoms
- Positive Symptoms
- Negative Symptoms

Cognitive Deficits (Problems Related to Thinking)

One of the most profound sets of symptoms experienced by an individual with schizophrenia are problems with cognition. Cognitive problems are various and can significantly impact the person's ability to interact with the world. The specific cognitive problems that an individual with schizophrenia might have are:

- Memory: Both short- and long-term memory can be affected.
- Attention and concentration: An individual can become easily distracted and have a difficult time focusing on things like conversations, games and television shows.
- Orientation: A psychotic or otherwise severely symptomatic person might have difficulties determining who he is, where he is, or even the current day, month and year.
- Logic: A person might have trouble recognizing natural relationships between actions or events ("If I don't take my medication, my symptoms might get worse" is a logical belief). Instead, an individual with schizophrenia might make decisions based on magical or nonsensical relationships ("If I take my medication the president will be killed" is not a logical belief).

- Learning: An individual can experience difficulties in absorbing new information or learning new skills.
- Speech: The person might create their own definition for certain words, and thoughts may be strung together in such a way that they seem only distantly related. In the extreme, the speech can be so disorganized that it is referred to as "word salad."
- Concrete thinking: An individual might interpret things so literally that her ability to recognize the subtlety in communication is reduced. Concrete thinking can impact her ability to comprehend humor or other subtle aspects of communication. A statement like "It's raining cats and dogs" could be confusing to someone who is extremely concrete in her thinking.

Mood Symptoms (Problems Related to Emotions)

In addition to myriad cognitive problems, an individual who has schizophrenia can intermittently have mood-related symptoms such as:

- Anxiety
- Depression
- Helplessness
- Demoralization

Positive Symptoms

The positive symptoms of schizophrenia are certainly not positive in the sense of somehow being good. Instead, positive symptoms are symptoms that are out of the ordinary and very noticeable by others. They are often bizarre and cause many of the unusual behaviors that we mentioned in the opening of this chapter. The most common positive symptoms include:

- Hallucinations: A hallucination is the person's perception of something that is not perceived by others. The two most common forms of hallucinations are:

  - Auditory: Individuals with auditory hallucinations report hearing voices. They often report that the voices are not just innocuous chatter, but can be frightening. The voices might be derogatory and can ridicule the individual or even tell him to hurt himself or someone else.
  - Visual: Visual hallucinations are less common than auditory hallucinations, but people do report seeing things no one else sees.

In addition to auditory and visual hallucinations, some individuals experience olfactory (smell), tactile (touch) and gustatory (taste) hallucinations.

- Delusions: Delusions are strongly held beliefs that are in contrast with the cultural mores or beliefs of the society. Delusions go far beyond beliefs that are debatable. Believing that a particular food tastes terrible, while others might perceive the food as tasting good, is an unshared opinion, not a delusion. Believing that an organized group is attempting to poison one's food is likely a delusion. There are six common types of delusions:

  - Paranoid: Belief that others (i.e. police, family, treatment team) are attempting to do harm to the individual.
  - Control: Belief that others can control the individual's thoughts. The person might actually believe that aliens have inserted a thought control electrode in his or her brain.
  - Grandiose: Belief that the individual has some special talents and/or is deserving of special favors and recognition.
  - Somatic: Despite medical evidence, a belief that he or she has some terrible illness that is destroying a part of his or her body.
  - Thought broadcasting: Belief that others can hear the individual's thoughts.

Negative Symptoms

Symptoms are referred to as negative if there is the absence of something normal or expected. While positive symptoms might lead to a person being noticed because he appears to be doing odd things, negative symptoms make a person appear odd because the individual is not doing things that are considered normal. Some negative symptoms are:

- Flat affect: Showing very little variation in facial expression, tone of speech or body language. Regardless of the objective situation, the person shows the same expressionless response.
- Alogia: Having very little to say and very little interest in engaging in a conversation.
- Anhedonia: The absence or lack of pleasure, even for those things that previously brought enjoyment.
- Social withdrawal: Showing very little interest in being with or interacting with others.

- Apathy: Having very little interest in doing anything for oneself or for others.

Consequences of the Symptoms

The symptoms described above, in addition to being problematic in and of themselves, have consequences. And it is often the consequences that families and others are most aware of:

- Self-care deficits: An individual might have problems with skills such as hygiene, shopping, preparing meals and money management.
- Social skills deficits: An individual with schizophrenia often has a difficult time socializing or interacting with others. He may feel ill at ease and do or say things that others find inappropriate or odd.
- Self-harm: Individuals with schizophrenia die of suicide at a much higher rate than the general population. See Chapter 10 for more information.
- Harm to others: Individuals with schizophrenia are generally not more dangerous than anyone else in society. However, if the individual is delusional or otherwise acutely psychotic, there is an increased likelihood of the person becoming dangerous.
- Job readiness deficits: Job readiness skills have both social and cognitive aspects. These are exactly the skills that are affected by schizophrenia. As you will read in Chapters 7 and 13, rebuilding skills is one of the most important aspects of rehabilitation and recovery.

SCHIZOAFFECTIVE DISORDER: A COUSIN OF SCHIZOPHRENIA

In discussing schizophrenia, we said that there could be intermittent mood symptoms. There will be other times when the individual has psychotic symptoms and no mood-related problems. However, when the individual has symptoms indicating the presence of schizophrenia, but mood symptoms are present for long periods of time, it is possible that the more accurate diagnosis is schizoaffective disorder. Schizoaffective disorder is closely related to schizophrenia, with the primary difference evolving around the mood symptoms. In some ways the distinction is not terribly important because the medications and approaches to rehabilitation that are appropriate for one are appropriate for the other. In cases where the schizoaffective disorder is more closely related to bipolar disorder (see below), the psychiatrist will likely prescribe medications used for bipolar disorder.

BIPOLAR DISORDER

Bipolar disorder, sometimes referred to as manic-depressive disorder, is a brain disorder that causes extreme shifts in a person's mood, energy and ability to function. Unlike the normal ups and downs that everyone goes through, the up and down symptoms of bipolar disorder are severe. They can result in damaged relationships, poor job or school performance, and even suicide.

Individuals with bipolar disorder who are not currently symptomatic often function at a higher level than do individuals with schizophrenia who are not symptomatic. An ironic consequence of the higher functioning is that a person with bipolar disorder may suffer for years before the illness is properly diagnosed and treated.

Symptoms of Bipolar Disorder

Bipolar disorder causes dramatic mood swings—from exaggerated good moods and/or irritability (mania) to sad and hopeless feelings (depression), and then back again. Between the mood swings there can be periods of normal mood. Along with the changes in mood, there are corresponding changes in energy and behavior. Some of the other signs of *mania* include:

- Increased energy, activity and restlessness
- Racing thoughts
- Speech that is very fast and jumps from one idea to another
- Distractibility
- Reduced need for sleep
- Exaggerated beliefs about one's abilities
- Poor judgment (i.e., impulsive spending, risky behaviors)
- Provocative, intrusive or aggressive behavior
- Delusions

The signs of depression are similar to those identified below under the Major Depressive Disorder heading.

One of the complications in treating a person with bipolar disorder is that the individual often denies that anything is wrong. In the initial stages, when there is a mild to moderate level of mania (referred to as hypomania), the symptoms might actually feel good and even be associated with good functioning and enhanced productivity. It is not long, however, before the hypomania turns into a full-blown manic episode. In a relatively short time the person can go from feeling good and having a positive sense of self-worth to spending money that he or she might not have, making very poor and risky decisions, and being delusional.

It may be helpful to think of the various mood states of bipolar disorder on a continuum. At one end is severe depression, above which is moderate depression and then low mood. (The low mood is often referred to as "the blues" when it is short-lived and "dysthymia" when it is chronic). Following low mood on the continuum is normal or balanced mood, above which comes hypomania and then severe mania.

MAJOR DEPRESSIVE DISORDER

A major depressive disorder is not the kind of depression that can be accounted for by a tragic life event such as the death of a loved one, the loss of a job, or a serious physical illness that one might be suffering. During and following the situations just described it is appropriate for a person to be sad. Ordinarily, however, when the situation changes or time passes the sadness lifts. Major depressive disorder, however, is an illness. The symptoms go far beyond what might be expected based upon an individual's life situation and include:

A low interest or pleasure in almost all activities
A feeling of being depressed most every day
Significant weight gain or weight loss when there is no purposeful attempt to gain or lose weight
Significant increase or decrease in amount of sleep
Psychomotor agitation or slowness
Fatigue and lack of energy
Feelings of worthlessness
Recurrent thoughts of death or suicide

Just as individuals with schizophrenia can have mood-related symptoms, individuals who suffer from major depressive disorder can have cognitive problems. The person can have a diminished ability to think, concentrate or make decisions. The distress and cognitive symptoms can be so severe that they can impair the individual's ability to care for him- or herself. Severely depressed individuals often find it overwhelming to even get out of bed to shower and eat a meal.

PERSONALITY DISORDERS
(PARTICULARLY BORDERLINE PERSONALITY DISORDER)

For most of the chapters in this book the topics addressed are relevant regardless of whether your family member has schizophrenia, schizoaffective disorder, bipolar disorder, major depressive disorder or a personality disorder. However, if you have been told that your family member has a personality disorder, particularly a borderline personality disorder, we recommend that you do some additional reading. There are numerous informative books and Internet Web sites (see Recommended Reading).

Our understanding about the cause of personality disorders is much less sophisticated than our understanding about the cause(s) of other mental illnesses. While there is possibly some predisposing biological component, we do not yet have consensus as to the nature of the biological component

In addition to having a biological component, personality disorders also appear to have a learned social component. That is, to some extent, personality disorders reflect learned (albeit ineffective) approaches to dealing with the world.

The Nature of Personality Disorders

Most people go through life observing situations, observing others and making judgments based on those observations. Our interactions with the world are, in turn, based on a combination of our personality style and the situation in which we find ourselves. For most people, our observations and corresponding ways we act are generally not black or white. We see the world in shades of gray and act accordingly. Our observations have some degree of objectivity. We trust some people and we are wary of others. In some situations we act quickly and in other situations we weigh our options more slowly. In some situations we might act aggressively and in others we tend to be submissive. In other words, while we all have an inclination to behave a certain way, we have a range of behaviors at our disposal.

Individuals with a personality disorder have a defect in the way they see the world and are often ineffective in how they deal with the world. Rather than viewing situations in shades of gray, they demonstrate little variability in their view of the world and very little flexibility in their repertoire of behavior.

There are ten different personality disorders, each with its own unique pair of "distorted glasses" through which individuals see the world. Of the ten, only two of the personality disorders –antisocial personality disorder and borderline personality disorder– tend to get much attention in the public mental health system. We are not going to discuss antisocial personality disorder because most state mental health authorities do not consider it to be a diagnosis that would qualify a person to be eligible for mental health services. An individual with an antisocial personality disorder is ordinarily eligible for services *only if the person has another diagnosis that would make the individual eligible*. Individuals with an antisocial personality disorder generally come to the attention of the mental health system through either law enforcement or the corrections system.

These individuals are often perceived as "hot potatoes." Neither the criminal justice system nor the mental health system feel equipped to meet the needs of both the individual and society. In any case, for the purposes of this book, we do not consider antisocial personality disorder to be a serious mental illness.

Many individuals with personality disorders other than antisocial and borderline disorder lead lives of quite desperation, and rarely come to the attention of the mental health system. They seem to get along on a day-to-day basis.

Borderline personality disorder is a very serious disorder, both in terms of the symptoms and the special way that individuals with borderline personality disorder are often perceived by mental health professionals. As we mentioned earlier, schizophrenia, schizoaffective disorder and bipolar disorder are Axis I illnesses, while borderline personality disorder is an Axis II disorder. The distinction between an Axis I illness and an Axis II disorder is important to understand for two reasons. First, the approach to rehabilitation for an individual with an Axis II disorder can be quite a bit different than the approach for an individual with an Axis I disorder.

Second, in some systems of care, the availability of experts to treat individuals with Axis II disorders is often less than the availability of expertise for treating individuals with an Axis I disorder. If you have been told that you family member has a borderline personality disorder it is especially important to ensure that members of the treatment team have the expertise that will be required.

In the following table we have identified how an individual with borderline personality disorder sees the world, and the consequent behaviors that she might display.

Distorted View of the World	Possible Behaviors and Descriptors
Individuals with a borderline personality disorder see the world as a place of rejection and abandonment. It is a place where they perceive they have been rejected in the past and will likely continue to be rejected and abandoned in the future.	Individuals with a borderline personality disorder exhibit extreme changes in mood, from intense neediness to equally intense anger and irritability. The changes are generally inappropriate, in that they do not have anything to do with what is objectively going on in the world around them. Instead, the mood changes are a function of their distorted view of the world. (The title of one of the recommended readings, *I Hate You - Don't Leave Me*, describes the essence of the borderline experience.)
They have an inconsistent self-image that often changes depending upon whom they are around at the time.	
Individuals with a borderline personality disorder often report feeling empty and in need of others for sustenance.	As a consequence of their extreme changes and intensity of how they see the world, their relationships are often characterized by instability.
	People who know someone with a borderline personality disorder often describe the individual as being "shallow."
	They tend to be impulsive and reckless. They can go on spending sprees, have numerous sex partners, drive recklessly and indulge in binge eating.
	It is though individuals with borderline personality do not have a "dimmer switch" for their emotions. What often brings individuals to the attention of the mental health system are recurrent suicidal behaviors, gestures, threats or self-mutilating behavior.

CHAPTER 5

Communicating and Resolving Conflicts Effectively

"Adversity is like the period of the rain... Cold, comfortless, unfriendly to man and to animal; yet from that season have their birth the flower the fruit, and the pomegranate."
—Sir Walter Scott

Eric E. Schindler, Ph.D.
Michael R. Berren, Ph.D.

Three ways to guarantee poor communication with your family member who has a mental illness.

BERREN

Don't listen to what he is saying.

Don't see the situation from her perspective.

Don't say anything positive.

Playing golf well requires mastering a number of skills, and then practicing and refining those skills. There is the grip, the correct motion for the backswing, the positioning of the head over the ball and the distribution of weight between the left and right side of the body. And that's just for starters. There are literally dozens of motions one needs to learn in order to become an even average golfer. As evidence of the fact that the required skills are numerous and can take years to learn, look at the golf magazines that are available. Monthly issues of the major magazines focus on dozens of tips for improving one's game. And that's just magazines. It doesn't count the individuals, both neophytes and long-time players, who are taking lessons to refine their skills.

Swimming, basketball and bowling (and all other sports) each require their own unique set of skills that must be learned. Even if someone has natural talent for a particular sport, he or she needs coaching and practice to excel. The same is true for playing a musical instrument or learning to cook. As a matter of fact, learning and practicing is required to become proficient in just about everything we do. When a parent teaches his adolescent son or daughter to drive, the parent is well aware that the child must learn certain skills and then practice those skills. The goal is to have the new driver so skilled that he or she can apply what has been learned under a variety of circumstances, such as heavy rain, mountainous terrain or narrow country roads.

What is true of sports, music, cooking and driving a car is also true of communication and problem-solving. Communication and problem-solving require special skills, and those skills must be practiced. This is especially true when the communication and problem-solving concern a stressful issue and involves someone with a serious mental illness. In this chapter we are going to address:

- Consequences of Poor Communication and Problem-Solving
- Barriers to Good Communication and Problem-Solving
- Approaches to Improve Communication and Problem-Solving Skills

One of the most significant frustrations for families is the communication problems they have with their family member who has a mental illness. Families often report that they have a difficult time just talking to their family member. The families indicate that their family member can be either nonresponsive or the discussions result in everyone feeling angry and unfulfilled. The angry discussions that seem to go nowhere are often those that revolve around treatment adherence and lifestyle. Some of the topics that are most likely to lead to unhappy and unproductive outcomes are:

- Requests for assistance with household tasks
- Discussions about compliance with medication
- Discussions about use of alcohol or other drugs
- Discussions about daily activities

Individuals with a mental illness also report frustration with the conversations they have with their family. They report that they often feel as though they are being criticized or interrogated, as opposed to participating in a conversation or discussion.

CONSEQUENCES OF POOR COMMUNICATION AND PROBLEM-SOLVING

Two Ships That Couldn't Get It Right

A supposedly true story from World War I described two ships that were supposed to meet at a predetermined coordinate somewhere in the Indian Ocean at a certain day and time. Yet, on the agreed-upon date and time only one of the ships turned up. The other ship was close by, looking forward to its scheduled rendezvous the *next day*! Why the mix-up? Because at the beginning of their communication one of the ships was on the eastern side of the International Date Line and the other was on the western side! (Remember that there is a one-day difference as one crosses the International Date Line. If it's Tuesday one mile to the west of the line, it's Monday one mile east of the line). The ships' commanders had not taken something as basic as the International Date Line into consideration when they planned the meeting.

In a number of the chapters of this book the point is made that families do not cause mental illness. Mental illness is a brain disease; it is not caused by bad parenting. That being said, the approaches to communication and problem-solving within the family can play a role in how an individual with a mental illness deals with his or her world, and the extent to which the individual's illness becomes a disability. To frame the preceding in a very positive way, families can play an important role in helping their family member cope with or minimize symptoms, and increase the likelihood of effective lifelong problem-solving.

The opposite is also true. Poor communication and poor problem-solving can lead to increased stress, no one in the family getting his or her needs met, and the individual with the illness having a greater likelihood of more severe symptoms.

BARRIERS TO GOOD COMMUNICATION AND PROBLEM-SOLVING

There are two major types of barriers to communication that families are likely to face. The first deals with the effects of mental illness itself. The second are classic barriers to communication that can occur for everyone.

Impact of the Mental Illness

As you have already read in chapters 2 and 4, mental illness is a brain disease and the symptoms can impact the individual's ability to think and communicate clearly. In this chapter, we want to help you develop skills that will allow you to communicate and problem-solve more effectively with your family member. As you improve your skills and provide your family member with opportunities to improve their skills, it may make a difference in the here and now. Skill-building might also make a long-term difference in how your family member learns to live with and recover from his or her mental illness.

As we begin this discussion, we want to make it clear that the information we are presenting is somewhat parallel to instructions in a golf magazine. That is, the information is important and useful, but nothing can take the place of practice. Get involved with a group where you can practice communication skills. There are a couple of options that you should consider. Many NAMI affiliates conduct a *Family to Family* program. In the *Family to Family* program you will have the opportunity to practice communication skills with other families who are likely dealing with situations and communication issues similar to your own. It is also possible that the agency providing your family member's treatment also provides family communication skills training.

There are four aspects of mental illness that can affect communication:

- Thinking (i.e., comprehension, concentration, logic, odd beliefs and delusions)
- Feelings (i.e., depression, anxiety, agitation and negative symptoms such as apathy and blunted effect)
- Perceiving (i.e., hallucinations)
- Behaving (i.e., social skills deficits and impulse control)

In addition to the four symptom-based problems, there is another issue that can impact how an individual with a mental illness might communicate and problem-solve. A young adult with schizophrenia might be seeing the world from a different perspective than that of his same-age peers. Friends from high school might have gone on to college, started rewarding careers and begun planning future lives with milestones, such as starting a family or purchasing a home. The young adult with a mental illness is less likely to be attending to concerns of the distant future. This is important for families to remember because the distance an individual attempts to see into the future, and the implications the person sees for the future, can affect his or her communication and problem-solving goals.

Other Common Barriers

There are barriers to communication that are above and beyond those associated with mental illness. They are barriers in that they generally put a halt to communication. They are the verbal equivalent of holding up a large red STOP sign. The barriers indicate a lack of interest in communication. In some cases the barriers are used with good intention and are designed to reassure the other person. In some cases the barriers are used out of frustration and serve only to make the other person feel bad. In either case, the barriers serve to hinder communication and problem-solving. They are presented here as things to watch for and try to avoid when you are communicating with your family member (or anyone else for that matter).

Communication Barrier	Example
Criticizing	"You are always getting into trouble by not thinking ahead. You've got nobody to blame but yourself."
Name-calling	"You're a fool. You are always making bad choices."
Analyzing (making judgments about why the person is doing what they are doing)	"Obviously you don't want to get better. If you did you would be taking your medication like the psychiatrist told you to."
Ordering or threatening (particularly if you are in a position of power)	"You better go to your appointment today if you want to stay in this house."

Moralizing (telling the other person that they *should* do because it is the right thing)	"If you had any sense of what was good for you, you would be taking your medication faithfully."
Excessive/Inappropriate Questioning (particularly if you use questions that can be answered "yes or no")	"Did you take your medication?" "Did you take all of your pills?" "Are you sure you took them all?"
Advising (giving solutions too early in the problem-solving process)	"If I were you I would be going to a program where I would learn some job skills."
Reassuring (ignoring the legitimate concerns of others)	"Don't worry about it. Things will work out and everything will be all right."
Use of logical arguments (using logic before coming to an understanding of the other person's real concerns)	"If you follow the instructions on the bus route map you are not going to get lost. The maps are printed to that they are very understandable."

To add a third layer to communication problems that might occur, there is the natural stress and conflict that can beset a family coping with *any* chronic illness. Patience, understanding and good intentions are sometimes difficult to come by, particularly when there is a long-term illness. Keep this in mind and try to avoid problem-solving when stress is at a high level. Obviously this cannot always be done and sometimes the situation demands problem-solving at times of heightened stress. When possible however, problem-solving should be practiced as a proactive rather than a reactive activity.

Family members need to be aware of the context of their problem-solving and make sure to take care of themselves. As indicated in Chapter 3, if you do not take care of yourself, you will not be as able to be of assistance to your family member.

Problems Are Inevitable

Do not blame your family member or yourself for having problems. A problem is a challenge to be confronted, not a threat to be avoided. It is better to try to solve a problem and fail than to never try to solve the problem at all.

There is a solution to every problem, or at least every problem situation can be improved upon. If you set your mind to it, you can find a solution and carry it out.

APPROACHES TO IMPROVE COMMUNICATION AND PROBLEM-SOLVING SKILLS

One of your roles as a family member is to model good communication and problem-solving skills for your family member with a mental illness. If you can do this, two things will happen. First, you will find that you feel better, your family member may feel better, and things may get resolved more easily. Second, you will hopefully find that as your family member develops communication and problem-solving skills, other parts of his or her life will likely improve.

Two important aspects to improving communication and problem-solving with your family member are to remember who it is that you are talking to, and remain vigilant to the barriers to communication that can be avoided.

If your family member has poor communication and problem-solving skills, it is quite likely a consequence of his or her illness. Do not expect your family member to be someone that he or she is not, or to have skills that he or she does not have. This does not mean that your family member's opinions should be minimized, or that the individual's point of view should not be respected. What it does mean is that problem-solving might require a great deal of patience and understanding. Be supportive and attempt to be a mentor.

Once you accept that poor communication and problem-solving is largely a function of an illness as opposed to your family member being stubborn or defiant, you might feel less stress. This acceptance might not make the communication go any better, but the acceptance can help the process from breaking down. If you believe that your family member's poor communication is separate from the individual's illness and he is just being obstinate or difficult, you will likely get frustrated and have a harder time being a mentor.

Problems and Growth

A wise man once noted that a life without any problems would eventually be quite boring. It is through solving problems and overcoming challenges that we grow and develop, and get satisfaction from life. Much of what we know about problem-solving can be applied to the challenge of living with or being a relative to a person with a serious mental illness.

Four Things You Can Do to Improve Communication

In addition to accepting the role of the illness in communication, and being vigilant to the barriers to communication, there are four skills that can increase the likelihood of effective problem-solving. As you become a better communicator, try to model the skills so that they can be learned and used by your family member.

Skills That Can Improve Communication	Specifics of What to Do
Get to the point. Avoid long sentences and introductions to topics.	• Clearly state an issue or concern. • Keep your points brief. • Do not get off track and discuss things that do not relate to the topic at hand. If there are other things that you want to discuss, wait until the first issue is resolved.
Express how you feel as opposed to what you think your family member would or should not do. Do not find fault or make evaluative statements.	Use "I" statements such as "I feel good when you take your medication properly," as opposed to a statement such as "You're not taking your medication properly; you need a better way to remember to take your pills."
Be clear and specific. Focus on behaviors rather than perceptions of personality traits.	Make statements such as "You have not helped to clean up after dinner for three days in a row," as opposed to statements such as "You are a slob and you never help around here. You are always making a mess and never cleaning up after yourself."
Control emotions and speak in a calm voice.	Try not to get angry or agitated. If you do feel angry, express your feelings calmly, using "I" statements. Do not yell or act in manner that implies that you "have given up" on problem-solving. If you feel as though your family member is not cooperating, do not take it personally. It is most likely an aspect of the individual's illness.

Seven Steps to Effective Problem-Solving

The four communication skills identified in the table above may help the communication process with your family member. In addition to those four skills, there are seven strategies you can use to structure situations that may make problem-solving go more smoothly.

Strategy	Specific Activities
Decide on a time and place where all involved will be able to discuss the problem without distraction or interruption.	• Do what you can to find a setting where phones will not be ringing, the television will not be on and people will not be coming and going. • Make sure that enough time has been set aside to discuss and hopefully resolve the problem.
Define the specifics of the problem. Do not go to the next step until you are certain that everyone understands the issue that needs resolution. Remember that you are here to find solutions, not to win an argument.	• Do not proceed to finding solutions until there is agreement as to the nature of the problem.
Brainstorm possible solutions. Make sure that your family member's opinions and feelings are listened to.	• Actively invite participation from all members. A rule of thumb is that in brainstorming there is no criticizing of opinions or attempts to censure any point of view or idea is legitimate. • Ask questions if you do not understand, but keep questions brief and to the point.
Select the best solution.	• Evaluate the possible consequences of each solution. • Based on the consequences (both good and bad), come to a consensus as to the best solution. Do not bully your family member into accepting your beliefs. • Everyone should realize that there is no perfect solution. The task is to find solution with the most positives and the fewest negatives.
In order to carry out the plan, identify who will do what, and when they will do it.	• Identify all of the steps necessary to carry out the solution. (This can be detail work and require identifying roles for everyone involved.) • Before ending the problem-solving session, check back to make sure there is agreement on what has transpired and future directions.

nplement the plan.	• Take the steps that have been agreed upon by the group. • One of the steps will be to set a time when the outcomes of the plan can be evaluated. • Everyone involved should meet at a predetermined time to discuss whether the solution has been effective.
valuate the plan.	• Everyone involved should meet at a predetermined time to discuss whether the solution has been effective. • If the solution has not been effective, the group needs to go back to the drawing board, determine what went wrong and, based on what has been learned, continue with the problem-solving.

The Trouble Tree

The carpenter I hired to help me restore an old farmhouse had just finished a rough first day on the job. A flat tire made him lose an hour of work, his electric saw quit, and now his ancient pickup truck refused to start. While I drove him home, he sat in stony silence. On arriving, he invited me in to meet his family. As we walked toward the front door, he paused briefly at a small tree, touching tips of the branches with both hands.

When opening the door, he underwent an amazing transformation. His tanned face was wreathed in smiles and he hugged his two small children and gave his wife a kiss.

Afterward he walked me to the car. We passed the tree and my curiosity got the better of me. I asked him about what I had seen him do earlier. "Oh, that's my trouble tree," he replied. "I know I can't help having troubles on the job, but one thing's for sure, troubles don't belong in the house with my wife and the children. So I just hang them up on the tree every night when I come home. Then in the morning I pick them up again.

"Funny thing is," he smiled, "when I come out in the morning to pick 'em up, there ain't nearly as many as I remember hanging up the night before."

Reprinted with permission of Afterhours Inspirational Stories

It's Not So Much What You Say, But How You Say It

A sultan called in one of his seers and asked how long he would live.

"Sire," said the seer, "you would live to see all your sons dead." The sultan flew into a rage and handed the prophet over to his guards for execution. He then called for a second seer and asked him the same question. "Sire," said the prophet, "I see you blessed with long life, so long that you will outlive all your family." The sultan was delighted and rewarded this seer with gold and silver jewelry.

Both prophets knew the truth, but one knew how to communicate, and the other did not.

Reprinted with permission of Afterhours Inspirational Stories

Obstacles? Deal with Them Now

An old farmer had plowed around a large rock in one of his fields for years. He had broken several plowshares and a cultivator on it and had grown rather frustrated about the rock.

After breaking another plowshare one day, and remembering all the trouble the rock had caused him through the years, he finally decided to do something about it.

When he put a crowbar under the rock, he was surprised to discover that it was only about six inches thick and that he could break it up easily with a sledgehammer. As he was carting the pieces away he had to smile, remembering all the trouble that the rock had caused him over the years and how easy it would have been to do something about it earlier.

Reprinted with permission of Afterhours Inspirational Stories

CHAPTER 6

Treatment Part I: Psychotropic Medication (Effectiveness and Side Effects)

"You can complain because roses have thorns,
or you can rejoice because thorns have roses."
—"Ziggy"

Martha P. Fankhauser, M.S.
Michael R. Berren, Ph.D.

It is only within the past 50 years that mental illness has been effectively treated with medications. For centuries prior to the 1950s, individuals with mental illnesses were forced to live with very little relief from their often terrifying symptoms.

Today psychotropic medications are among the most commonly prescribed of all medications. Newer-generation psychotropic medications work differently from older medications. They are more effective and have fewer side effects than medications that were considered "first line" only a few years ago. We are in an era of tremendous progress and the availability of newer medications that have fewer side effects will continue to grow. For individuals with a mental illness and their families, the newer medications are something for which to be grateful. They hold great promise with respect to treatment of mental illness.

As with any medication, psychotropic medications also come with their own set of precautions. Some can require careful monitoring, both to minimize the risk of side effects and to maximize the benefit. In order to familiarize you with the issues, this chapter is divided into eight topics:

- How Psychotropic Medications Work
- Psychotropic Medication is Generally a Lifelong Proposition
- What Psychotropic Medications *Can Do* and *Cannot Do*
- Nonadherence: Medication Is Not Effective If It Is Not Taken
- Approaches to Increasing Adherence
- Possible Medication Side Effects
- Classification of Psychotropic Medications
- Information That Should be Communicated to Your Family Member's Psychiatrist[1] and Treatment Team

HOW PSYCHOTROPIC MEDICATIONS WORK

Mental illnesses such as schizophrenia, bipolar disorder and major depression are generally thought to be due to chemical imbalances in the brain. While there may be disagreement as to the origin of the imbalances, there is no question that mental illness is a disease of the brain. As discussed in Chapter 2, while a number of situations that cause stress can play a role in worsening the symptoms of schizophrenia, stress alone can not cause mental illness.

The chemicals in the brain that play a role in mental illness are called *neurotransmitters*. The neurotransmitters are essential for communication between different parts of the brain. They act as messengers between the

---

[1] Psychiatrists are not the only professionals who prescribe psychotropic medications. In many systems of care nurse practitioners are the primary prescribers. So when we use the term "psychiatrist" we are referring to all professionals who might prescribe psychotropic medications for your family member.

millions of neurons in the brain. Millions of messages pass from one neuron to the next by traveling the length of the neuron, then crossing a tiny channel to the next neuron (referred to a *synapse*). It is the neurotransmitter that crosses the channel from the end of one neuron to the beginning the next neuron. If the message (i.e., the neurotransmitter) is not sent correctly from one neuron to the next, it is likely that the individual will experience symptoms of a mental illness. Sometimes there are disturbances or imbalances in the functioning of these neurotransmitters[2]. As a result, communication within the brain can be disrupted or incomplete. Simply put, many of the symptoms of mental illness are a result of the disrupted communication in the brain.

One of the neurotransmitters in the brain is called *dopamine*. Dopamine plays a major role in schizophrenia. If there is too much dopamine in certain areas of the brain, there is an increased chance of psychotic symptoms, such as hearing voices or having extremely irrational beliefs.

Norepinephrine and *serotonin* are two other important neurotransmitters that play a role in depression. If there is too much norepinephrine passing from one neuron to the next there is the increased probability that the individual will have a depressive illness. Other neurotransmitters include *acetylcholine* and *gamma-aminobutyric acid*.

As a simple example of the role neurotransmitters play in mental illness, imagine a relay race. The first runner receives a message and his role is to run to the next runner and pass along the message—similar to passing a baton. Each new runner, in turn, runs to the next runner and passes along the message until it is delivered to some end point. In an ideal relay, the message received at the end point is the same as was given to the first runner. This is to some extent how messages are sent through the brain. If, however, along the way each runner passes only part of the message, or an exaggerated or an incorrect message, the message at the end will no doubt be something very different than what was sent.

The psychotropic medications target problems that occur at the synapse of the neurons that prevent accurate messages from getting through. The science of psychopharmacology is to find the best approach to make sure that the message between the neurons is passed and received accurately, and at the same time making sure there are as few side effects as possible.

One model of how psychotropic medications work is shown in Figure 1A and 1B. Figure 1A depicts the problem of too little of the neurotransmitter passing from the first neuron to the second neuron. There is too little neurotransmitter to correctly stimulate the second neuron because some of the neurotransmitter returns to the first neuron rather than crossing

[2] Something that you should be aware of is the fact that neurotransmitters are made from protein. People who do not have enough protein in their diet are at risk of not being able to make enough neurotransmitter. Additionally, certain medications are less likely to be effective if the person does not eat a balanced diet. (Chapter 10 provides useful information about diet.)

the synapse. A remedy, shown in Figure 1B, is to block the neuro-transmitter from re-entering the first neuron (the process of neuro-transmitters was also discussed in Chapter 2, if you would like a review).

Psychotropic medications work by helping to correct the imbalances of neurotransmitters and restore more normal brain communication. In some cases the medication serves to increase the amount of neurotransmitter (an agonist effect). In other cases, the medication works by blocking or decreasing (an antagonist effect) the amount of neurotransmitter between the neurons.

Figure 1

Figure 1A. Some of the neurotransmitter returns to the first neuron (called reuptake) at the point of the synapse.

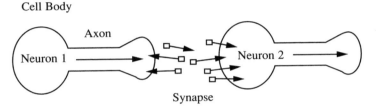

Figure 1B. A solution to block or inhibit the neurotransmitter from returning to the preceding neuron.

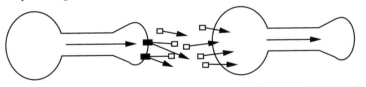

PSYCHOTROPIC MEDICATION IS GENERALLY A LIFELONG PROPOSITION

The medications that your family member will be taking are prescribed to help reduce or eliminate symptoms of their mental illness. From the beginning, however, you need to be aware that the relationship between psychotropic medications and mental illness is more like the relationship between insulin and diabetes, than the relationship between penicillin and an infection. That is, for schizophrenia, medications are something that individuals will likely take for their entire life. And, at times, over the course of their illness, they might even need additional medications for short-term, acute symptoms. The medications control the symptoms by stabilizing the neurotransmitter malfunction in the brain. The medications do not cure the illness. If the medication is stopped, the malfunctioning will likely begin again. While there is no cure for mental illness, individuals can recover and lead very productive lives. They can be symptom-free, have meaningful roles with family, friends and society, go to school and hold permanent employment. But like someone with diabetes, who must continue to take medication, an individual with schizophrenia must also continue taking their medications while continuing to be involved in recovery activities.

WHAT PSYCHOTROPIC MEDICATIONS *CAN DO* AND *CANNOT DO*

For most individuals with schizophrenia or other serious mental illnesses, medications are going to be a very important part of their ongoing treatment and recovery. As stated above, it is likely that they will need to take medication for quite some time, if not their entire life. The medications that they take will often be quite effective in reducing, if not eliminating, many of their symptoms. The following table identifies some of the symptoms for which medications will be effective.

Symptoms That Are Improved With Antipsychotics,
Antidepressants and Mood Stabilizers

Antipsychotics	Antidepressants	Mood Stabilizers
Positive Symptoms Delusions Hallucinations Bizarre behavior Disorganized thinking Agitation Paranoia Hostility	Physical Symptoms • Weight Change • Psychomotor agitation or retardation • Fatigue • Decreased libido • Aches and pains • Unprovoked crying	Mood • Mood swings • Expansive • Euphoric Cognitive • Racing thoughts • Grandiose delusions • Paranoia
Negative symptoms (not generally improved with typical antipsychotics) Feels no pleasure Social withdrawal Apathy Attention impairment	Cognitive symptoms • Concentration • Indecisiveness Behavioral/emotional symptoms • Poor hygiene • Feeling of worthlessness • Suicide attempts	Physical • Insomnia • Hyperactivity Behavioral • Recklessness • Manipulativeness • Disinhibition

But unlike some illnesses where medication might be the only source of treatment, the psychotropic medications are not going to be all that your family member needs. While the medications can help control many of the symptoms of mental illness, the medications are not going to provide your family member the skills that they might need to get back into a competitive job market. The medications are not going to help them with conversation or other social skills that they need to get along with others. They also will not help with many of the normalization activities that are at the core of recovery. By helping relieve many of the symptoms, however, the medications do help make your family member better able to work on recovery issues. In the next chapter many of the psychosocial programs that your family member will need, in addition to their medication, are discussed.

THE FIX

There is the story of a salesman who was driving through the Great Plains. He pulled into a service station and a young attendant came running up to the car. The man in the car indicated that he was headed for Omaha and was having some trouble. The young attendant immediately opened the hood and began fiddling with wires. He checked the oil and all of the fluids. After working on the car for about fifteen minutes he told the traveler that he was good to go. The young attendant then went off to help another customer. After the young attendant went off to the next car, the traveler went into the office to speak to the manager. He told the manager that the young attendant was very polite and quite a hard worker. "But I still have a problem," said the traveler. "I need to get to Omaha and I am lost. I can't make heads or tails out of my map."

The story above, which is based on a debate between two famous psychologists, illustrates an issue similar to that your family member has to deal with. On the one hand they need someone to "look under the hood." They need a thorough evaluation to determine their diagnosis and appropriate medication. But that is part of the picture. They also need someone to help them along the path to recovery.

NONADHERENCE: MEDICATION IS NOT EFFECTIVE IF IT IS NOT TAKEN

The following statement makes a fairly obvious point, but one worth making:

> Psychotropic medications, regardless of how effective they might be in the laboratory, are ineffective if they are not taken. These medications are also not likely to be effective if they are not taken as directed.

Medication adherence is not just an issue for individuals with a mental illness. Nonadherence is often cited by physicians as a significant health care problem. The reason that adherence is so important for an individual with a mental illness is that up to 40 percent of all episodes of decompensation are a result of individuals not taking their medication, either correctly or at all.

Adherence is more than just taking the prescribed medication; it is *taking the medication as directed*. So before we talk about the classification of medications it is important to address the issue of adherence—reasons for nonadherence, and strategies that can be used to increase adherence.

Reasons for Nonadherence

• Side effects: For many individuals, the side effects caused by psychotropic medications can be uncomfortable and unwanted. Thus, while the medication usually reduces the symptoms of the illness, the individual might consider the side effects in deciding whether or not to take their medication. As a result, the individual's decision to continue to take their medication may change over time. At times the symptom improvement might be reinforcing enough to ensure adherence. At other times the side effects might be severe enough to lead to nonadherence.

• Inconvenience/nuisance: Inconvenience covers a wide range of issues, including storage of medications and having to carry pills around if they must be taken at various times during the day. While storage and toting pills might not seem like a major issue, it can be an issue for someone living in an unstable living situation or another setting where they might not have private storage. Having to take any medication can be a nuisance no matter what type of illness a person might have.

- Remembering and other cognitive issues: If you read health care magazines or look on the Internet under the topic *of medication adherence* you will find a number of products available to help individuals remember to take their medications. "Just forgetting" is one of the most common reasons that the general public gives for nonadherence.

  Given the fact that memory and other cognitive problems are often symptoms of mental illness, remembering to take medication is even more of an issue for individuals with a mental illness.

- Part of the illness: There are two parts to this issue. The first might be represented by the statement "I don't need to take medication, I'm okay without it." One of the hallmarks of mental illness is often denial, or refusing to accept one's illness. If there is denial, it will certainly play a role in the person's willingness to comply faithfully with taking his or her medication. If your family member does not believe that they have an illness, why should they comply with taking their medication?

  A second way that the illness itself can lead to nonadherence is the situation where the person recognizes that the medication might help, *but at the time, they do not want help.* For example it is not uncommon for individuals with major depression who begin to experience increased depressive symptoms to choose to stop taking their medication. They stop taking the medication because the increased depression leads to a snowballing phenomenon. Increased depression leads them to feel that they are not worthy of feeling good. Feelings of worthlessness can lead them to stop taking their medication. When they stop taking their medication they become even more depressed, feel even less worthy and the process of ever-increasing symptoms continues.

- Reacting to the medication not working: In some cases the medication might actually not be working. But rather than going to the psychiatrist or another member of the treatment team to discuss the problem, the person just stops taking the medication.

- Negative symptoms: As discussed in Chapter 4, there are a number of negative symptoms of schizophrenia. Negative symptoms such as apathy and withdrawal can certainly play a role in an individual not complying with medication.

- Sometimes some symptoms are hard to give up: It is not uncommon for individuals with bipolar illness to report that they actually miss some of the symptoms of their illness. Some individuals report that the medication seems to dull their creativity and enthusiasm. They might feel that they are less productive. And even though the individual might realize that the medication protects them from the extremes of the illness, there is often a feeling of loss. Some individuals who have bipolar disorder actually stop taking their medication so that they might experience some sort of mild "high." The problem is that without medication the individual can go from the mild high to severe symptoms fairly quickly.

• Medication is an admission that they have an illness: This reason for nonadherence rests on a faulty logic of cause and effect. The individual might make the argument with himself that "If I take the medication it must mean that I have an illness. Therefore, if I don't take the medication, I am not ill."

APPROACHES TO INCREASING ADHERENCE

There are a number of interventions that can increase the likelihood that your family member complies with taking the medication. Some of the suggestions listed below are things that you can do. Others are strategies that involve the psychiatrist and members of the treatment team.

• Be informed about the medications your relative is taking: People should always be fully informed about the purpose of the medication they are taking. They should also be informed about possible side effects. This is the case whether the medication is for the treatment of a mental illness or a physical illness. If your family member is taking a combination of medications, they should be informed about the purpose of each medication and how the medications might relate to each other. In most situations the person should participate in discussions about the advantages and disadvantages of various medications, and participate in the decision about which medication(s) to take. If and when the medication regime changes, the individual should be informed about why there needs to be a change and what the new medications are expected to do. Even if the individual is cognitively impaired, attempts should always be made to keep them as fully informed as possible.

The prescribing practitioner should spend time discussing the medication with your family member. This should be done in the context of how the medication relates to the entire treatment plan, not just the symptoms that might be targeted by the medication. You and your loved one should always be vigilant to make sure that the psychiatrist and others on the treatment team see your family member in a holistic manner.

Pharmacists who fill the prescription are also wonderful resources and should also be called upon to spend time with your family member discussing the medication(s).

• Set up cues: Given the fact that many individuals are taking multiple medications and that the medications can change over time, we recommend that your family member have a sheet like the one below. Such a grid can both help them to remember when to take medications and also why they are taking each medication.

Medication Reminder Sheet

Name of the Medication (s)	Medication Routine		Purpose of the Medication(s)	Possible Side Effects
	Number of pills to be taken	When the pills should be taken		

• The medication routine should be as simple as possible: The more complex the routine, the more likely it is that there will be a lack of adherence. So do what you can to ensure that those who are working with your family member keep the routine as simple as possible. This might mean taking the medications once a day as opposed to more often. There will be times, however, for some individuals that certain medications need to be taken at multiple times during the day. But when at all possible, try to keep things simple.

• Monitoring: For a number of different reasons there might be times that your family member is not reliably taking their medication. If this is the case you might want to consider increasing levels of supervision. If you believe that some level of supervision is necessary, discuss the issue with your family member and search for ways to use the least amount of supervision necessary to ensure adherence[3]. That is, don't be more controlling than you need to be. If a moderate level of supervision might be effective, don't employ a more extreme level. At a very low level of supervision you might have your family member keep a log of when they take their medication. Your role would be to regularly check the log. Increasing levels of supervision include pill counting to actually having someone store and dispense the medication.

- Consider the use of injectable medications: If adherence appears to be impossible, the treatment team might consider injectable medication (called depot) rather than pills. However, the problem with injectable medication is that there are very few medications that are available as injectables, which limits medication choice.

- Medication should be tied to a treatment plan: Perhaps most importantly, make sure that the treatment team discusses each part of the treatment plan with your family member. The team should work with your family member to understand the importance of each part of the plan and how the parts fit together. The medication should be seen by both the treatment team and by your family member as only one part of the treatment plan. If medication is seen as one part of a bigger picture leading to recovery, the chances of adherence are greater than if adherence is merely a goal in and of itself.

- Some final issues about adherence:

  - Medication should always be taken as directed on the prescription label. An individual should never take more medication than is prescribed or double up on dose, even if a previous dose was missed.
  - A person should never stop taking their medication without first consulting their psychiatrist. Some medications can cause a withdrawal reaction if abruptly discontinued.
  - Medications should be stored in the original bottle in a cool, dry place.
  - Be aware of special precautions such as diet, driving a car, drinking alcohol or taking other medications.

---

[3] Make sure you read about the approaches to problem-solving in Chapter 5.

POSSIBLE MEDICATION SIDE EFFECTS

Side effects may be worse early in therapy when the body is adjusting to chemical changes caused by the medication. Most side effects are short lived, decrease over time, and are not bothersome. However, if a side effect is a possible allergic or toxic reaction; persists; is uncomfortable, distressing or causes impairment in functioning; your family member's psychiatrist should be notified immediately. The table below contains a list of common side effects that can be associated with psychotropic medications. The likelihood of each side effect for each specific medication is presented in Tables 1 - 4, at the end the chapter.

Obviously, as with all medications, side effects with specific medications vary from person to person. Some individuals will experience very minimal side effects. Some individuals will experience some short-term, mild side effects. Still others will unfortunately have some fairly significant problems with side effects. If your family member is one of the individuals to suffer from side severe side effects make sure that their psychiatrist is informed immediately.

Possible Side Effects of Psychotropic Medications

Side Effect	What might be experienced	
Allergic Reactions or Toxicity	Difficulty breathing, itching, ringing in ears, skin rash, sores in mouth	
Anticholinergic effects	Blurred vision; dry mouth, throat or nose; increased thirst, constipation, problems with urination	
Appetite, Sleep	Significant increase or decrease in appetite or sleep	
Cardiovascular/ Orthostatic hypotension	Dizziness, lightheadedness or fainting, especially upon going from a sitting to standing position. A rapid or pounding heart	
Central Nervous System	Drowsiness, headache, increased sweating, nervousness, poor memory or difficulty concentrating, slurred speech, unsteady or feeling a lack of balance when walking	
Extrapyramidal Reactions (EPS)	Akathisia	Restlessness and pacing, or inability to sit still. It is often accompanied by anxiety or agitation.
	Dystonia	An infrequent but severe muscular reaction characterized by painful muscle spasms of the face, neck and extremities
	Akanisia	Characterized by a zombie-like, shuffling gait, and a mask-like expression.
Gastrointestinal or Urinary	Nausea or vomiting Diarrhea, frequent or difficult urination	
Sexual Problems	Decreased libido	
Tardive Dyskenesia	Lip smacking, facial and lingual masticatory movements, trunk rocking and restless foot.	

CLASSIFICATION OF PSYCHOTROPIC MEDICATIONS

There are five medication classifications that are important to the treatment of serious mental illness:

• Antipsychotics
• Antidepressants
• Mood stabilizers
• Antianxiety (anxiolitics and hypnotics)
• Anticholinergics

As indicated earlier, the psychotropic medications work to reduce symptoms by restoring chemical (neurotransmitter) balance in the brain.

They do not cure an illness. Because the medications target symptoms, as opposed to specific illnesses, you might find that your family member is prescribed an antidepressant or antianxiety medication even if their primary diagnosis is schizophrenia. This is because depression is commonly associated with schizophrenia. (Imagine if you were hearing voices and having difficulties with your thoughts, wouldn't you be depressed and anxious?) Likewise, individuals with major depression might be prescribed an antipsychotic medication if their depression was so severe that it was leading to problems with thinking.

Antipsychotic Medications

Antipsychotic medications (sometimes referred to as *neuroleptics*) are used to block psychotic symptoms such as hallucinations and delusions. Newer antipsychotic medications (referred to as atypical antipsychotics) have also been demonstrated to have some effectiveness in the treatment of negative symptoms such as emotional and social withdrawal and decreased motivation. (See Chapter 4 for a discussion of positive and negative symptoms.) Because antipsychotic medications treat symptoms and not a specific illness, they can also be used to treat psychotic symptoms that are caused by major depression and other mental illnesses. The older antipsychotic medications can often be very effective in reducing positive symptoms. They do not, however, seem to have any effect on negative symptoms. They also can produce side effects that cause problems with movement. These are referred to as extrapyramidal symptoms (EPS) and are described in the table entitled "Possible Side Effects of Psychotropic Medications" presented earlier in this chapter. The primary EPS symptoms include acute dystonia, akathisia and akanisia.

The newer, atypical, antipsychotic medications are an improvement over the older medications not only because they are very effective in treating both positive and negative symptoms, but because they are much less likely to produce EPS side effects.

Early-onset EPS (the person gets the symptoms relatively soon after starting the medication) can usually be controlled with medications called anticholinergics. A later-onset movement disorder that may occur is called tardive dyskinesia. Tardive dyskinesia is characterized by involuntary rhythmic movements, especially of the tongue, lips and jaw. There can also be trunk rocking and restless foot. The best treatment for tardive dyskinesia is prevention. While there can be improvement with treatment, a remission can take up to two years. The risk of tardive dyskinesia increases with age, in postmenopausal women, and with high-dose therapy. There is no known treatment for tardive dyskinesia except to discontinue the antipsychotic treatment or switch to an atypical antipsychotic agent.

Atypical Antipsychotics: More About How They Differ from Typical Antipsychotics

The *atypical antipsychotic* medications did not exist prior to the 1990s. They are referred to as atypical because they are different from the older medications. There are four primary differences:

- As indicated above, the atypicals do not cause the movement disorder side effects associated with the older medications.
- They affect different neurotransmitters than the older medications.
- They have some impact on negative symptoms, while the older medications do not.
- They seem to decrease symptoms of mental illness in some individuals who have not been helped by the older medications.

The atypicals are also much more expensive than the typicals. A month's supply of an atypical antipsychotic can cost hundreds of dollars compared to well under a hundred dollars for an equivalent supply of a typical antipsychotic. Some professional literature has pointed out, however, that if all of the costs associated with treatment, such as reduced need for inpatient care, emergency room use, productivity etc., were factored in, the costs might not be that different. I mention cost because it can be an issue in publicly funded agencies. And because cost can be an issue, it is important that you pay attention to the medication that your family member is being prescribed, and why they are receiving that particular medication. The antipsychotic medications, along with side effects are listed in Tables 1a and 1b.

Antidepressant Medications

Antidepressants work by increasing the amount of three neurotransmitters (norepinephrine, dopamine and serotonin) that pass from neuron to neuron in the brain. Tricyclic antidepressants and monoamine oxidase inhibitors (MAOIs) have been available since the late 1950s. However, this medication class has more side effects and is more dangerous when compared to newer antidepressants. They still have a role in difficult-to-treat individuals who have not responded successfully to some of the newer medications. Currently, serotonin reuptake inhibitors, which are sometimes referred to as selective serotonin reuptake inhibitors (SRIs or SSRIs), are the most commonly prescribed antidepressants. Like the atypical antipsychotics, the SRIs are an improvement over the older anti-depressants because they have fewer side effects. One of the primary side effects of the older antidepressant medications is anticholinergic effects. These include dry mouth, blurred vision, constipation, othostatic hypotension (decreasing blood pressure when standing up quickly), seizure risks and toxicity with overdoses.

MOAIs, while quite effective in treating depression for many individuals, is also a class of medication that can cause severe problems if taken with other drugs. It is very important that the psychiatrist know about all medications that your family member is taking if they are being prescribed an MAO inhibitor. There are also important dietary restrictions when taking this class of medications. Some foods to avoid while taking an MAOI include cheeses, certain processed meats such as bologna and salami, hot dogs, and red wine. The psychiatrist will help your family member avoid prescription drugs. Your family member needs to make sure that they also do not take certain over-the-counter (OTC) medications. Pharmacists are a good source of information when purchasing OTC medications. He or she will be able to make recommendations on OTC therapy and consult with your doctor if necessary. Some of the more important over-the-counter medications to closely monitor while taking an MAOI include diet pills, cold preparations and nasal sprays. Even the dentist should be aware if your family member is taking an MAO inhibitor because some anesthetics used in dental procedures can be problematic.

Antidepressant medications are usually started at lower doses with a gradual increase until a therapeutic effect is achieved. Antidepressants generally take several weeks before they begin to have an optimal effect and should be taken for a minimum of six months after depression has lifted. Some individuals may need to continue on the medication for a year or more to prevent relapse even though the symptoms of depression may have resolved and the person reports "feeling better." Although antidepressants are not addictive, when they are discontinued it is important to taper off them slowly in order to prevent a withdrawal syndrome and to prevent a return of symptoms. The antidepressant medications along with side effects are listed in Tables 2a, 2b and 2c.

Mood Stabilizers

Mood-stabilizing medications help to reduce the symptoms of mania, hyperactivity, exaggerated elation, rapid speech, grandiose ideas, poor judgment, aggressiveness, and hostility associated with bipolar disorder. They also help to restore normal sleep patterns and stabilize the mood so the individual does not switch to another mood state, such as depression.

This explains the name "bipolar"—switching from one extreme state such as elation or excitability to the other extreme of depression and lethargy. Lithium, a naturally occurring compound, is a common mood stabilizing medication. Certain anticonvulsant medications (medications that are often prescribed for individuals with seizure disorders) are more effective than lithium for treating rapid-cycling mood swings (meaning a short time frame between being depressed then being excitable) and mixed-states (coexistence of mania and depression). At times, lithium is combined with anticonvulsants and antipsychotics. Additionally, anti-convulsants may be combined with antipsychotics for persons who cannot be stabilized on one medication.

Mood-stabilizing agents can cause a wide variety of side effects and some of them require fairly regular blood level monitoring. As with antidepressants, mood-stabilizers are generally started at lower doses and then gradually increased to achieve a therapeutic effect. The mood stabilizing medications and their side effects are listed in Table 3.

Antianxiety Medications (Hypnotic and Anxiolytic Agents)

Antianxiety medications or tranquilizers are also referred to as anxiolytics. At higher doses they are referred to as hypnotics. Many of these medications have a risk of causing dependence (physical and psychological effects that can produce addiction), tolerance (requiring higher doses for the same therapeutic effect), and withdrawal reactions if the medication is abruptly stopped. The most common antianxiety medications are benzodiazepines; one of the best-known benzodiazepines is Valium.

The common side effects of benzodiazepines are sleepiness, drowsiness, reduced coordination and alertness, and impaired judgment and memory. When taking benzodiazepines, a person should not drink alcohol or take other sedating medications such as tranquilizers, sleeping pills, barbiturates, narcotics, antihistamines or anticonvulsants unless specifically prescribed by a practitioner. Alcohol and other central nervous system depressants increase the sedative effect of benzodiazepines and may cause severe intoxication and even death. Newer nonbenzodiazepine agents have a potential for dependence and should not be used long-term. The antianxiety medications along with side effects are listed in Tables 4a and 4b.

Anticholinergic Medications

Anticholinergics are often prescribed in combination with the typical antipsychotic medications to decrease the risk and severity of extrapyramidal side effects. Anticholinergics are not routinely prescribed, however, as there is some evidence that they can reduce therapeutic effect of neuroleptics. Thus, the anticholinergics are prescribed to treat EPS, but not as a preventive measure.

INFORMATION THAT SHOULD BE COMMUNICATED TO YOUR FAMILY MEMBER'S PSYCHIATRIST AND TREATMENT TEAM

It is important that the psychiatrist knows about other medications your family member might be taking, possible food or drug allergies, and illnesses. It is also important that the psychiatrist is aware of how the prescribed psychotropic medication is working. Some specific information to discuss with the psychiatrist includes:

- Allergies that your family member might have to drugs or foods
- Other medications, over-the-counter products, vitamins, herbal products, and dietary supplements that are currently being taken
- Medical conditions, particularly diabetes and kidney, liver or heart disease
- Special diets
- Use of caffeine, alcohol, nicotine, marijuana and other drugs
- The effectiveness of the psychotropic medication in controlling symptoms
- Side effects experienced
- Possible barriers to adherence

Christina J.

I was 17 years old when I went to the pharmacy to fill my first prescription for an antidepressant. I was apprehensive, but also a little hopeful. It did, however, seem unfair. Seventeen-year-olds should be going to the drugstore for makeup and magazines, not to get a prescription for an antidepressant medication. If you needed a prescription it should be for acne or the flu.

That was eight years ago. Over the past eight years I have been on more medications than I care to count. I have taken antidepressants, antipsychotics, mood stabilizers and even medications to control side effects that the other medications might cause. Sometimes the medications seem to work and sometimes they don't work. There have been times that I stopped taking my medication because it didn't seem to be working. There are other times that I have not been compliant, not because the medication is not working, but for my own personal reasons.

For me, psychiatric medications are symbols. They represent the sadness and terror that I sometimes feel. They remind me of the hospitals and doctors. But mostly they represent the fact that I have a mental illness. It is a reminder that I have an illness that somehow makes me different from the friends who I grew up with and went to school with. Four times a day I gulp my pills down and each time it's a hard slap across the face. Sometimes I feel like it's a no-win situation. When I'm depressed I want so badly not to be depressed. I'm willing to take any medication that will make the pain go away. Then when I'm not depressed and I'm taking my medication, I'm constantly being reminded that I have an illness. When I'm feeling well I don't want that reminder hanging over my head.

Fortunately the part of me that wants to be well is usually stronger than the part of me that doesn't want to take the medication. You see, I would rather be reminded of my illness four times a day than have my life dominated by the illness. It's a sacrifice I must make in order to live a fruitful life. I still have difficult times, but the good times are finally starting to outnumber the bad. It may take a long time for my doctor to find the "right mix" of medications, but it's a process that is headed in a positive direction.

Tables 1 through 3, EPS= Extrapyramidal, ACH= Anticholinergic, GI= Gastrointestinal,
= Cardiovascular (Extrapyramidal and Anticholinergic effects are discussed in the narrative portion
he chapter.)
"X" in the cell indicates a High or Very High relationship between the medication and the side
ct.

le 1 Antipsychotic Medications
Typical Antipsychotics

dication *(Trade Name)*	EPS	ACH	Sedating	CV	Other side effects and concerns
lorpromazine *(Thorazine)*	X	X	X	X	Photosensitivity (sensitivity to sunburn), dermatitis
phenazine *(Permitil, Prolixin)* ailable as an injectable)	X				
loperidol *(Haldol)* ailable as an injectable)	X				
xapine *(Loxitane)*	X				
soridazine *(Serentil)*		X	X	X	
lindone *(Moban)*	X				
phenazine *(Trilafon)*	X				
oridazine *(Mellaril)*		X	X	X	Impaired sexual functioning
othixene *(Navane)*	X				
luoperazine *(Stelazine)*					

Atypical Antipsychotics

dication *(Trade Name)*	ACH	Sedating	CV	Other side effects and concerns
zapine *(Clozaril)*	X	X	X	Seizures at high doses, increased salivation, weight gain
nzapine *(Zyprexa)*		X		Weight gain
etiapine *(Seroquel)*		X	X	
peridone *(Risperdal)*			X	High doses can cause EPS
rasidone *(Geodon)*			X	Initial nausea and vomiting, dizziness

e 2. Antidepressant Medications

Tricyclic/Tetracyclic Antidepressants

dication *(Trade Name)*	ACH	Sedating	CV	Sexual Functioning	Other side effects and concerns
itriptyline *(Elavil)*	X	X	X	X	Potential Risk if pregnant
oxapine *(Asendin)*	X	X		X	Risk of EPS, NMS, and TD; seizure risk with overdose
mipramine *(Anafranil)*	X	X	X	X	Seizure risk at high doses
ipramine *(Norpramin)*					
xepin *(Sinequan, Adapin)*	X	X	X	X	
pramine *(Tofranil)*	X	X	X	X	Potential risk if pregnant
protiline *(Ludiomil)*	X	X		X	Increased risk of seizures at high doses
triptyline *(Pamelor)*	X	X		X	Potential risk if pregnant
triptyline *(Vivactil)*	X			X	
nipramine *(Surmontil)*	X	X	X	X	

2b. Monoamine Oxidase Inhibitors

Medication (Trade Name)	ACH	Sedating	CV	Sexual Functioning	Other side effects and concerns
Isocarboxazid (Marplan)	X		X	X	Agitation and insomnia, withdrawal reactio
Phenelzine (Nardil)	X	X	X	X	Withdrawal reactions
Tranylcypromine (Parnate)	X		X	X	Agitation and insomnia, withdrawal reactio

2c. Serotonin Reuptake Inhibitors (SSRIs)

Medication (Trade Name)	Sedating	Sexual Functioning	GI	Other side effects and concerns
Citalopram (Celexa)		X	X	
Fluoxetine (Prozac)		X	X	Agitation and insomnia, many drug interactions
Fluvoxamine (Luvox)	X	X	X	Withdrawal reactions
Paroxetine (Paxil)	X	X	X	Withdrawal reactions, weight gain, many drug interactions
Sertraline (Zoloft)		X	X	Nausea, diarrhea, agitation insomnia, increased blood pressure at high doses

2d. Other New Antidepressant Medications

Medication (Trade Name)	ACH	Sedating	CV	Sexual Functioning	GI	Other side effects and concerns
Venlafaxine (Effexor)				X	X	Nausea and diarrhea, agitation, insomnia withdrawal reactions
Nefazodone (Serzone)		X				Drug interactions
Trazodone (Desyrel)		X	X			
Mirtazapine (Remeron)	X	X	X			Sedation and weight gain at higher dose
Bupropion (Wellbutrin, Zyban)						Agitation, insomnia, possible seizure ris at high doses

Table 3. Mood-Stabilizing Medications

Medication (Trade Name)	Potential Side effects and Concerns
Carbamazepine (Tegretol)	Dizziness, unsteadiness, nausea, vision problems, fatigue, liver functioning, rashes, bloo disorder, water intoxication
Lithium carbonate (Eskalith, Lithobid)	Nausea, diarrhea, abnormal taste, fatigue, weight gain, tremors, increased urination, thirs hypothyroidism, acne, rashes, slurred speech, confusion, potential risk if pregnant
Valproic acid and derivatives (Depakene, Depakote)	Drowsiness, cramps, eating disorder, diarrhea, nausea, change in menstrual cycle, pancre atitis, prolonged bleeding time, liver functioning, tremors, hair loss, weight gain, potenti risk if pregnant
Gabapentin (Neurontin)	Drowsiness, dizziness, fatigue, lack of coordination, upset stomach, nausea, weight gain
Lamotrigine (Lamictal)	Dizziness, sedation, fatigue, weight loss, rashes, vision problems, photosensitivity (sensitiv to sunburns), lack of coordination
Oxcarbazepine (Trileptal)	Dizziness, sedation, fatigue, headache, nausea, vision problems, abdominal pain, abnorm gait, rash, water intoxication
Topiramate (Topamax)	Fatigue, dizziness, lack of coordination, memory problems, confusion, speech problems, nausea, abnormal sensations, tremor, vision problems, anxiety, kidney stones, depression abdominal pain, weight loss, muscle weakness, leg and back pain

le 4. Antianxiety Medications

Benzodiazepines

ızodiazepines have the potential side effects of dizziness, fatigue ataxia, memory impairment, depression, ıal problems, blurred vision, and lack of coordination.

neric Name *(Trade Name)*	Potential Side Effects	Additional Concerns
razolam *(Xanax)*	Typical Profile for Benzodiazepines	Potential risk if pregnant, severe withdrawal reactions if abruptly stopped
ordiazepoxide *(Librium)*	Typical Profile for Benzodiazepines	Potential risk if pregnant
nazepam *(Klonopin)*	Typical Profile for Benzodiazepines	
razepate *(Tranxene)*	Typical Profile for Benzodiazepines	Potential risk if pregnant
zepam *(Valium)*	Typical Profile for Benzodiazepines	Potential risk if pregnant
azepam *(Paxipam)*	Typical Profile for Benzodiazepines	Potential risk if pregnant
azepam *(Ativan)*	Typical Profile for Benzodiazepines	Potential risk if pregnant
ızepam *(Serax)*	Typical Profile for Benzodiazepines	
pirone *(BuSpar)*	Nausea, lightheadedness, headache restlessness	
ızolam *(ProSom)*	Typical Profile for Benzodiazepines	Contraindicated if pregnant
azepam *(Dalmane)*	Typical Profile for Benzodiazepines	Contraindicated if pregnant
zepam *(Doral)*	Typical Profile for Benzodiazepines	Contraindicated if pregnant
ıazepam *(Restoril)*	Typical Profile for Benzodiazepines	Contraindicated if pregnant
zolam *(Halcion)*	Typical Profile for Benzodiazepines	Contraindicated if pregnant

Nonbenzodiazepine (Hypnotics)

benzodiazepines have the potential side effects of headache, drowsiness, dizziness, nausea, diarrhea, muscle , memory confusion, falls and tremor

eric Name *(Trade Name)*	Potential Side Effects
plon *(Sonata)*	Typical Profile for nonbenzodiazepines
idem *(Ambien)*	Typical Profile for nonbenzodiazepines

CHAPTER 7

Treatment Part II: Psychosocial Rehabilitation and Components of a System of Care

"Success is not a doorway, it's a staircase."
—*Dottie Walters*

Beth C. Stoneking, Ph.D.

Before we talk about psychosocial rehabilitation, we need to discuss what is meant by a *system of care* and how the concept emerged. Having this historical perspective will be helpful in understanding the service system available in most communities for individuals with a serious mental illness.

WHAT IS A SYSTEM OF CARE?

Recognition of the need for a system of care grew out of *deinstitutionalization*, the release of thousands of individuals from state mental hospitals back to their local communities beginning in the 1960s.

Deinstitutionalization was based on the principle that a person with a mental illness should be treated in the least restrictive environment possible, in the community close to their families and friends. (See chapters 12 and 14 for additional discussion about deinstitutionalization.)

By the early '70s, however, newspaper articles, television documentaries and professional journal articles were reporting on the negative consequences of deinstitutionalization. Many individuals with a mental illness who had been discharged from state hospitals back to the community ended up homeless, in jail or in local psychiatric hospitals. They often received inadequate or no mental health care in the local community.

The problem with deinstitutionalization was not the concept itself, but rather the absence of supportive and rehabilitative programs in communities. The sad truth is that funding for community-based services did not follow those individuals who were discharged from state hospitals and sent back to the community.

In 1974, the National Institute of Mental Health (NIMH) responded to the problems by convening a task force to promote the development of organized, community-based systems of facilities and services. The overall goal of the new systems was to enable people with serious mental illnesses to remain in the community and to function at optimal levels of independence. The end product of the task force (which included administrators, high-level professionals, line staff, parents, family members and other key stakeholders) was the Community Support System. The Community Support System concept recognized that medications and inpatient treatment alone were not enough to achieve the goal of integrating individuals with a serious mental illness into the community. More community support was needed. Subsequently, the task force identified ten components of a community support system that were essential in order to effectively integrate individuals into the community.

- Medication
- Outreach
- Assistance in meeting basic human needs
- 24-hour crisis services
- Psychosocial and vocational services
- Rehabilitative and supportive housing
- Training and education
- Natural support systems (families, friends, churches, civic groups, etc.)
- Grievance procedures to protect the rights of individuals
- Case management

WHAT IS PSYCHOSOCIAL REHABILITATION?

Psychosocial rehabilitation focuses on teaching and supporting a person with a mental illness to develop the physical, emotional, social and intellectual skills necessary to live, work and manage their psychiatric symptoms in the community. The goal is for the person to function at his/her highest possible level in normal roles (e.g., employee, friend, student, mother/father, husband/wife).

Psychosocial rehabilitation programs operate under a core set of principles and values. Its cornerstones are that the service approach should be strength-based and the individual is considered an expert in their treatment.

A Strength-Based Recovery Approach

A strength-based approach focuses on identifying and then building on an individual's strengths and resources, as opposed to focusing on symptoms and problems. Symptoms and problems are more effectively addressed in the long run when the initial engagement begins by identifying the individual's strengths. Focusing on symptoms and problems is not only ineffective, but it also creates a paternalistic system in which individuals are made to feel dependent upon a mental health system.

Consumers as Experts in the Recovery Process

Having an individual participate as an expert in their treatment is critical if they are going to take responsibility for, and participate actively in, their recovery. Active participation is important because it is highly correlated with motivation. We know that when someone takes an active role in their treatment they are more motivated to achieve the goals that have been established. The process of having people become active in, and take responsibility for, their own recovery takes time and requires

85

patience on the part of the treatment team and family.

In addition to the two cornerstone principles, the International Association of Psychosocial Rehabilitation Services has identified other principles important to effective psychosocial rehabilitation. They are presented below to give you something against which to compare the principles of your family member's treatment provider.

- Recovery is the ultimate goal
- Every person has the capacity to learn, grow and change
- People are treated with dignity and respect
- Services are individualized to meet the unique needs of each person
- Involvement and partnership of the individual and the family is essential
- Practitioners should make conscious efforts to eliminate labeling, discrimination and stigma
- Culture and ethnicity are sources of strength and enrichment
- Services should be coordinated, accessible, and available for as long as needed
- Involvement in "normal" community activities is actively encouraged and supported

Now that we have talked about systems of care and philosophies underlying psychosocial rehabilitation, let's look at what makes up a system of care. The system that we are going to describe might not be exactly like the system in your community. Every community is unique. If however, yours is very different, it is important to find out why. Perhaps there is a very good reason, and your questions and the agency's response will be instructive. If you are not satisfied with the answers, Chapter 13 discusses the best approaches to addressing your dissatisfaction.

COMPONENTS OF A SYSTEM OF CARE[1]

There are eight parts to effective systems of care, and remember the parts are woven within the values and principles that were discussed above.

- Treatment planning
- Case management
- Housing
- Employment and education
- Counseling
- Crisis care
- Inpatient treatment
- Consumer-run programs

[1] This list does not include components necessary to deal with the issues of a dual diagnosis or medication. Those components are discussed in chapters 8 and 6 respectively.

Treatment Planning: The Foundation for All That Follows

The treatment plan is the foundation for all other parts of the system. It cannot be emphasized enough how important the treatment plan is. The plan is essentially a contract between your family member and the mental health system. The treatment plan, which is developed with the case manager and/or treatment team, should identify goals, and the services that need to be provided so that your family member can achieve those goals.

The plan should be very specific and indicate who will be doing what, as well as what the anticipated outcomes are. If you want to evaluate the quality of a system of care you generally don't need to go any further than the treatment planning process. If it is not taken seriously it is doubtful that an effective system of care can follow.

The staff in high-quality systems of care works with individuals to develop clear, concise plans where goals and strategies are targeted, thoughtful and measured. The staff in lower-quality systems develops plans that are general rather than specific and don't identify the strategies to achieve them.

The *process* of developing the treatment plan is often as important as the content. Your family member should take an active role in its development. The goals should be *theirs*, not goals that they accepted because a case manager or other staff member told them they were good goals.

People's needs and situations change over time. Consequently, treatment plans should be updated as changes occur. A rule of thumb is that the plan should be reviewed at least every six months and should become more sophisticated as the rehabilitation process progresses. It should address activities such as work exploration, social skills, housing, social supports, employment and member-run programs or self-help/peer support.

Case Management: The Glue That Holds It All Together

Case management is the glue that holds the components of the system together. A case manager (or sometimes a treatment team) is responsible for helping your family member make informed choices about the opportunities and services available. The case manager helps assure timely access to needed supports and coordinates services to meet the individual's goals.

The first step for the case manager is to engage or connect with your loved one in a way that fosters trust. Without a trusting relationship, outcomes and goals are rarely attained. The case manager should listen to your loved one's unique concerns, experiences, desires and goals. The case manager should also listen to the family. After all, you know your family member better than anyone else. Make it clear to the treatment team, and case manager in particular, that you want to participate in treatment planning. This will require your loved one's permission, and it is important to obtain this permission early in the treatment/rehabilitation process.

Several different models of case management exist, but those that use a treatment team approach tend to be the most effective because they use resources more effectively and have greater problem-solving capability.

The treatment team is most effective when its composition is multi-disciplinary, is culturally diverse and reflects the ethnic ratios of the community. Teams are often available to members 24 hours a day, seven days a week, allowing for intervention and support before a situation becomes a crisis. The best case management models provide services whenever and wherever they are needed. Thus if your family member cannot (or will not) go to the clinic, the clinic will go to him or her. A typical treatment team consists of the following:

- Case manager
- Housing specialist
- Rehabilitation specialist
- Vocational specialist
- Psychiatrist
- Nurse

Housing

Because of the significance of housing services, we have devoted an entire chapter to the discussion (Chapter 9).

Employment and Education

When we look back over our life experiences, we likely recall that we have met many of our friends, mentors and acquaintances at places we have worked or attended school. Recognizing that many persons with a mental illness experienced their first symptoms in their teens or early twenties and have had their education and early work experiences interrupted by mental illness, we realize they likely have a deficit that goes beyond the illness. For example, they have probably missed opportunities to develop supportive relationships and lifelong friendships.

Employment and education settings provide opportunities for meeting people and getting involved in activities that are both enjoyable and provide a social role beyond that of a person with a mental illness. These settings allow an individual to practice social skills, participate in sport activities and holiday celebrations, and serve on various boards and committees. Numerous studies have shown that involvement in normal activities increases self-esteem and overall life satisfaction. It also reduces psychiatric symptoms and the need for other costly mental health services. Typical employment and education activities within the system of care often include:

• Pre-vocational Services. Pre-vocational programs include work exploration experiences designed to develop job preparation skills. Pre-vocational opportunities include touring job sites, "job shadowing," volunteering and conducting informational interviews with employers. Some of the job preparation skills that are taught include completing job applications, interviewing techniques, appropriate work attire, appropriate manners in the workplace and conflict resolution.

• Employment Approaches and Models of Employment. Successfully obtaining and maintaining employment is not a straight line for a person with a mental illness. The person might require access to a wide range of support services to accommodate their needs. Fortunately, a variety of employment programs are available.

  - Sheltered workshops occur in structured program settings and generally involve contract work (often the assembly of products). The wages are paid by the sheltered workshop, not the company for whom the work is being completed. Sheltered Workshops are an older approach and have recently been excluded from receiving federal dollars.
  - Work adjustment has several levels and focuses on fostering positive work habits and attitudes, developing basic work skills (e.g., attendance, punctuality, task completion), and building work stamina. Work adjustment programs provide training in doing real work. As with sheltered workshops, participants receive wages from the work adjustment program, rather than from the company that contracts with the program.
  - Transitional employment opportunities generally, but not always, occur within the context of the *Clubhouse* model. The *Clubhouse* is a community of staff and members who work together on a daily basis to provide and receive services such as meals, companionship and skills training. Paid work is also an important aspect of the clubhouse. The clubhouse secures jobs in the community that are in turn filled by members of the clubhouse. Transitional employment is transitional in that it is ordinarily time limited, usually six to nine months. During transitional employment, members receive support (skills training and job coaching) as they acclimate to the work environment. In most

transitional employment programs there is an agreement with employers that someone on the clubhouse staff will fill in for an individual who, for whatever reason, is unable to work a particular shift. Because the clubhouse ordinarily has contracts with a number of employers, members have the opportunity to try out various types of employment opportunities to find where they have the best fit.

- Employment enclaves are also commonly known as supervised "work crews." They generally involve a community agency contracting with an employer to perform a specified job that is done by a group of members who are supervised by employment enclave staff. Examples of the type of work done by enclaves include janitorial work, landscaping and washing cars at a dealership.

- Supported employment programs assist individuals in identifying their strengths, areas of interest and goals. The programs work with individuals to develop the skills necessary to find employment opportunities, fill out applications and interview for jobs. Learning to cope with stress and work-related problems is also a focus of supported employment programs. The jobs that individuals get generally pay minimum wage, but are competitive jobs in that they are open to anyone in the community. The better supported employment programs help people recognize that they may have to try a number of different jobs before they find one they like.

• Supported Education and Training. Further education might be appropriate for some individuals. This might be completion of a GED or perhaps attending a trade school, junior college or even a university. The supported education programs function much like the supported employment programs in providing the individual with the skills and supports that they will need to be successful.

Counseling: What, When and When Not?

Many individuals with a mental illness also have problems and concerns (i.e., loneliness, suicidal behavior, substance abuse, depression) that respond to specific kinds of group or individual therapy. Some therapeutic approaches have proven to be more effective than others for individuals with a serious mental illness. The approaches that have been demonstrated to be the most effective are those that avoid exploration of psychological issues and focus psychosocial skills, emotional regulation skills, and distress tolerance skills. The behavioral and cognitive behavioral approaches that are the most effective often require the individual to do homework (practice the skills that are taught), thus involving him in the recovery process.

Crisis Care

A crisis system integrated into the rest of the system of care can lead to fewer hospitalizations and an increased ability to live independently in the community. An effective crisis system can also reduce the number of calls to police and sheriff's departments, avoiding trauma for all involved (see Chapter 12 for more about criminal justice system involvement). A comprehensive crisis system should include:

• Case Management: Teaching relapse prevention and support strategies before an individual has a psychiatric crisis can prevent or substantially reduce the magnitude of a crisis if one were to occur. An important role of the case manager is to work with you and your family member to come up with a crisis plan.

• Warmlines: Warmlines provide phone support to individuals who want to talk to someone. They have been demonstrated to be successful in helping individuals deal with situations before they become a crisis. Generally warmlines are operated by trained individuals who themselves have a mental illness. Individuals report feeling good about calling warmlines because they know that the person on the other end of the phone line understands what they are talking about.

• Mobile Crisis Teams: Calling the police or the sheriff's department is potentially dangerous for everyone involved. Having trained Mobile Crisis Teams with 24-hour availability for assessment and brief intervention is a better alternative.

• In-Home Supports: Having staff available to go into an individual's living situation has prevented many hospitalizations. The in-home support team usually consists of a nurse and another staff member or peer support specialist. The nurse will remain on site until the person is physically stable and medication concerns have been addressed. After the nurse leaves the staff person or peer-support specialist will stay to provide support and develop a crisis stabilization plan.

• Urgent Care (Crisis Stabilization Facilities): Urgent care facilities exist either as stand-alone programs or as programs located in hospital type settings. Urgent care and crisis stabilization programs focus on reducing the individual's symptoms, and ensuring that they are not dangerous to themselves or anyone else, and can provide for their basic needs. The time spent in urgent care facilities is generally less than 23 hours.

• Crisis Residential Facilities: Crisis residential facilities are less institutional than hospitals. They are designed to help individuals resolve an immediate crises, become stabilized on their medications and then, as soon as possible (few days to a couple of weeks), get back to their daily routine. A number of research studies have demonstrated that individuals treated in crisis residential care facilities for short-term crisis resolution improve more quickly than individuals with similar problems who are admitted to hospitals.

Inpatient Treatment

Improvements in medication and improved systems of care have resulted in fewer inpatient admissions. And when an individual is hospitalized the stay is relatively short (generally less than a week). If someone is hospitalized, however, it is an indication that their symptoms are acute enough that nothing less intensive is appropriate. And because someone believed that the symptoms were severe enough that a protective environment was necessary, it is important that your family member is not discharged before they are safe to be discharged. This means that they are safe both in terms of the symptoms that caused the hospitalization and the availability of a setting appropriate to go upon discharge. (See Chapter 9 for more about housing options.)

Consumer-run Programs

Consumer-run programs are becoming more and more important within the system of care. Consumer-run programs are programs that have consumers as staff, a consumer as the executive director and a board of directors whose majority membership consists of consumers of mental health services. While consumers fill the majority of positions, at times the consumer management may hire a professional manager who has specific credentials necessary to meet the requirements of a funding agency or credentialing body.

The consumer-run programs are important to your loved one for two reasons. First, they are run by peers, and the individuals working in the programs are likely to be very understanding of your family member's needs. Secondly, consumer-run programs provide a great opportunity for individuals to model positive behaviors. One of the most important messages a person learns in consumer-run programs is that in spite of mental illness individuals can be productive members of society.

Over the next decade we will likely see a significant increase in the number of consumer-run programs. We will also see more consumers having the opportunity to complete their education and obtain required credentials, and then be hired to fill more executive positions within the programs.

Dealing with Adversity

A daughter complained to her father about her life and how things were so hard for her. She did not know she was going to make it and wanted to give up. She was tired of fighting and struggling. It seemed as one problem was solved a new one arose. Her father, a chef, took her to the kitchen. He filled three pots with water and placed each on a high fire. Soon the pots came to a boil. In one he placed carrots, in the second he placed eggs, and in the last he placed ground coffee beans. He let them sit and boil, without saying a word. The daughter sucked her teeth and impatiently waited, wondering what he was doing. In about twenty minutes he turned off the burners. He fished the carrots out and placed them in a bowl. He pulled the eggs out and placed them in a bowl. Then he ladled the coffee out and placed it in a mug.

Turning to her, he asked, "Darling, what do you see?" "Carrots, eggs and coffee," she replied. He brought her closer and asked her to feel the carrots. She did and noted that they were soft. He then asked her to take an egg and break it. After pulling off the shell, she observed the hard-boiled egg. Finally, he asked her to sip the coffee. She smiled, as she tasted its rich aroma. She humbly asked, "What does it mean, father?" He explained that each of them had faced the same adversity, boiling water, but each reacted differently. The carrot went in strong, hard and unrelenting. But after being subjected to the boiling water, it softened and became weak. The egg had been fragile. Its thin outer shell had protected its liquid interior. But after sitting through the boiling water, its inside became hardened. The ground coffee beans were unique, however. After they were in the boiling water, they had changed the water. "Which are you?" he asked his daughter. "When adversity knocks on your door, how do you respond? Are you a carrot, an egg or a coffee bean?"

How about YOU, my friend?

Are you the carrot, which seems hard, but with pain and adversity do you wilt and become soft and lose your strength?

Are you the egg, which starts off with a malleable heart? Were you a fluid spirit, but after a death, a breakup, a divorce or a layoff have you become hardened and stiff? Your shell looks the same, but are you bitter and tough with a stiff spirit and heart?

Or are you the coffee bean? The bean changes the hot water, the thing that is bringing the pain, to its peak flavor when it reaches the boiling point. When the water gets the hottest, it just tastes better. If you are like the bean, when things are at their worst, you get better and make things better around you.

How do you handle adversity? Are you a carrot, an egg or a coffee bean?

Reprinted with permission of Afterhours Inspirational Stories

CHAPTER 8

Mental Illness and Substance Abuse: Making Matters Worse

"When you come to the end of your rope, tie a knot and hang on."
—Franklin Delano Roosevelt

Michael Franczak, Ph.D.
Christina Dye

As discussed in Chapter 3, when a loved one is diagnosed with schizophrenia or other serious mental illness, families go through a number of feelings and stages including denial, bargaining, anger and depression. Because of the stigma associated with mental illness, guilt and shame might also be experienced. For parents, learning that their son or daughter has a serious mental illness can also bring about a curious sense of relief.

While the diagnosis can be both frightening and overwhelming, there is relief in finally having an explanation for their child's odd, and sometimes even bizarre, behavior and for the problems he or she was having.

The diagnosis puts a name and label to a previously confusing set of behaviors and symptoms. The diagnosis also implies that their loved one has an illness, and because it is an illness there is a good chance he can be treated.

Then for some families the other shoe drops. There might be the late-night call from the police informing them that their loved one has been taken to a local detoxification facility with a cocaine overdose, or is in jail on a drug possession charge. For other families there might be signs of progressively problematic drinking.

The initial diagnosis of a serious mental illness can feel like a cold slap across the face, but the added revelation that their loved one also suffers an addiction disorder is more than many parents can bear. Mental illness is bad enough, but alcoholism and drug addiction are definitely *things that happen to other people*. While society has become more aware that mental illness is a brain disorder, substance abuse is still often associated with personal choice, criminal and/or moral issues.

Until recently, systems of care for mental health and substance abuse were designed as if the two disorders never met. Treatment was different in terms of funding sources, admission criteria and treatment philosophies. At times the differing philosophies led to treatment approaches that conflicted with each other. Professionals were trained to provide mental health services or substance abuse services, but rarely trained to provide both.

Yet, while professionals continued to work within their traditional areas of expertise, people referred for treatment were increasingly displaying symptoms of both mental illness and substance abuse. In fact, it's generally recognized today that in both treatment systems, *co-occurring disorders are the expectation, not the exception*. Estimates are that at least half of the individuals who have a serious mental illness also have a co-occurring addiction disorder.

This blurring of the lines between mental illness and addiction is the hallmark of a co-occurring disorder. Persons with a co-occurring disorder experience a magnification of social, health and behavioral problems compared to individuals with a mental illness alone. Not only are they far more likely to be homeless or victims of violence, but they have higher rates of HIV, syphilis and other sexually transmitted diseases. Among women who have a mental illness with a co-occurring addiction disorder, 85 percent have been victims of violence.

Individuals with co-occurring disorders are also a treatment challenge. They are hospitalized more frequently, use mental health crisis services more often and attempt suicide more often than individuals with a mental illness only.

This chapter is intended to serve as a guide to help you understand the dynamics of co-occurring disorders. We will discuss both the issues underlying co-occurring disorders and the interventions and treatment options. We will discuss the family's role in working with treatment providers, and practical steps you can take to assist in your family member's recovery. Our bottom line for dealing with co-occurring disorders is that families must ensure that their loved one is working with a team of professionals that is expert in dealing with both illnesses.

WHAT IS A CO-OCCURRING DISORDER?

Typically, a co-occurring disorder is defined as "the simultaneous presence of two primary conditions or diagnoses: substance abuse (or substance dependence) and a mental health disorder." And as mentioned above, a co-occurring disorder should not be considered an exception to the norm. It is quite common. We have just used a lot of jargon. Here is what we mean by some of the terms:

- The conditions are *simultaneous* in that treating one does not preclude active treatment for the other.
- The conditions are also both *primary* in that one is not more important than the other in developing treatment plans.
- *Substance abuse* is a pattern of maladaptive use of alcohol and other drugs. A characteristic of substance abuse is the continued use of substances in situations which continuously place the individual at risk of harm to themselves or others.
- *Substance dependence* is a disorder of the brain resulting in thought, behavior and emotional dysfunction, as well as physical reliance on continued doses of a drug. The tendency or vulnerability for substance dependence can be hereditary or result from excessive exposure to the substance. The hallmark of substance dependence disorders is the inability to control or curtail use despite severe, potentially fatal, consequences.

For families of a person with a co-occurring disorder, the message is clear – their family member suffers from two primary brain disorders that interact in complex ways. Symptoms of one disorder can trigger a relapse of the other. Individuals with a co-occurring disorder are a vulnerable population, and without intervention experience high mortality rates.

ASSESSMENT FOR CO-OCCURRING DISORDERS

At the heart of good treatment is a meaningful treatment plan. The heart of a meaningful treatment plan is, in turn, a comprehensive, accurate diagnosis. Herein lies a dilemma. The condition is difficult to diagnose. The diagnosis of a mental illness is much more difficult when an individual is also abusing drugs or alcohol. It is not uncommon for an individual's first contact with the mental health system to occur when the police bring her to the emergency room because she is acting odd and causing a disturbance. If she is intoxicated, the effect of the drugs and or alcohol must be ruled out as a cause before she can be diagnosed as having a mental illness. If she is dismissed as "just a substance abuser," without an adequate evaluation for a co-occurring mental illness, it is quite likely that she will not receive the appropriate services.

The clinician doing the diagnostic assessment will attempt to obtain a detailed history. This includes the age when symptoms of a mental illness first appeared and the pattern of symptoms during any period of sustained abstinence or reduced use of alcohol and drugs. The clinician doing the assessment will also try to identify those substances that are capable of producing the symptoms exhibited and determine whether the individual used them in the recent past.

While sources of information for the assessment are varied and can include your family member's self-report, past treatment records and urine screening tests, the role of the family in assisting the assessment process is critical. You are the best historian both in terms of your loved one's symptoms and any family history of alcoholism or drug abuse. If discussing family substance abuse is uncomfortable, it's okay to present it as an issue for a distant relative—a cousin, or great-aunt or grandfather.

The specific of *who* was affected by substance disorder is not as important as identifying whether a family pattern exists.

The consensus of experts is that the presence of one of the co-occurring disorders is a risk factor for the other. Certain substances, most notably stimulants (such as cocaine or crack methamphetamine), alcohol and narcotics (heroin), can trigger full-blown psychotic states or magnify particular symptoms of mental illness. Cocaine, for example, can worsen the delusions of an individual with schizophrenia. Additionally, alcohol and other drugs can interact with prescribed medications and reduce their therapeutic effects. Likewise, mental illness can lead to substance abuse, as the person begins to use substances to self medicate (in an attempt to relieve the symptoms of mental illness or the side effects of medications).

Unfortunately, in the long run, substances make both psychiatric symptoms and medication side effects even worse.

Attempting to sort out the interactions of mental illness and substance disorder symptoms to arrive at an accurate clinical profile is neither rapid nor simple. In most cases, the disorders are simultaneous and jointly contribute to the individual's symptoms.

In a large number of cases, even the best and most detailed assessment will not fully support the diagnosis of a serious mental illness, and if the individual does not abstain or reduce substance use, it might be impossible to isolate the symptoms of one disorder from the other.

INDIVIDUALS WITH CO-OCCURRING DISORDERS CAN RECOVER

Early assessment and focused treatment for co-occurring disorders is critical to your loved one's health, safety and well-being. More than 30 years of research supports the fact that treatment for substance abuse disorders effectively reduces drug and alcohol consumption, improves social and occupational functioning and lessens criminal involvement. However, research is equally clear that individuals with co-occurring disorders are among the most challenging populations to treat. Studies consistently indicate that this population is non-compliant with treatment. As a consequence, the individuals frequently relapse in both substance use and psychiatric symptoms.

COMPONENTS OF HIGH-QUALITY INTEGRATED TREATMENT

If your loved one is enrolled in services for a co-occurring disorder, the system of care should consist of several ingredients. While not all programs meet all of the criteria described below, the more criteria it meets, the greater the likelihood of a positive outcome.

• A Welcoming and Accessible Treatment System. The system should not treat individuals as if they are the blame for their illness. There should also be an acceptance of relapse. Relapse happens, and individuals should not be made to feel as though they have failed.

• Integrated Service Delivery. Individuals should receive both mental health services and substance abuse services concurrently within one comprehensive system of care. The treatment plan should be very specific in addressing how the individual will be simultaneously treated for both disorders. A rule of thumb is that whenever a psychiatric disorder and substance disorder coexist, *both disorders should be considered primary* and receive customized, simultaneous treatment.

- Assertive Outreach and Intensive Case Management. The case manager working with your loved one should have the qualifications to work with individuals who have a dual diagnosis. They should also work tirelessly to maintain routine contact. Since both substance and psychiatric relapse can occur quickly, the case manager should have frequent face-to-face contact and rapidly intervene when signs of relapse appear. A single treatment team for both illnesses is very important. It should focus on a long-term relationship with your loved one. The team must have experience dealing with individuals who have difficult, complex problems including homelessness and non-compliance.

- Comprehensive Range of Services. For people with co-occurring disorders, the risk for recurring psychiatric symptoms and relapse is quite high. Treatment plans and treatment agencies must be flexible in identifying and providing services to match your family member's ever-changing needs.

- An Emphasis on Engagement and Motivation. Too often treatment programs demand that individuals show up ready for treatment on the first day, as if they were appearing for a job interview. Instead, the first task for the treatment team should be helping the individual prepare for treatment. This can be done by helping her identify reasons for not using substances, attending treatment sessions, and taking her prescribed medication. Engagement in treatment is a combination of coaxing, coaching and consequences. The staff should be prepared to spend a great deal of time helping people with co-occurring disorders understand and manage their illnesses. This can be a slow process, and families need to be aware that there is no quick fix.

- Awareness That People Pass Through Stages of Treatment. Treatment should be viewed as a process, rather than an event. It begins with engagement and initial stabilization, moves on to active intervention and support, and is followed by recovery. Individuals may move in and out of stages, and even move backward. Change takes time and requires hard work by both the treatment team and your loved one. The treatment team and family should accept relapse as well as success. People with co-occurring disorders may spend months just in the stage of initial engagement.

- Frequent Review of Medications. Prescribed medications should be reviewed frequently and adjusted based on observed effects and individual comfort level. When possible, the psychiatrist should select medications for both their anticraving and psychotherapeutic effect.

- Ongoing Assessment and Treatment Plan Updates. Treatment teams should regularly review the treatment plan with the individual. Both progress and relapse should be documented and treatment evaluated in the context of how specific services contributed to either outcome.

The above principles are to some extent dependent upon a system of care, not just qualified, caring staff. An area where families can get involved is ensuring that the system of care in their community supports the above principles.

Finally, an empathic, hopeful and long-term relationship is a key principle of co-occurring disorder treatment. The single most important strand in the web of relationships supporting a person with a co-occurring disorder is maintaining ties unconditionally over time. This unconditional support is necessary even though the individual may not follow treatment recommendations, may experience multiple crises and may vary in his or her degree of success in maintaining sobriety.

FAMILIES MUST BE INVOLVED AND TREATMENT TEAMS MUST HAVE EXPERTISE

Families can play an active role in the treatment and recovery of their loved one simply by being aware of his or her special needs and the increased risk for relapse. Four areas where families can have an impact are:

- Advocating for Expertise on the Treatment Team
- Participating Actively in Treatment Planning
- Creating Timelines
- Having a Long-Term View

Advocating for Expertise on the Treatment Team

Families should do all they can to make sure that psychiatrist and other treatment staff address both disorders in their loved one's treatment plan and treatment. Your family member's clinical team should demonstrate competence in treating individuals with a co-occurring disorder. Look for the presence of a certified substance abuse counselor on the treatment team. Chapter 14 provides information and tips about how to work with treatment teams and the steps you can take if you believe that your family member is not getting the care you believe they should receive.

Participating in Treatment Planning

Any treatment plan for co-occurring disorders should be framed around outcomes that are fully supported by you and your loved one. Initially, outcomes may be focused on "discovery" activities that assist your loved one in understanding that her use of substances is problematic and tends to escalate her symptoms. Initially, outcomes might be incremental. That is, there will likely be many small steps along the path to reducing substance use patterns. The initial step in changing substance use patterns is reducing harm to the individual. Defining the pattern of use that is non-harmful might require numerous successive attempts. The treatment plan should consider the severity of the mental illness and your loved one's symptoms when she is using drugs and when she is not. In all cases, regardless of specifics, your family member must be an active member of the team.

Treatment plans should, when appropriate, include strategies that the family can employ at home for improving medication compliance and reducing the use of alcohol and other substances. It is often helpful to set daily or weekly goals for reducing drinking and drug use and assisting your loved one in identifying skills and strategies for achieving abstinence. "Contingency contracting" is an approach to intervention that has been demonstrated to be effective in substance abuse treatment. It involves your loved one agreeing to specific rewards for achieving a goal and specific consequences for not achieving it. This technique can be used both at home and at the clinic. Even goals that are not met can bring about discovery and deeper understanding. A philosophy underlying co-occurring disorders is that people do not fail. Success might not come quickly, but when it does the individual is rewarded.

It is important to understand that there is a big difference between *not yet succeeding* and *failing*.

Creating Timelines

It may be helpful to create a timeline with your loved one that identifies serious events, such as a hospitalization or an arrest, and map the conditions that led up to the incident. Conditions to consider include a change in the type or frequency of substance use, health issues and periods of increased stress. Timelines are useful in creating a visual picture that pieces the various parts together. With the information derived from a timeline, the individual has a better chance of controlling or managing his behaviors.

Having a Long-Term View

A long-term view is at the heart of successful interventions and recovery. Family members should assume that multiple treatment episodes are the norm. An individual with a co-occurring disorder frequently requires gradually increasing amounts of treatment as she becomes more accepting. She also needs extensive case management and community support on her road to recovery. For the most seriously disabled, treatment interventions must be simple, concrete and use role rehearsals and other repetitive activities. Involvement in peer recovery groups such as Alcoholics Anonymous, Double Trouble and Dual Recovery can be helpful for many individuals. Such programs help maintain stability and support relationships with non-substance-abusing friends. Most recovery groups also offer support for family members for sharing concerns and identifying solutions in an environment of hope and empowerment. Your family member's treatment team should be able to connect you with family support groups in your community.

Letter to My Case Manager

I thought I would drop you a few lines to let you know about someone that I have come to know intimately. She is pleasing to the eye and can be found at the AA meetings. I'm very glad I got to know her. I have been looking for her all my life and can't help but believe God has put her in my life. I don't think I can live without her because she brings so much peace into my life and makes living more rewarding. When I embrace her, which I love to do, I feel love like I have never felt before.

When I look in her eyes it seems like I have known her before; how strange.

I can't believe it took so long to find her. I just know she was somewhere out there waiting for me. All of the staff here know her well and feel that she will be good for me.

It's nice to have their support in this special relationship and they are happy for me, I am sure. I feel I can trust her endlessly. She will always be there for me—or so she says. All I have to do is reach out to her. Her popularity in the AA circle is uncanny. You might have heard of her—her name is sobriety.

Submitted by T.L.

Just Keep Planting

Paul Rokich is my hero. When Paul was a boy growing up in Utah, he happened to live near an old copper smelter, and the sulfur dioxide that poured out of the refinery had made a desolate wasteland out of what used to be a beautiful forest. When a young visitor one day looked at this wasteland and saw that there was nothing living there—no animals, no trees, no grass, no bushes, no birds...nothing but 14,000 acres of black and barren land that even smelled bad—well, this kid looked at the land and said, "This place is crummy." Paul knocked him down. He felt insulted. But he looked around him and something happened inside him. He made a decision: Paul Rokich vowed that someday he would bring back the life to this land.

Many years later Paul was in the area, and he went to the smelter office. He asked if they had any plans to bring the trees back. The answer was "No." He asked if they would let him try to bring the trees back. Again, the answer was "No." They didn't want him on their land.

He realized he needed to be more knowledgeable before anyone would listen to him, so he went to college to study botany.

At the college he met a professor who was an expert in Utah's ecology.

Unfortunately, this expert told Paul that the wasteland he wanted to bring back was beyond hope. He was told that his goal was foolish, because even if he planted trees, and even if they grew, the wind would only blow the seeds 40 feet per year, and that's all you'd get because there weren't any birds or squirrels to spread the seeds. And the seeds from those trees would need another 30 years before they started producing seeds of their own. Therefore, it would take approximately 20,000 years to revegetate that six-square-mile piece of earth. His teachers told him it would be a waste of his life to try to do it. It just couldn't be done.

So Paul tried to go on with his life. He got a job operating heavy equipment, got married, and had some kids. But his dream would not die. He kept studying up on the subject, and he kept thinking about it. And then one night he got up and took some action. He did what he could with what he had. This was an important turning point. As Samuel Johnson wrote, "It is common to overlook what is near by keeping the eye fixed on something remote. In the same manner, present opportunities are neglected and attainable good is slighted by minds busied in extensive ranges."

Paul stopped busying his mind in extensive ranges and looked at what opportunities for attainable good were right in front of him. Under the cover of darkness, he sneaked out into the wasteland with a backpack full of seedlings and started planting. For seven hours he planted seedlings. He did it again a week later. And every week, he made his secret journey into the wasteland and planted trees and shrubs and grass. But most of it died. For 15 years he did this. When a whole valley of his fir seedlings burned to the ground because of a careless sheepherder, Paul broke down and wept. Then he got up and kept planting.

Freezing winds and blistering heat, landslides, floods and fires destroyed his work time and time again. But he kept planting. One night he found a highway crew had come and taken tons of dirt for a road grade, and all the plants he had painstakingly planted in that area were gone. But he just kept planting. Week after week, year after year he kept at it, against the opinion of the authorities, against the trespassing laws, against the devastation of road crews, against the wind and rain and heat...even against plain common sense. He just kept planting. Slowly, very slowly, things began to take root. Then gophers appeared. Then rabbits. Then porcupines.

The old copper smelter office eventually gave him permission, and later, as times were changing and there was political pressure to clean up the environment, the company actually hired Paul to do what he was already doing, and they provided him with machinery and crews to work with. Progress accelerated. Now the place is 14,000 acres of trees and grass and bushes, rich with elk and eagles, and Paul Rokich has received almost every environmental award Utah has.

He says, "I thought that if I got this started, when I was dead and gone people would come and see it. I never thought I'd live to see it myself!" It took him until his hair turned white, but he managed to keep that impossible vow he made to himself as a child. What was it you wanted to do that you thought was impossible? Paul's story sure gives a perspective on things, doesn't it?

The way you get something accomplished in this world is to just keep planting. Just keep working. Just keep plugging away at it one day at a time for a long time, no matter who criticizes you, no matter how long it takes, no matter how many times you fall. Get back up again. And just keep planting. Just keep planting.

Reprinted with permission of Afterhours Inspirational Stories

CHAPTER 9

Housing Issues

"In the middle of difficulty lies opportunity."
—Albert Einstein

Barbara Montrose, BSBA

For nearly all families who have a member with a serious mental illness, housing becomes an issue at one time or another. For some families, housing seems like a never-ending concern. One day their family member is living in a group home. The next day, they are missing and later found in a homeless shelter. The family works hard to secure new housing arrangements. But the new housing lasts for just a short time and their family member is again living in the streets.

For other families, housing is an intermittent problem. When housing is the issue, however, it is a major problem. There is no such thing as a minor housing crisis. Lack of adequate housing, or worse yet, homelessness can be a primal fear for families. It is hard to imagine many things more troubling than wondering if your loved one has a roof over his/her head. Some specific thoughts may run through a family member's mind:
Is he living in a safe environment? Will he do something to get himself evicted from his apartment? How is she going to take her medication if she doesn't have anyplace to store it? How is she going to afford a rent increase? How can we have him live with us, when all we do is fight and argue when he lives at home?

Unstable housing and homelessness are more than idle worries.

Homelessness and mental illness are related. Between 20 and 25 percent of the adult homeless population suffers from a serious mental illness. At any one time, approximately 200,000 individuals with a serious mental illness are also homeless. Other individuals with a serious mental illness live in substandard housing, unsafe situations or are barely hanging on to not being homeless.

On the positive side, there are far more housing options for individuals with a mental illness than there were only a few years ago. As systems of care have moved to strengthen community-based services, numerous housing alternatives have been developed. In this chapter we will identify the types of issues that should be considered when evaluating various housing options. After addressing the issues, we will review the housing options that exist. Keep in mind that no one option is necessarily better than any of the others. All have pros and cons depending upon an individual's needs at the time…and needs can fluctuate.

ISSUES TO BE CONSIDERED

There are five important issues to consider when thinking about housing options for someone with a severe mental illness.

• Safety: While safe housing is important for everyone, it is especially important for someone with a mental illness. Some of the specifics to consider in evaluating housing safety include the presence of smoke detectors, cleanliness, locks on doors and an environment where the individual is less likely to be victimized.

• Structure/Support: Some individuals require a great deal of structure in their living arrangements to remain compliant with treatment and have the ability for self care. For other individuals, too much structure can either scare them away from systems of care, or stifle and hinder their own recovery.

• Socialization: Socialization is important for both pure enjoyment of life, as well as for learning and practicing social skills. Individuals who lack outlets for social activities might do well in a living environment where such activities are included.

• Location: Location is important particularly if the individual does not have access to private transportation. Location does not necessarily mean a particular part of town, but rather convenience to bus routes, shopping, parks and possibly a library and other sources of recreation.

• Cost: The cost of housing is always an issue. Programs to help cover costs are addressed later in this chapter. (Much of Chapter 11 is also devoted to the issue of obtaining entitlements to help your loved one with finances.)

HOUSING OPTIONS

There are a number of alternatives for housing, none of which are necessarily better or worse than any other. At different times, different housing choices might be appropriate. The option that is most appropriate today might not be the most appropriate option tomorrow. Housing options include the following:

• Living With Family
• Housing as Part of a Treatment Program
• Board and Care Homes
• Transitional Housing
• Independent Living

Living With the Family

One option for some families is to have the loved one live with the family. This might mean living with parents, siblings or with someone in the extended family. There are advantages to living with family, but there are also complications. The obvious advantage of an individual with a mental illness living with family is the increased likelihood of safety, support, the availability of nutritious meals, medication monitoring and the opportunity to socialize with people who are understanding. Living with family is also going to cost less than many other options.

There are, however, potential concerns. Some of the concerns would exist for any adult living with his/her family of origin. Problems that go along with not separating from family, such as lack of privacy and potential over-involvement, are possible. There are also issues of the individual's mental illness. There may be times when the family member is too disruptive or the tension in the household becomes intolerable. If the individual with a mental illness is going to live with the family, it is important to have a frank discussion concerning household rules and privacy. (Chapter 5 can help with this process.)

Housing as Part of a Treatment Program

There can be times that an individual might need the added support of a treatment program to assist them with day-to-day living skills. This is an option for someone who does not need the protection or intensity of a hospital, but is too vulnerable to live independently. Without the daily support and monitoring of a system of care, the individual would quite likely have an extreme exacerbation of his illness.

Within the context of treatment programs, there are housing options that vary in structure, from quite restrictive to significant independence. In most systems of care, individuals can move up and down a continuum of restrictiveness depending upon their needs. Some of the specific programs to discuss with your family member's treatment team include the following:

• Safe Havens: Safe Havens were developed by the Department of Housing and Urban Development (HUD) to provide housing and other support (such as food, clothing and personal care items) to individuals who are homeless, have a severe mental illness and have been unwilling to accept treatment. There is usually no cost associated with Safe Havens, and they provide safety and stability while being non-intrusive, low-demand environments. A goal of the Safe Haven is to prepare the individual to move to more independent levels of housing in the future.

• Short-Term Crisis Residential: There are numerous crisis residential treatment programs that can help provide stability when an individual is in crisis. After the crisis has been resolved, the individual can return to a previous residence or move to a supervised or semi-supervised setting.

• Supervised and Semi-Supervised Settings: In supervised and semi-supervised living arrangements, individuals live with other individuals under the supervision of a treatment program. This housing option is appropriate for an individual who might not be totally safe if living independently, who requires structure to care of daily needs, and/or who needs assistance with medication monitoring. The difference between supervised and semi-supervised setting is the number of staff available and the number of hours during a 24-hour period that staff are available.

Board and Care Homes

Board and Care homes were once an important housing option in our country. While they have lost their popularity with the general population, they remain a critical option for many people with a serious mental illness. Some of the better homes provide social activities and medication monitoring as well as a room and food. In almost all cases, however, Board and Care homes are separate from the mental health system. In most communities, there are no licensing requirements to operate a Board and Care home. Consequently, it is incumbent upon you to make sure that the facility is safe and clean.

Even though Board and Care homes are not part of the official mental health system, your family member's treatment team is likely to know of the better homes, and which homes to avoid.

Transitional Housing

HUD's transitional housing programs are designed for individuals whose behavior has resulted in them being homeless. If your family member has been kicked out of various residential settings and even asked to leave emergency shelters for the homeless, he might be appropriate for transitional housing. The goal of transitional housing is to help the person learn the skills necessary to maintain housing and be able to move to permanent housing within 24 months. Transitional housing programs do require the individual to pay a portion of their income toward their rent.

Independent Living

Another housing option for your family member is to live independently. The advantage of independent living is "normalization," which is a major step toward recovery. If independent living is the best option and finances are an issue, there are programs that can provide assistance. HUD Offices, City and County Public Housing Authorities, and your family member's treatment team can help you to connect with the various programs.

• Emergency Household Assistance: Most communities receive federal Community Services Block Grants to fund emergency household financial assistance programs. Some local governments operate these programs themselves while others allocate funds to community agencies. These funds can help with rent and deposits, utilities and emergency housing repair.

• Shelter Plus Care: Shelter Plus Care is another HUD program. It is designed to link rental assistance and supportive services for low-income persons with disabilities who are at risk of being homeless. (If your family member is living with you, but the situation is no longer tenable, an "eviction" letter from you should serve as notice they will soon be homeless—thus making them eligible for Shelter Plus Care.)

As with the transitional housing, the Shelter Plus Care resident must pay a portion of her income toward the rent. The major difference between Shelter Plus Care and transitional housing is that transitional housing is available for up to 24 months, whereas Shelter Plus Care is considered permanent housing.

• Public Housing: The housing authority in most cities maintains an inventory of affordable housing, which is provided to an individual for a percentage of his income. In some communities additional services, such as food stamp sign-up, delivery of food boxes and transportation might be provided at the housing sites.

• Section 8 Housing Assistance: Section 8 is funded by HUD and is probably the largest rental assistance program in the country. Although the majority of Section 8 units are for any low-income individual, many communities allocate some units specifically for low-income persons who are disabled.

Section 8 units may be "place-based" or "tenant-based." Place-based means that the assistance is tied to a specific building or units within a building. Tenant-based means that assistance is portable and the individual can move from one approved facility to another. Tenant-based is often a good option and can make an important difference to someone who likes to move; they would lose their Section 8 housing if it was place-based.

The most important things for you to remember about independent living housing assistance programs are:

- There can be long waiting lists so find out what is available and get on the lists.
- For some programs, applications are accepted only on certain days and only at certain times on those days.
- Your local HUD office (and the HUD Web site) and city and county public housing authorities can provide you with information about the programs.
- Your family member's treatment team should be knowledgeable and have expertise concerning housing programs.

Our Thanksgiving

Thanksgiving is my favorite time of year. I'm not sure if it's because of crispness in the air, the food, the opportunity to visit with family, or a combination of everything. All I know is that I love it. And of all the Thanksgivings we have had, the one we had five years ago will stay with me forever.

My niece has schizophrenia. She is one of the fortunate ones. From the time she was first diagnosed, she has always done fairly well. She takes her medication faithfully and works very hard to maintain an apartment.

She has a cat she calls MFP (for My Fuzzy Pill). There have been some rough times with her illness, but on the whole she has really done very well. She is the person whom her psychiatrist turns to when he needs someone with schizophrenia to meet with parents who have just had a son or daughter diagnosed. This new family is usually over-whelmed, and she helps them feel reassured by showing them that schizophrenia does not mean "no hope." People with schizophrenia can be "normal."

The consumer-run day program where my niece is a peer mentor was planning a large feast. Turkeys, stuffing, mashed potatoes, cranberry sauce—all the trimmings. There would be enough food to feed between 20 and 30 people. Two weeks before Thanksgiving Day, an electrical short caused a minor fire and damaged the electrical system. The damage was not extensive. No one was hurt, but the repairs and inspection by the fire marshal were going to take longer than expected and would not be completed by Thanksgiving.

I had never discussed my niece's illness with our neighbors. I live in a condominium community, and while I share pleasantries with others, we are somewhat private people. But I was so upset about the fire and about my niece missing Thanksgiving with her friends that I shared my feelings with some of the women with whom I play bridge. To my surprise I learned that one woman has a son living in another state who has schizophrenia and another woman has a daughter who is a psychologist.

Well, things moved quickly, and within 24 hours of my sharing my niece's plight, five of us who live in the complex made plans. We decided to invite my niece and her friends to our activity/recreation room for a feast. I talked to my niece and two other peer mentors, as well as the administrator of the program. We assigned tasks, prepared a menu and were on our way. Word spread fast, and within a couple of days we had more volunteers than we had jobs. We had a retired couple whose children live out of state who wanted to join in. We had other neighbors who just wanted to do something for someone else.

On Thanksgiving Day we had 12 individuals from the consumer-run program, nine of their family members and 12 residents of the condominium community sharing a wonderful time. The room was filled with joy. It was a big hit. In fact, our dinner created so much interest that the following year there were more people who wanted to participate than we would have room for. With less than adequate room in our activity room, we turned our "new tradition" into a progressive dinner.

Next year will be our sixth annual "Progressive Thanksgiving," as we call it. We have more than 100 participants. Some are patients, some are family members, some are employees and volunteers of the day program, and others are residents of the condominium community and their families.

Submitted by B.B.

CHAPTER 10

Health Care and Wellness

"Health always seems much more valuable after we lose it."
—Unknown

Thank you to Eli Lilly and Company for allowing us to make use of their publication, *Solutions to Wellness*, in the preparation of this chapter.

Michael R. Berren, Ph.D.
Kathleen A. Oldfather, MSN, ANP, GNP

The good news is that your health is about the same as someone in your age group who does not have a mental illness. The bad news is that means you are overweight and have high cholesterol.

The initial concerns that a family ordinarily has about a loved one with a mental illness generally revolve around the psychiatric symptoms and related behaviors. After dealing with the immediate issues of the illness, the financial and legal concerns (addressed in Chapters 12 and 13) often become a priority. Over time, many families get involved in the recovery of the family members and improving systems of care in the community.

It is only later that the family begins to learn that their loved one with a mental illness might also have more physical problems than does the general population. Individuals with a mental illness are more likely than the general population to get ill, to have accidents, and to have serious complications from their illnesses and accidents. And in spite of their needs, individuals with mental illness are also less likely to get appropriate health care.

As a consequence, individuals with a mental illness tend to die nearly 15 to 20 years younger than do their peers in the general population. A review article summarizing over 60 professional publications indicates that the rate of mortality for individuals with a mental illness ranges from two to four times that of the general population. A number of studies suggest that the mortality rate of individuals with mental illness is *10 times higher* for non-natural causes of death such as accidents, suicides and homicides than it is for individuals without mental illnesses.

In this chapter, we will discuss some of the reasons for the poor health status and high mortality rate of individuals with a mental illness. More importantly, we will address interventions and wellness activities that can result in better physical health and improve the likelihood of a long life.

Quite honestly, we were somewhat hesitant to include this chapter in the book. The argument for not including it is that dealing with the psychiatric symptoms of mental illness is difficult enough. To tell families, "By the way, in addition to the mental health problems, lifestyle consequences and stigma that your family member is going to be facing, your family member is likely to have health care problems," seemed a heavy burden. On the other hand, because problems with health and difficulty receiving health care is a reality for many individuals with a mental illness, avoiding the topic and not taking the opportunity to provide some strategies for dealing with health-related issues seemed unfair. So as you read about the health and health care problems, please remember that we are presenting the information not to raise concerns that cannot be dealt with, but to help you understand the problem and be prepared to handle it.

The model for this chapter (and really the model for many other chapters in this book) parallels the story of Charles Dickens' Scrooge in "A Christmas Carol." As you likely remember, Scrooge was taken on a tour of Christmas Past, Christmas Present and Christmas Future. In his visit to Christmas Future, he witnessed his employee Bob Cratchit and his family having a sparse and sad Christmas dinner. Their son Tiny Tim was not present. His crutch, sitting over by the side of the room was the only reminder that he had once existed. At the end of the visit to Christmas Future, Scrooge wanted to know if the future was cast in stone or if things could be changed? He indicated that after this long night he was a new man and wanted a chance to help the Cratchit family. The ghost of Christmas Future informed him that he *could in fact* do things that would change what he had witnessed in the Christmas dinner scene where Tiny Tim had died. The visit to the future wasn't a picture of things that had to be, only things that might be.

Likewise is the threat for the potential health-related problems of individuals with a mental illness. While the data is quite clear that the likelihood of poor health is much higher for an individual with a mental illness, steps can be taken to ensure the best health status possible for the individual. Individuals and families have it within their power to promote good health. I am not saying that you can help in all areas. But you might be able to in some.

A question that you might be asking yourself is "Why do individuals with a mental illness have a greater incidence of illness and accidents?"

First, mental illness in and of itself is probably not a direct cause of poor health status. It is unlikely that a gene or other abnormality that causes mental illness also causes poor health status. Rather, it is likely that the poor health status and higher mortality rate are caused by other factors that are in turn related to mental illness. That is, while mental illness does not directly cause persons to be unhealthy, factors that are associated with mental illness are likely to *predispose* the individual to poor health. Said another way, mental illness is an *indirect* cause of poor health status — it can result in a number of problems that in turn play a role in negatively impacting the person's health. The good news is that steps can be taken to help ensure that those other problems do not become problems for your family member. To assist your journey to help ensure good health for your loved one, we discuss these three topics in this chapter:

• Health Status Risk Factors Associated With Mental Illnesses
• Individuals Who Have a Mental Illness Receive Inadequate Health Care.
• Living a Healthy Lifestyle: Nutrition and Exercise.

HEALTH STATUS RISK FACTORS ASSOCIATED WITH MENTAL ILLNESS

There are a number of risk factors that negatively impact the health status of individuals with a mental illness. There is also a relationship between the risk factors. That is, there is a good likelihood that if someone were to score high for one of the risk factors, she would likely score high for certain other factors. Obviously, not all individuals with a mental illness will be impacted by these risk factors. Some individuals might score low on all of them. On the average, however, individuals with a mental illness are more likely to score higher on at least a couple compared to the general population.

Health Problems Go Hand-in-Hand With Poverty

We mention poverty first, because it is frequently an unfortunate consequence of mental illness. While newer medications and improved systems of care have significantly improved the chances of individuals with schizophrenia and other mental illnesses being competitively employed, the rates of poverty are still remarkably high. And with poverty comes issues such as living in unsafe conditions. Research tells us that individuals with schizophrenia are four times more likely to die as victims of violence than people without a mental illness.

Exposure to Communicable Diseases

Persons with mental illnesses who live in supervised residential settings have a much higher likelihood of being exposed to a variety of illnesses (including infectious diseases) than does the general population. Some examples are colds and flu, tuberculosis, pneumonia, hepatitis, urinary tract infections, and sexually transmitted diseases such as herpes and HIV.

Poor Judgment

When an individual has a problem with thinking clearly, it is not unreasonable to assume that he might use poor judgment. This can include participating in unsafe sex, being in areas or situations where he will be abused, deciding not to take an important medication such as insulin, and spending limited money on cigarettes, alcohol or drugs instead of food.

Self-Harm and Suicide

One obvious and significant concern is self-harm. While most individuals with a mental illness are not inclined to hurt themselves, there is a much higher incidence of self-harm and possible suicide than the general population.

Victimization

Individuals with a mental illness are more likely to be victims of crime and abuse. This is one of those factors connected to the other risk factors. Quite often, an individual who has a mental illness and is also living in poverty has no option other than to live in less desirable sections of town and, at times, in specific housing complexes with a high crime rate. In such an environment, unclear thinking or poor decision-making skills can make such a person an "easy target."

Poor Hygiene

In addition to the obvious negative social consequences, poor physical and dental hygiene can result in serious physical problems. Poor dental hygiene results in tooth decay, gum disease and tooth loss, which can seriously affect eating habits. Lack of personal cleanliness can result in infections including urinary tract infections or lice infestation.

Side Effects of Medications

Some medications that individuals take for their mental illness can cause side effects that make them more vulnerable to accidents. As was pointed out in Chapter 6, dizziness can be a side effect. When I was reviewing mortalities in a large mental health system, there was a three-month period in which a number of individuals died, who just should not have died. One young man fainted, face first, into a fountain in the front of his apartment complex and drowned. Another young man stepped off of a bus and in his confusion ran in front of the bus as it was leaving the curb. Side effects of medication can cause problems other than just accidents. There are also medical consequences that are discussed in Chapter 6.

Tobacco Use

The information about tobacco is clear. It is the cause of numerous health-related problems, including many cancers and heart disease. Individuals with a mental illness tend to smoke at a far greater rate than individuals who do not have a mental illness. A recent study suggests that persons with mental illnesses are twice as likely to smoke as is the general population.

Poor Diet

Americans as a whole do not eat the kinds of food that promote good health. We eat too few vegetables and fruits and too many fried foods, potato chips and desserts. As bad as most of us are at healthy eating, individuals with a mental illness are worse. Often they live in situations where good diets are difficult if not impossible to maintain. Because of its importance and because it is something that can be impacted, we have devoted an entire section of this chapter to diet.

Lack of Exercise and Recreation

As with diet, many of us do not get enough exercise. And as with diets, individuals with a mental illness are worse at keeping physically fit. Because of its importance we are devoting a whole section of this chapter to issues of exercise.

INDIVIDUALS WHO HAVE A MENTAL ILLNESS RECEIVE LESS ADEQUATE HEALTH CARE

In addition to the health risk factors associated with mental illness identified above, the health care (really, the *lack of health care*) that individuals with mental illness receive plays a major role their health status. Quite often, individuals who have a mental illness do not receive the same level of health care as others do. They do not have the same access to care, do not receive the same level of screening and preventative care, and definitely do not receive the same type or level of treatment for certain physical illnesses as does the general population.

I was involved in a study where the health care services of individuals with a mental illness were compared to the services of individuals who were poor but did not have a mental illness. There were some important findings.

- Fewer Resources for Treatment: For every dollar spent on medical services for individuals without a mental illness, 82 cents was spent for individuals with a mental illness.

- Resources Used for Emergency Services and Hospitalization: While the total expenditure for individuals with a mental illness were 18 percent less, there was also a difference in how the resources were used. Individuals with a mental illness had less of their health care dollar going toward outpatient care than did individuals without a mental illness, but had far more of their health care dollar spent going toward

121

ambulances and emergency room care.

A good example can be illustrated in the treatment of urinary tract infections. Urinary infections accounted for a good portion of the outpatient treatment dollar for individuals without a mental illness compared to next to nothing for individuals with a mental illness. On the other hand, urinary tract infections accounted for a good portion of hospital costs for individuals with a mental illness compared to next to nothing for individuals without a mental illness. In other words, while urinary tract infections are common, individuals without a mental illness received fairly routine treatment in outpatient settings. Individuals with a mental illness often did not receive care until it required treatment in more urgent, more expensive settings.

PATIENT AND PRACTITIONER ISSUES

There are patient, practitioner and health care systems issues that interfere with individuals with a mental illness receiving appropriate health care. Some of the more important problems are:

- Physician Consistency: Some physicians have negative attitudes about treating individuals with a mental illness. Even when attitudes are not a problem, many physicians do not have the background necessary to understand the special needs of individuals with a mental illness. As a consequence, individuals with a mental illness are less likely to have a consistent primary care provider.
- Awareness: Psychiatric symptoms can interfere with an individual's ability to detect health problems and communicate those problems to her doctor.
- Compliance: Individuals with a mental illness are less compliant with follow-up treatment. There are a variety of reasons for lack of compliance, including inadequate transportation, cognitive problems and living situations that can make compliance difficult.

Systems Barriers

In addition to patient and practitioner issues, there are systems barriers to delivering effective heath care to individuals with a serious mental illness. Public services for mental health and physical health are often provided through separate systems of care. This creates a number of obstacles, including communication between providers and individuals having to go to multiple sites to get lab work done or fill prescriptions.

We introduced this chapter by saying we wanted to provide strategies to help to make sure that your family member stays healthy. Some of the ways that you can be of assistance include:

- Make sure health care is a part of your family member's treatment plan.
- Do what you can to be supportive of your family member getting health care.
- Discuss risk issues with your family member.
- Try to get to know your family member's physician. Given the limited access to many health care professionals, if you can't get to know the physician, at least know their name, should you ever need to get in touch with them.

LIVING A HEALTHY LIFESTYLE: NUTRITION AND EXERCISE

The next two sections provide information you can use yourself and to help improve the quality of life of your family member. Perhaps you already eat nutritious foods, exercise and relax. If you do, great. If not, you are like the vast majority of Americans and you might want to think about how you could modify your own lifestyle. As was discussed in Chapter 3, if you are going to be of help to your family member you need to make sure that you take care of yourself.

A healthy lifestyle includes choices and actions. A person needs to balance physical fitness, stress, work, medication and nutrition. Making a long-term commitment to a healthy lifestyle can give someone more energy, increase self-esteem, as well as reduce the risk of chronic mental diseases, and reduce the risk of increased symptoms of schizophrenia or a relapse.

THE ROLE OF NUTRITION IN A HEALTHY LIFE STYLE

The typical American diet, *not just the diet of individuals with mental illness*, is too high in fat, salt and sugar, and too low in fiber and vital nutrients. At times, it is not that individuals don't have healthy food options, but instead they tend to make poor choices about food. Obviously, it is not always that simple. For individuals with a mental illness, options are not always available. Poor dietary habits, in combination with lack of exercise and high stress, have been connected to such health problems as:

- Obesity: An individual is overweight when their weight is 10 percent greater than ideal body weight and obese when their weight exceeds the ideal body weight by 20 percent. Excess weight can cause a strain on the heart, bones and joints. It also increases the likelihood of diabetes and related complications.
- Coronary heart disease and stroke: Excess cholesterol, a fat-related

substance in the blood, can clog arteries and blood vessels. Depending on where the vessel leads, the result can be a heart attack or stroke.

• High blood pressure (hypertension): Excess sodium and sugar in the diet can cause high blood pressure. Over a long period of time, high blood pressure can, in turn, lead to an increased risk of heart disease, stroke and kidney problems..

In order to eat healthy and avoid the problems associated with poor nutrition, here are some guidelines and strategies that you should consider:

Eat a Variety of Foods

There are over 40 known nutrients that the body needs. To be well nourished, it is important to eat a variety of foods that contain balanced amounts of these nutrients. Nutritionists often point to a food list (pyramid) like the one that follows to show the recommended balance among food. The diet should include more of the foods at the bottom of the list, and less of the foods at the top.

Fats, Oils and Sweets
Milk, Yogurt and Cheese
Meat, Poultry, Fish, Dry Beans, Eggs
Fruit and Vegetables
Whole Grain Cereal, Rice, Pasta

Balance Diet with Physical Activity

It is fairly simple, if an individual eats food containing more calories than the body needs for energy, the extra calories are stored as fat. In order to lose weight, more calories must be burned than consumed and physical activity is the only healthy way to burn calories.

People with schizophrenia and other mental illnesses may face special obstacles in balancing their eating with exercise. For example, negative symptoms (apathy, lack of motivation, withdrawal) can reduce activity level. Medications can also play a role. Some medications taken to relieve psychiatric symptoms can cause muscle stiffness and involuntary movements that make it difficult to exercise. (See Chapter 6.) Another problem is that some of the newer medications can increase appetite and cause weight gain.

Eat Grain Products, Vegetables and Fruits

Fruits, vegetables and grains are loaded with vitamins and minerals and have little or no fat. Increasing the amount of fruits, vegetables and grains in the diet can play a significant role in helping to do the following:

- Lower blood pressure and reduce the risk of heart disease and stroke
- Reduce the chances of getting certain types of cancer
- Make the immune system stronger
- Slim and trim the waistline

An additional benefit from eating grains, fruits and vegetables is that they contain large amounts of soluble and insoluble fiber. *Soluble fiber* absorbs water and the resulting swelling can give a full feeling and result in eating less. *Insoluble fiber* is sometimes called roughage because of the bulk it adds to the diet. Fiber is important to good nutrition because it does the following:

- Helps alleviate constipation (a possible side effect of certain medications)
- Reduces cholesterol levels
- Helps control blood sugar levels
- Reduces the risk of bowel disorders and colon cancer

Avoid High-Fat, High-Cholesterol Foods

While some dietary fat (unsaturated fat) is needed for good health, diets high in saturated fats are associated with high cholesterol, heart disease and high blood pressure. Saturated fats (those fats that are generally solid at room temperature) also have twice as many calories as proteins and carbohydrates for the same amount of nutrition.

Avoid Foods High in Salt and Sugar Content

Foods made with simple sugars consist of empty calories and provide very little in terms of vitamins or minerals. Excess sodium is directly related to high blood pressure. Some of the foods that are the highest in sodium include snack foods and processed meats such as ham, bacon and bologna.

Avoid Alcohol and Drugs

Alcohol is high in calories and has few or no nutrients. Additionally, drinking alcohol can lead to high blood pressure, liver damage, added risk for heart disease, increased risk for stroke, inflammation of the pancreas, as well as impaired judgment. This is in addition to the impact of drugs and alcohol on mental illness, which was addressed in Chapter 8.

Drink Plenty of Water

The importance of water in the diet cannot be overstated. More than 75 percent of the human body is made up of water, and water is necessary to maintain many bodily functions. A person should drink at least eight 8-ounce glasses of water daily, and more when they are outside in hot weather or exercising.

Set Goals Toward a Healthy Diet

In order to make healthy dietary changes, it is important to first identify areas that need improvement, and then set goals and take action. When making changes in dietary habits, it is probably best to make a few changes at a time. Trying to make too many changes at once can be over-whelming and may cause feelings of frustration and can result in giving up. In setting goals, it is important to identify barriers to achievement of the goals as well as steps that can be taken to overcome the barriers. For example, if an individual lives in a facility where they have no ability to store food, which is certainly a barrier that will need to be overcome.

Ways to Control Hunger

There are times people eat, not because they need food, but because of the comfort associated with eating, or because of a learned habit of eating out of boredom. Here are some alternative behaviors that can be used to help curb overeating or eating at times when food is serving a purpose other than for nutrition:

- Take a walk when feeling hungry. While exercising, the digestive system "takes a break" and allows the energy it would normally use to go to the exercising muscles. As a result, hunger is reduced .
- Drink a glass of water. Liquids fill the stomach and can "trick it" into feeling as if food has been eaten.
- Eat a rice cake or raw vegetables. Drinking water with these high fiber snacks is even better because the fiber expands to, again, "trick the stomach."

THE ROLE OF EXERCISE IN A HEALTHY LIFE STYLE

The second component of a healthy lifestyle is a program of regular exercise. Exercise has both physical and mental benefits. The muscles, the heart and other parts of the body grow stronger and more efficient when they are called upon regularly for the effort required in exercise. Exercise can help emotionally by increasing a sense of well-being and self-esteem.

The amount of exercise is to some extent an individual matter, but most experts agree that in order to be beneficial at least 30 minutes, 3 to 4 times per week is essential. Even though one can benefit significantly from only two hours of exercise a week, most individuals do not get enough exercise.

If you or your family member is not getting enough exercise, it is important to assess the roadblocks that are preventing participation in regular exercise. Planning for how to overcome roadblocks is an important first step.

Exercise Helps Normalize Blood Pressure and Prevents Heart Disease

Exercise helps to normalize blood pressure and prevent heart disease by slowing down the buildup of plaque in the arteries. Aerobic exercise increases the "good" cholesterol (HDL) and decreases the "bad" cholesterol (LDL). Exercise offers other positive outcomes:

• Regulates blood sugar
• Reduces bone loss and support of body structure
• Promotes weight loss
• Promotes flexibility
• Provides pleasure and increases the ability to relax

An active life also tends to encourage other health-promoting habits, like avoiding tobacco and alcohol and developing healthy eating habits.

While most people in reasonably good health are probably able to begin an exercise program, it's always a good idea to check with a doctor before starting or changing an exercise routine. Always be sure the doctor is aware of the medications being taken, since some medications may affect the ability to exercise.

Exercise can be grouped into Three Major Types

Type of Exercise	Benefits
Cardiovascular ("Aerobic")	Stimulates the heart and lungs, and builds endurance
Flexibility	Lengthens, stretches and flexes muscles
Strength-developing	Increases muscle strength and stamina

While all three types of exercise have some overlap, cardiovascular and flexibility are the most important for basic fitness.

Aerobic Exercise

An aerobic exercise is one that is active enough to increase the heart and breathing rates for a sustained period of time. In order to improve cardiovascular fitness, exercise must be aerobic. If the main goal of exercise is to lose weight, the exercise does not need to be aerobic.

Exercises to Increase Flexibility

Flexibility has to do with range of motion and can help prevent low back pain, posture problems and minor injuries associated with everyday life. The primary flexibility exercise is stretching. Consider the following points when exercising for flexibility:

- Stretch just far enough to feel a little "pull" or mild pain in the muscles.
- Do not stretch to a point of excessive pain.
- Flexibility exercises must be done at least three to four days per week for improvement to occur.
- Include flexibility exercises as part of warm-up or cool-down.
- Do stretches gently; do not bounce up and down.

Strengthening Exercises

Strengthening exercises generally involve weight training, the goal of which is to change body composition by increasing muscle mass and decreasing body fat. It is not as beneficial to a healthy lifestyle as the cardiovascular and flexibility exercises, so it is not recommended by itself. However, strengthening along with aerobics and flexibility exercising can be beneficial.

Tips for Getting Started With an Exercise Program

- Talk to a physician before getting started.
- Start slow. Ease into an exercise program. Overdoing it may result in

feeling discouraged or cause strain, pain or injury.
- Give it a one-month trial period. Make a commitment to stay with the exercise program for one month, despite minor aches and pains. The discomfort will pass as strength and endurance increase.
- Set realistic goals. Getting in shape takes months not days. Set short-term and long-term goals that are challenging yet reachable. If possible find a way to reward your family member (and yourself) for reaching goals.
- Fit exercise into your daily routine. Find daily activities, such as taking stairs instead of elevators and escalators, that increase activity level.
- Take advantage of community resources. There are a number of facilities in most every community where individuals can exercise inexpensively or for free. There are parks, recreation centers and the YMCA. There is even the mall, which is great in hot or cold weather.

The Relationship Between Mental Illness and a Hysterectomy

This is a fairly simple story. I am telling it because I'm angry. I'm angry at my daughter. I'm angry at her primary care physician. I'm angry at the mental health center, her case manager and her psychiatrist. I'm also mad at myself. I'm mad at our whole healthcare system. I hope if I tell our story, I will somehow feel better.

My daughter, who is in her early 40s, had a surgical procedure about three months ago. It is a procedure that with better healthcare she would not have needed. If she didn't have a mental illness she would not have needed the surgery.

She began having symptoms about six months earlier. Her case manager knew that she was having physical symptoms and told her to go see her physician, but she didn't. Somehow the case manager must have assumed that if it was a physical problem, it was not his concern. She didn't have a physician to see, and the case manager didn't even know it.

The doctor she had used earlier once got angry with her for not following his advice. She felt embarrassed and refused to see him again.

Unfortunately, her case manager never checked to see if she still had a primary physician.

As her symptoms got worse, I knew something was wrong but I didn't do anything. By the time she finally could no longer deal with the excessive bleeding she had a friend take her to the emergency room. The ER exam revealed that she needed a hysterectomy. She was in the hospital for three days and left without a uterus. I'm really not sure who is to blame, or if anyone is to blame. My daughter should have made a better decision and gotten treatment earlier. But her treatment team should have done something. Her doctor shouldn't have made her feel so unwelcome. And society should find a better way of providing healthcare.

But mostly I'm angry with myself. I should have taken a more active role in making sure that she was getting good healthcare. I was wondering if I would feel better by telling my story. And you know what? I do.

Submitted by J.L.

On Giving Up Too Soon

A man meets a guru on the road. The man asks the guru, "Which way is success?" The bearded sage with a long white robe does not speak.

Instead he points to a place off in the distance. The man, thrilled by the prospect of quick and easy success, rushes off in the appropriate direction. Suddenly, there comes a loud "Splat!"

Eventually, the man limps back, tattered and stunned, assuming he must have misinterpreted the message. He repeats his question to the guru, who again points silently in the same direction.

The man obediently walks off once more. This time the splat is deafening, and when the man crawls back, he is bloody, broken, tattered and irate. "I asked you which way is success," he screams at the guru. "I followed the direction you indicated. And all I got was splatted! No more of this pointing! Talk!"

Only then does the guru speak, and what he says is this: "Success is that way. Just a little after the splat."

Reprinted with permission of Afterhours Inspirational Stories

Caught Between a Rock and a Hard Place

The story that I am about to tell you is absolutely true. But it's so bizarre that it challenges all logic. My daughter has bipolar disorder. She also has diabetes. Both of her illnesses have been hard on her and her family. She developed diabetes as a youngster, long before she was diagnosed with bipolar disorder. Even though we know there is no relationship between the two illnesses, and they are really quite different, they both bring with them tremendous social and peer relationship issues.

As a teenager she felt as though her diabetes kept her from being able to "fit in." She often avoided social situations where food and drink were involved because she felt embarrassed about her diabetes. She didn't want to deal with explaining why she wasn't eating pizza and drinking soda (or when she was older, beer). I know it sounds trivial, but to a teenage girl, any sign of being different is hard to deal with.

Today her problems with diabetes and bipolar disorder are more severe than the mere problems of a teenager wanting to fit in. First, the medications for her bipolar illness and diabetes seem to interact in a negative way, because she has a very difficult time regulating her blood sugar level. When she has a manic episode she will eat foods that she shouldn't eat and have even greater problems with her sugar level. When she feels bad she might stop taking one or both of her medications.

She was recently hospitalized when she stopped taking her lithium and insulin. She became extremely psychotic and ultimately had to be taken to the hospital by the police. Once hospitalized she was placed back on her lithium and seemed to make quick progress…with her mental illness.

Her blood sugar level, however, was way out of whack. Unfortunately, her diabetes did not respond as quickly to treatment as did her mania. Within a few days, her psychiatrist felt as though she was stable and could be transferred to a medical floor for a couple of days until her sugar level was stabilized. He believed that given the fact that she lived in a boarding home, it wouldn't be prudent to release her until her diabetes was well controlled.

Here is where the story gets bizarre. She lives in Arizona, where Medicaid patients receive mental healthcare from one health plan and physical healthcare from another. The two health plans are totally separate. The psychiatrist informed the hospital that my daughter no longer needed the psychiatric unit, and instead needed to be transferred to a medical floor for a couple of days. Unfortunately the health plan that is responsible for her medical care said that her diabetes problems were not at a level that would suggest that there was a medical necessity requiring hospitalization. The health plan that was responsible for her physical health said that she could go home and take her insulin on an outpatient basis. Her psychiatrist, who worked for the mental health plan, called the physical healthcare plan and explained the situation. He informed them that because of her living situation and current fragile state she needed to remain in the hospital for a few days. The physical health plan responded by stating that if her mental illness was causing her to need hospitalization, the health plan that is responsible for her psychiatric care should pay for the extended stay. The psychiatrist indicated that she needed hospitalization, not for her bipolar disorder, but rather for her diabetes. She needed hospitalization because if she were to go home she would likely not take her insulin correctly and within a very short time would require hospitalization for an even more serious diabetes complication. The debate went on for two days. The stress was tremendous. The psychiatrist kept her on the psychiatric floor as the debate between two health plans occurred.

Was this a bipolar problem or was it a diabetes problem? The two health plans also debated about outpatient care for her diabetes. If someone could monitor her insulin, she could safely go home. But who was responsible for the monitoring? The mental health program said that they did not have the resources to monitor her insulin. The physical health plan said it could not send someone to her home on a daily basis.

Submitted by D.A.

CHAPTER 11

Taking Care of Business: Understanding and Obtaining Entitlements

"Do not go where the path may lead,
go instead where there is no path and leave a trail."
—*Ralph Waldo Emerson*

Michael R. Berren, Ph.D.

Previous chapters in this book have addressed many of the more important clinical issues of mental illness, including symptoms, diagnoses, medications and the continuum of care. In Chapter 15, the idea that recovery is a definite possibility is addressed. But what if, for either a short or more extended period of time, your family member's illness results in the person being unable to work? Where is the individual going to get money? How will he/she be able to afford food, housing, and other life necessities? Just as important, if your family member is not able to work and therefore unlikely to be able to obtain health insurance, how will he/she access health care for both physical and psychiatric needs?

These are the questions that we answer in this chapter. This is the *workhorse* chapter of the book. It provides practical information about securing benefits and entitlements for individuals with serious mental illness.

While it is important for families to understand medications and treatments and systems of care, it is dealing with eligibility for benefits and entitlements that is often of primary concern to most families. If you are worried about financial issues, it is going to be difficult to focus on issues of rehabilitation. Benefits and entitlements are areas where family involvement and active participation can have a significant payoff. The important specific areas addressed in this chapter are:

- Benefit Programs That Provide Income
- Handling Your Family Member's Income Benefits If He or She Is Incapable
- Benefit Programs That Provide Health Care Coverage
- If Your Family Member Is Not Eligible for Income or Health Care Benefits
- Primary Source Documents

BENEFIT PROGRAMS THAT PROVIDE INCOME

There are two federal programs that provide income for individuals with severe disabilities, including serious mental illnesses: Social Security Disability Insurance (SSDI) and Supplemental Security Income (SSI). Estimates by the Social Security Administration (SSA) indicate that one-third of the SSI rolls and one-quarter of the SSDI rolls consist of individuals with schizophrenia, bipolar disorder, and major depression. Both SSDI and SSI are administered by the Social Security Administration. And while both programs provide monthly income for people with disabilities, the non-medical eligibility requirements for the two programs are quite different.

The discussion of SSDI and SSI income can be divided into four specific areas:

- The Basics of SSDI and SSI
- The Basics of Disability and Substantial Gainful Activity
- The Duration of Benefits
- Work Incentives Programs

Because the issues are fairly technical and specific, we decided to present much of the information in a set of tables that follow.

The Basics of SSDI and SSI

opic	SSDI Funded through the Social Security Trust Fund.	SSI Funded through general tax revenues.
e acronym stands for:	Social Security Disability Insurance.	Supplemental Security Income.
gibility:	To be eligible for benefits an individual must: • Have a work history and have earned a minimum number of credits from work covered under Social Security; • Have a disability; and • Not be working (or working but earning less than the Substantial Gainful Activity [SGA] level).	To be eligible for benefits an individual must: • Have little or no income; • Have few or no resources; and • Have a disability. Work history is *not* a factor for SSI eligibility.
types of records ded when applying benefits:	Documentation is *very* important. Some of the required documents include: social security card, birth certificate, current medications and names, phone numbers and addresses of doctors that have provided treatment. For SSI, information concerning rent, income and any assets is also required.	
efit amount:	Based on the individual's lifetime average earnings covered by Social Security.	Based on all sources of income, living expenses, and the state in which the individual lives.
ting Periods:	Five months after a disability occurs. The first two years of the entitlement *comprises* the waiting period for Medicare health insurance. (Medicare is discusses below.)	There is no waiting period.
at Goes With It:		State and county often provide supplements; food stamps
ated Health Care:	• Medicare • Low-income Medicare recipients are eligible for Medicaid benefits to help pay a portion of the Medicare premium and deductables. See Medicare discussion following.	• Medicaid See Medicaid discussion following.

135

The Basics of Disability and Substantial Gainful Activity

Issue	The issues are the same for SSDI and SSI.
Definition of disability:	• The inability to engage in any Substantial Gainful Activity (SGA) because of a physical or psychiatric problem. (In 1999, SGA was defined as "earning over $700 per month.") • The disability must be expected to last for at least 12 months.
Criteria that determine whether an individual has a disability:	• The impairment must significantly limit the individual's ability to work. • If the individual is working, earnings must be below the SGA level. • The impairment must be included on an approved list of disabling illnesses. Serious mental illnesses, such as schizophrenia, bipolar disorder and major depression, are included on that approved list.

The Duration of Benefits

Issue	SSDI	SSI
Benefits are discontinued when:	The individual is determined to no longer have a disabling impairment because either: • He/she is working at the SGA level, or • There has been medical improvement to the point enabling the individual to work.	• The individual does not meet disability eligibility requirements for income and resources, or • The individual no longer has a disablin impairment. Individuals are generally inelig for SSI while in a Medicaid facility or a public medical or psychiatric facility. (Individuals eligible under Section 1619 can continue to receive cash benefits for up to two months if the facility allows th individual to keep all of the SSI paymen
Frequency of eligibility reviews:	Depends on the expectation of recovery; the more likely the recovery, the more often the review.	

Work Incentive Programs

Historically, there has been a disincentive for individuals with a disability to seek employment. The disincentive rests on the dilemma that going to work and being productive would ordinarily lead to losing benefits that might provide more income than the employment. Even worse, there is the possibility that an individual might attempt to go back to work, become ineligible for benefits and then find out, after a short time, that they are not yet ready for competitive employment. Recognizing the dilemma, some programs allow individuals to test their ability to work without risking the loss of benefits. The essence of the work incentive programs are:

• SSDI: Provides income and Medicare support over several years, allowing individuals to test their ability to work. This includes full cash payments during the first 12 months followed by a 36-month period in which cash benefits can begin again without a new application.

• SSI: Provides income and/or Medicaid coverage while the individual works. Once an individual receives SSI, disability status continues until he/she medically recovers, *even if the individual works.* If the individual is not eligible for SSI benefits because earnings are too high, eligibility for Medicaid might still continue.

The table that follows lists the most important Work Incentive Programs.

Important Work Incentive Programs

...me of Program	Who is Eligible		What the program offers
	SSDI	SSI	
...airment Related Work ...enses (IRWE)	Yes	Yes	Because of impairment, individuals may have to pay for items in order to enable them to work. In most cases, SSA can deduct the costs of these items from the amount of the earnings used to figure your family member's SSI payment. This means that the SSI payment will not be reduced as much because SSA will not count all of the earnings.
...uccessful Work ...empts	No	Yes	When the individual attempts to work and due to the impairment is unable to continue at the SGA level at any time within the first six months, those earnings are not counted when determining the SSI payment amount.
...tinued Payment Under ...ocational Rehabilitation ...gram	No	Yes	While benefits usually stop when an individual no longer has a disabling impairment, benefits will continue if the individual is participating in a vocational rehabilitation program.
...l Work Period (TWP)	Yes	No	Allows an individual to test his/her ability to work for at least nine months. During the Trial Work Period (TWP), as long as the individual has a disabling impairment, full SSDI benefits will be received regardless of earnings. At the end of a TWP, an evaluation is made to decide if the individual can work at the SGA level. If it is determined that the individual can work at the SGA level, SSDI benefits are discontinued and the individual is moved to the Extended Period of Eligibility program.
...nded Period of ...bility (EPE)	Yes	No	For 36 consecutive months following a TWP, benefit payments can automatically be reinstated with no new application if the individual continues to have a disabling impairment and earning fall below SGA level.
...tinuation of Medicare ...erage	Yes	No	An individual can receive up to 39 consecutive months of hospital and medical insurance after a TWP with no premium for hospital insurance. (See Medicare below.)
...for Achieving Self ...port (PASS)	No	Yes	Allows an individual to set aside income or resources over a reasonable period of time under a plan designed to help the individual become financially self-supporting. SSI does *not* count the income or resources set aside under a PASS when deciding whether an individual is eligible for benefits and in what amount.
...Payments for ...viduals Who Work – ...ion 1619	No	Yes	An individual can receive SSI cash payments and Medicaid even when earned income is at or above the SGA level. (This eliminates the need for the TWP or EPE that is available for SSDI eligible individuals.) To qualify, the individual must: • Have been eligible for an SSI payment for at least one month before beginning to work at the SGA level; • Still have a disability; and • Meet all other eligibility and resource requirements.

Continued Medicaid Eligibility for Individuals Who Work - Section 1619	No	Yes	Medicaid coverage can continue even when earned income is too high for SSI cash payments. To qualify, the individual must: • Have been eligible for SSI cash payment for at least one month; • Still have a disability; • Still meet all other eligibility requirements, including the resources test; • Have gross earned income that is insufficient to replace SSI and Medicaid

Ticket to Work: An Important New Work Incentive Program

An important innovative program, Ticket to Work, was initiated in January 2001. It will be phased in over a three-year period. (As with other federal programs, states must pass enacting legislation that puts key provisions of the program into effect.) The goals of the Ticket to Work Program are to:

• Increase an individual's choice in obtaining rehabilitation and vocational services; and
• Remove some of the barriers that have forced people with disabilities to choose between the security but fruitlessness of disability benefits and the risk but personal rewards of work.

The Ticket to Work Program should lead to some positive benefits for individuals with severe mental illness including:

• More providers and providers who are more motivated. Both SSDI and SSI disability beneficiaries will receive a "ticket" that they can use to obtain vocational rehabilitation services from their choice of approved providers. More agencies will be funded to provide vocational services that will in turn increase the amount of choice an individual has. As an incentive to motivate providers to help individuals become employed, the Social Security Administration will pay providers bonuses as individuals reach certain milestones, such as completing training programs.
• Less pressure regarding disability reviews and returning to work, specifically.
  - The Social Security Administration *will not* review the medical condition of a person receiving disability benefits if that person is using a Ticket to Work.
  - If someone has been on SSDI for at least two full years, the Social Security Administration will be barred from using his or her return to work as a basis for scheduling a disability review/evaluation.
  - If an individual's SSDI or SSI benefits have ended because earnings from work exceed the SGA, but he/she is now unable to continue work because of his/her medical condition, the individual has 60

months from the termination of the benefits to file for reinstatement of benefits. Further, while a new disability determination is being made, the individual is eligible for up to six months of provisional benefits, including Medicare and Medicaid, as appropriate.

- A pilot program to test gradual reduction in benefits. Currently, once an individual earns more than the SGA level for nine months, his/her benefits are abruptly terminated. A pilot project for SSDI beneficiaries will test a gradual reduction of SSDI benefits by $1 for every $2 the beneficiary earns at work.
- Medicaid Buy-in. The Ticket to Work Program allows states to implement one or both of two optional medical insurance eligibility programs:
  - Individuals with a disability can earn up to 2.5 times the federal poverty level (each state sets its own earning limits) and still be eligible for Medicaid Buy-in Programs.
  - Individuals with a disability whose earnings disqualify them for SSDI benefits can receive continuing Medicare coverage for an extended period of time. Prior to the Ticket to Work Program, if an individual's earnings exceeded the SGA level for nine months (a Trial Work Program) they would lose their Medicare benefits. The Ticket to Work Program allows states to extend Medicare Part A coverage for an additional 4.5 years. After that time, the individual can continue Medicare coverage but will be required to pay the full premium.

HANDLING YOUR FAMILY MEMBER'S INCOME BENEFITS IF HE OR SHE IS INCAPABLE

What if your family member's symptoms and/or functioning level is such that he/she is unable to appropriately handle the SSDI or SSI income being received? If the individual is incapable, the Social Security Administration has the authority to appoint Representative Payees to handle the finances. It is the Social Security Administration's preference that the Representative Payee be a family member. When that is not possible, Representative Payee responsibility can be assigned to friends, third parties or organizations. Once assigned, it is the Representative Payee's legal responsibility to ensure that the payments are for the use and benefit of the beneficiary only. Families should be cautioned, however, that while the Social Security Administration has some basic safeguards to ensure that Representative Payees do not misuse benefits, they do not perform credit or security background checks on prospective organizational Representative Payees. Thus if the family chooses not to be the payee, the family should consider direct involvement in determining the appropriate payee.

A major portion of Chapter 14 is devoted to describing specific strategies for helping your family member handle his/her finances.

BENEFIT PROGRAMS THAT PROVIDE HEALTH CARE COVERAGE

Just as there are two programs that provide income, there are two distinct health insurance programs for individuals with disabilities including serious mental illnesses.

Medicare

Medicare is a health insurance program for individuals who receive SSDI income. Individuals become eligible for Medicare after qualifying for SSDI disability benefits for two years. There are two parts to the Medicare health insurance program:

- Hospital insurance: This is often referred to as Medicare Part A and is generally provided at no cost to the individual.
- Supplementary medical insurance: This is often referred to as Medicare Part B and is available to most Medicare recipients. However, the recipient is responsible for paying an insurance premium.

Low-income Medicare recipients with minimal resources are also eligible for one of three programs in which Medicaid (discussed below) can help with some or all of their out-of-pocket Medicare costs. To be eligible for any one of the three programs, the individual must be entitled to Medicare Part A. The three programs are:

- Qualified Medicare Beneficiary (QMB): Pays the Medicare Part B premiums, deductibles and co-insurance for individuals who have very minimal resources.
- Special Low-Income Medicare Beneficiary (SLMB): Pays Medicare Part B premium for individuals who have minimal resources but still exceed the limit for QMB eligibility.
- Qualified Individual (QI): Pays a portion of the Medicare Part B Premium for individuals with minimal resources but who still exceed the resource limit for SLMB eligibility.

Medicaid

Medicaid is a jointly funded, federal-state health insurance program for low-income individuals. Unlike Medicare in which eligibility is the same nationally, Medicaid allows each state to determine the level of poverty that enables an individual to be eligible. In some states, an individual can earn twice the Federal Poverty Level (FPL) and still be eligible for Medicaid, whereas in other states an individual can earn less than the FPL and still *not* be eligible. All SSI recipients are, however, automatically eligible for Medicaid in all states.

Medicaid Buy-In Program for Qualified Disabled Working Individuals (QDWI)

In addition to the special programs to cover Medicare Part B listed above, the QDWI program can pay Medicare Part A premiums for individuals who continue to have a disability but are no longer entitled for Medicare Part A benefits because they have returned to work.

IF YOUR FAMILY MEMBER IS NOT ELIGIBLE FOR INCOME OR HEALTH CARE BENEFITS

It is an unfortunate reality that not every individual with a disability will be eligible for SSDI, SSI and/or Medicare or Medicaid. If your family member is not eligible for SSDI or SSI income, or Medicare or Medicaid health care, there are places to look for assistance. These other programs do not, however, provide the same level of support as the federal programs.

General Assistance (GA)

These are cash assistance programs financed and administered by states and counties. GA programs are designed to meet the short-term or ongoing needs of low-income persons who are ineligible for (or awaiting approval for) federally funded cash assistance such as SSI. The income requirements are much more stringent than for SSI and are designed for the severely poor–individuals whose income is less than one-half of the FPL. GA benefits are also lower than benefits for SSI. On average, the GA monthly cash benefit is less than 50 percent of SSI benefits.

Medically Needy/Medically Indigent (MNMI)

Many states have, what are referred to as programs for the Medically Needy/Medically Indigent (MNMI). MNMI programs are designed to provide health care for individuals who are not eligible for Medicaid or Medicare. The best place to find out about MNMI programs is through the local mental health program or county health care office.

Food Stamps

The National Food Stamp Program, operated by the Department of Agriculture, provides poor individuals with resources that they can use to purchase food. As with Social Security Administration benefits programs, there are income and resource eligibility requirements. For SSI recipients, the amount of SSI benefit is *not* counted, making them automatically eligible for food stamps. Individuals can use their food stamps just like cash at most stores that sell food. Food Stamps do have some limitations.
The first limitation is that food stamps can *only* be used to purchase food. They *cannot* be used to purchase non-food related items such as such as soaps, paper products, household supplies, grooming items, toothpaste, and vitamins etc. They also cannot be used to purchase food that is ready to eat, such as food that might be purchased from a market's deli counter or in a restaurant.

PRIMARY SOURCE DOCUMENTS

As with anything that is government-based, the programs we have described in this chapter are based on hundreds of pages of rules and regulations. In distilling those hundreds of pages, we may not have addressed some of the specific information that might be relevant to your specific issue. Recognizing that more specific information might be needed, we have listed below some of the more important publications and Web sites that provide specific information. Additionally, you should always keep in mind that benefits programs are constantly changing. Legislation is often rewritten and Web sites should be consulted for up-to-date information.

Primary Source Documents

Who	What	How to Contact
Social Security Administration	Phone Number	1-800-772-1213
	Web sites	www.ssa.gov Vast amounts of information and links
		www.ssa.gov/search/index.htm A comprehensive search of the SSA site, publications and related sites; information presented in easy-to-understand format as well as in-depth
		www.ssa.gov/odhome Information on disability benefits
		www.ssa.gov/pubs/ Lists all SSA publications
	Publications	www.ssa.gov/work Information about rehabilitation programs, work incentives and health care
		Understanding The Benefits (Publication No. 05-10024)
		Disability Benefits (Publication No. 05-10029)
		Food Stamps And Other Nutrition Programs (Publication No. 05-10100)
		Redbook on Work Incentives: A Summary Guide to Social Security and Supplemental Security Income Work Incentives for People with Disabilities. Social Security Administration SSA Pub. No. 64-030, January 2000
USDA and the Food Stamp Program	Publication	*A Guide for Representative Payees* (Publication No. 05-10076)
Food and Nutrition Service; Food Stamps	Web site	www.fns.usda.gov/fsp/menu/apps/apps.htm Facts about the food stamp program, including benefits, eligibility, how to apply, a toll-free number for food stamp information, as well as information about other nutrition assistance programs
Americans with Disabilities Act, Civil Rights Division of the U.S. Department of Justice	Web site	www.usdoj.gov/crt/ada/adahom1.htm Information on how ADA is being enforced and where you can go for help
Center for Independent Living	Web site	www.ciberkeley.org Help and referrals from an activist disabled citizens action group
Service Enhancement Associates	Web site	www.wallinginc.com Wonderful manual for understanding the ins and outs of Social Security, SSI, Medicare and Medicaid

My Mom

She is articulate, cunning and poised for acquiring knowledge of what to do next for her loved ones. She exercises her mind thinking of the next best thing to do. She always has the future on her mind. She sits like a beautiful feline, alert to any situation and ready to protect her family. She is always grooming herself to look and feel and be the best she can, sometimes hissing at the daily routine and life's little idiosyncrasies.

Quiet moments are filled with concerned thoughts of how to be the best supporter she can be at all times. God blessed her with a rich and fulfilling life using her time to the fullest.

You may think I am talking about my cats: no, it's just my mom!

Submitted by A.D.

Diligence

We have learned, over the years, that there are those who seem to receive benefits and those who seem not to. We made a decision a number of years ago that we were going to make sure that our son received every benefit that he might legitimately be eligible for. The key has been diligence and persistence.

—Comment made by a parent at a focus group meeting

Too Late

Susan related the painful details of the death of her son. He was diagnosed with a serious mental illness during an incarceration for drug dependency–related crimes. He was released without any type of treatment plan for his mental health needs. All he was given was a three-day supply of antipsychotic medications. He was not Medicaid eligible and as a consequence had to endure long waits in hospital emergency rooms and pharmacies just to get a five-day renewal of his medication. Despite or because of these limited measures, his mental health deteriorated. Within a month of his release from jail, he attempted suicide. Because of his mother's insistence, he was admitted to a psychiatric inpatient unit. He was discharged two weeks later, again with no treatment plan and no appointment at a mental health program. Left with no necessary supports and services, he returned to drug use. Within a short period of time, he committed suicide at the age of 24. Five days after his suicide, his mother was notified that her son's Medicaid application had been approved.

Reprinted with permission of New York City Voices

CHAPTER 12

The Legal System: Family Law, Civil Commitment, and Criminal Justice

"People are always blaming their circumstances for what they are. I don't believe in circumstances. The people who get on in this world are the people who get up and look for the circumstances they want, and if they can't find them, make them."
— *George Bernard Shaw*

Charles L. Arnold, J.D. and Michael R. Berren, Ph.D. (Introduction)
Charles L. Arnold, J.D. (Section 1: Guardianship, Conservatorship, Power of Attorney and Trusts)
Suzanne Baldwin Hodges, J.D. (Section 2: Involuntary Treatment/Civil Commitment)
Michael S. Shafer, Ph.D. (Section 3: Criminal Justice Issues)

Introduction

There is a time and place for everything. There are times when you will likely be involved in issues concerning the medications that your loved one is taking. There are times when you will be focused on your family member's treatment and hopefully his/her recovery. There are times when housing might be the issue. There are times when your family member will be doing well, and other facets of your life will take a priority over the individual's mental illness. There are also times, however, when very practical issues surrounding mental illness will come to the forefront. We made this same point in Chapter 11 when we addressed the issue of entitlements.

Like Chapter 11, this is a "workhorse" chapter. Having a comprehensive understanding of the impact of your loved one's mental illness requires knowledge of more than the illness itself. It requires an understanding of the legal issues associated with obtaining treatment at times when your family member might be refusing treatment. It requires an understanding of the legal issues associated with assets and how those assets might impact the individual's entitlements. It also requires an understanding of the criminal justice system. Some of the questions and issues within the legal arena that families often have to deal with include:

- How can we provide for our son or daughter when we are gone?
- How can we make sure that any inheritance we might leave is protected and used to benefit our son/daughter?
- Can we help provide resources for our son or daughter without affecting our child's eligibility for government benefits and entitlements?
- What happens if our son or daughter becomes acutely ill and is unwilling to accept treatment or medication? What can we do to help ensure that he/she receives treatment?
- What do we do if our son or daughter is arrested for some minor crime?

To a great extent the legal strategies identified in this chapter can be seen as tools. They are tools that can be used in conjunction with your family member's rehabilitation services and medication. They are tools to be used to help ensure the best quality of life for your family member.

SECTION 1 DEALS WITH THREE FAMILY LAW CONCERNS

- Helping your family member receive treatment at those times when he/she might be refusing treatment over the course of the illness. The approaches discussed in this section can help prevent the more intrusive civil commitment process discussed in Section 2.

- Providing monetary assistance to your family member without compromising his/her entitlements such as SSI or Medicaid.
- Protecting an estate that you leave your family member.

SECTION 2 DESCRIBES THE CIVIL COMMITMENT PROCESS

- Explains when and how to use the legal system to ensure that your family member receives needed treatment at those times that he or she is in desperate need of treatment, but refuses to accept treatment because of the illness.

SECTION 3 ADDRESSES THE CRIMINAL JUSTICE SYSTEM

- We talk about the relationship between mental illness and the criminal justice system. This section contains information about steps that can be taken to make sure that your family member does not become involved in the criminal justice system and what to do if he or she gets arrested.

Chapter 12 Section 1

Guardianship, Conservatorship, Power of Attorney and Trusts: Tools for You to Use

Charles Arnold, J.D.

BERREN

*These legal tools certainly have made a
difference in my level of comfort.*

I am a mental health lawyer. It wasn't so long ago that those words would require a lengthy explanation. It was always difficult for others, particularly for other lawyers, to understand the nature of my practice.

Traditionally, lawyers have always specialized by discipline — by the work they do such as bankruptcy, personal injury, patent law, criminal law, etc.

But my practice was (and is) different. We are involved in all types of law. Our work encompasses the variety of needs of the three groups that we serve: persons with mental illness and their families, persons with developmental disabilities and their families, and the elderly and their families. Some of the work we do is generic. That is to say, it doesn't matter what the nature of our client's disability is, the work we do as lawyers is essentially the same. In a guardianship case for example, we ask the court to make a finding of incapacity and to appoint someone to make substituted-judgment decisions for the incapacitated person.

Regardless of whether the incapacity was caused by a head injury, a developmental disability, Alzheimer's disease or schizophrenia, our work remains essentially the same.

Other work done in my office is not so generic. It is very much disability-specific. By that I mean we need to be knowledgeable about both the nature and extent of our client's disabilities, and the system of care within which they are receiving services. With that dual knowledge we can use legal processes to *help the treatment system* do the right thing for our client.

Formerly, I had the good fortune to serve as the Maricopa County Public Fiduciary (the Public Guardian) at a time when mental health law was in its infancy. That privilege provided me with the unique opportunity to grow up and mature as a lawyer, just as mental health law was doing the same. My public fiduciary experience gave me the opportunity to learn about both mental illness and the public mental health system. This knowledge allowed me to apply the legal training I had to assist in the advocacy of my clients. As a matter of fact, in many ways I see my practice of mental health law as that of an advocate who happens to have some legal tools not generally available to most other advocates.

Indeed, my purpose in writing this section of the legal system chapter is to help families understand the legal tools that are available to them in their role as an advocate for their family member.

It is important to recognize that the challenges faced by family members and advocates do not come with sets of instructions. As a result of various social, political and economic dynamics, the very systems that we, as advocates, recognize as vital to our loved ones' care are becoming more and more difficult to access. The maze of systems is confusing and the doors to service are often manned by formidable "gatekeepers." The

153

role of these gatekeepers is often to limit access to the system. Regardless of the reason that you might be told (budgetary limitations, "triage," "entitlement," or "diversion") systems with limited resources are often forced to limit access.

My hope in preparing this section of the chapter is that you will:

- Understand the challenges you and your family member might face.
- Understand the legal tools available to you to help ensure both access to care and protection of resources.
- Actually apply the tools and take satisfaction with your success.
- Sleep better at night because you know you have done your planning.

Before getting to the specific legal tools, it is important to recognize some cornerstone concepts underlying mental health law, and the communities and contexts in which it is applied:

- Mental health law, like most other areas of law, is dynamic. It is constantly changing. The law seeks to reflect the values and mores of society. As the values and mores of the society change, so does the law. Mental health law didn't exist 50 years ago. Since the "deinstitutionalization" movement, when people who were previously institutionalized were released into the community without the necessary support systems in place, it has progressed at a frenetic pace.

- Mental health law, like other areas of law, represents a balance between individual and community rights. Often, a person with a serious mental illness chooses to exercise his rights in a way that is contrary to what appears to be in his or her own best interests. The statutes concerning involuntary civil treatment, which are discussed in Section 2 of this chapter, are good examples of this delicate balance. Every person has the legal right to have a mental disorder and still remain free from unwanted treatment. The law seeks to balance the individual's important, personal right to be free from unwanted treatment with the community's right to be free from undue harm. Further, while the person with an illness has the civil right to be free from treatment our society tempers that right with the person's right to be as free of symptoms as possible. And so when as a result of a mental illness a person is dangerous to himself, dangerous to others, or so disabled that he can't meet even his basic needs, then the community's rights and the person's rights to be symptom-free are deemed to prevail, and involuntary treatment occurs.

- "The price is right" concept. The law seeks, in meeting the needs of persons with incapacitating disorders, to come closest to meeting the person's needs without being more restrictive than is needed. That is, the law uses the minimum "clout" necessary to ensure that the needs of the individual and society are met.

The legal system can be imposing, intrusive and burdensome, but it doesn't need to be that way. The true purpose of mental health law, in any context, should be to respond to a situation involving a person with a disability by first identifying and defining the individual's deficit in a fair and impartial manner. Thereafter, the legal system should attempt to "fill in" or make up for that deficit with as little intrusion as possible. Again, "come closest to meeting the needs without going over." The three points made above are important to keep in the back of your mind, particularly when you become frustrated at what seems like obstacles being thrown in the way of your loved one receiving the services and care that the individual needs. Remember what the purpose of mental health law is, and that although it changes constantly, it's intent is to reflect our needs as advocates and consumers.

There are several areas of family law that you should also understand:

- Proactive and reactive approaches to ensure that your family member's health care and financial needs are met.
- Estate planning approaches to ensure that resources you provide your family member are not used by the government to determine that your relative is not needy and therefore not eligible for entitlement programs, and approaches to ensure that the resources are protected and used only to benefit your relative.

PROACTIVE AND REACTIVE APPROACHES TO ENSURE APPROPRIATE CARE AND FINANCIAL PLANNING

It is important to plan ahead. Planning for a person's own incapacity is important for everyone. Every adult should have a full set of planning documents reflecting his/her wishes, dealing with health care and financial issues, or other issues deemed important by that individual. These documents are often referred to as Advance Directives. When a person has a mental illness, the planning process becomes even more important.

It assures a way for the individual to communicate his/her wishes for some future time when he/she might be unable to do so. Said another way, leaving clear instructions at a time the person has capacity to make decisions, for use at a time when he/she doesn't, is the best way to assure that the individual's wishes are carried out.

The planning process should revolve around questions that begin with "What happens if." "What happens if the individual needs treatment and refuses it?" What happens if the individual is making bad decisions about resources and is at risk of squandering everything?" The "what if" questions should be clearly articulated and addressed with your family member in an open and frank manner.

One of the cruel ironies of mental illness that distinguishes it from other illnesses is that *when a person is the most ill and most in need of treatment, he/she is generally the most resistant to agreeing to treatment.* The resistance is not a well thought out decision, as it might be for someone in the final stages of cancer who opts for no chemotherapy because the person is unwilling to trade what little time the treatment might buy for its likely side effects and the resulting lower quality of life.

For individuals with severe mental illnesses, rejection of treatment is often a manifestation of the illness itself. For example, individuals with paranoid schizophrenia might believe that their medication is poisoned. Given that irrational belief, it is not surprising that they will refuse to take their medication. Individuals who are severely depressed might see treatment as something that will help keep them alive, and they want to die. Individuals who are acutely ill with Bipolar Disorder are often agitated or angry. They might see treatment as something they don't need because they believe that their insight and abilities are superior to those providing the treatment. Thus the dilemma – generally, it is the times when your relative is the neediest that the individual's illness will cause most resistance to any type of assistance or treatment, either from you or professionals.

At those times in life when individuals with a mental illness are not capable of making decisions, the legal system provides two approaches to making decisions for them, proactive (planned) and reactive (knee jerk and unplanned). You and your family member should understand that in critical situations one of the two approaches to making decisions, if not even a more extreme approach discussed in Section 2, would likely be used. The more planning that is done with your family member, the greater the role that the person will play in deciding what happens at times that he/she is unable to speak cogently for him/herself. You and your family member must decide which approach is more appropriate for your particular circumstances.

As a mental health attorney, my recommendation is to be proactive. Waiting until a crisis occurs, thus requiring a reactive approach, can be difficult, expensive and intrusive – none of which a family going through crisis needs.

The balance of this chapter section will provide a roadmap to using the legal system to get assistance and help for a person with a serious mental illness.

Power of Attorney: A Proactive Approach to Ensuring Mental Health Care

A power of attorney is a voluntary transfer of authority from one individual to another. It is established at a time when a person has the capacity to understand what the act accomplishes. It may be as broad or as limited as is needed to accomplish the intended goal. That is, it can be limited to health care issues or can be expanded to include transfer of authority to handle finances and financial decisions. Further, the power of attorney can be prepared such that it becomes active immediately or at some later time, if and when a person becomes incapacitated. When it is set up to become active at some later point in time, it is referred to as a "springing" power of attorney. In either case it is important that it is a durable power of attorney, meaning that it remains effective after the person becomes incapacitated.

A health care power of attorney is the best way for a person to leave specific directions about his or her wishes. It also empowers a specific trusted individual to carry out those directions. Thus, a mental health power of attorney can be established by a person with a serious mental illness at a time when that person is well and capable of giving specific direction about his or her mental health care. It may be used to designate someone to carry out the individual's wishes, including making him or her a voluntary inpatient at a psychiatric hospital. The wise use of such a document can avoid the need for more extreme measures such as guardianship or civil commitment (discussed below and in Section 2) both of which are reactive and intrusive proceedings, designed to accomplish the same goal as the power of attorney — getting necessary treatment.

Some of the strategies that are addressed in this chapter can be difficult to deal with because they might appear adversarial in nature. You might feel that by preparing for the times when your family member is too ill to adequately make decisions about care, you are giving up hope. Your family member might also initially express displeasure (anger or resentment) that you are anticipating problems and planning for ways to take control away from the individual. However, the fact is that this chapter describes strategies that you can use to support your family member.

Financial Power of Attorney: A Proactive Approach to Financial Planning

For financial concerns, the parallel process to the medical power of attorney is the financial power of attorney. In essence, it is a process whereby an individual appoints another person to act as his or her representative and make all of the individual's financial decisions. As with the health care portion of the power of attorney, the financial portion can become effective immediately or have "springing power" and become effective only upon the individual's incapacity. Using a planning tool such as the power of attorney can avoid the need for a conservatorship (described below), which is a court action designed to protect assets that are at risk when a person becomes unable to manage his/her affairs. Indeed, the judicious use of a financial power of attorney may even prevent much of the stress often associated with a mental health crisis. As such, the power of attorney is both a tool and a preventive measure.

Although I strongly urge power of attorney planning, families and friends of persons acutely ill with mental illness don't always enjoy the luxury of being able to plan ahead. More often than not their initial contact with the legal system is because of an urgent, if not crisis situation, that is a consequence of the individual's mental illness. In the absence of a mental health power of attorney, gaining access to treatment when an individual needs it the most but is unable to act in his own best interest will require a more reactive approach.

Guardianship: A Reactive Approach to Ensuring Mental Health Care

A guardianship is essentially a court-imposed power of attorney. It is based upon a finding that the individual does not have the capacity to make responsible health care decisions. The essential difference between a guardianship and a power of attorney is that the latter allows the individual to participate in making decisions for the time when he or she does not have the capacity to do so. The former is the court's response to a crisis created by the person's inability to make responsible health care decisions. A guardianship creates a substitute decision-maker, appointed by a court, and authorizes the guardian to make appropriate health care and mental health care decisions for the protected person, referred to as a "ward." In many states, if necessary and appropriate, a guardian may be given authority to obtain inpatient mental health treatment for a ward.

Once a guardian is appointed, he/she remains as guardian until further order of the court. When the need no longer exists, the guardianship may be terminated by the court.

Conservatorship: A Reactive Approach to Financial Planning

A conservatorship is court response similar to a guardianship except it relates to financial decisions. The conservator becomes a substitute decision-maker, and is empowered to make financial decisions for the protected person. A conservator is appointed when the person's assets are at risk and in need of protection, and there have been no prior arrangements made, such as a financial power of attorney.

A conservator is responsible to the court to file an inventory, annual accountings, and to post a bond to insure faithful performance as conservator. Like a guardianship, a conservatorship remains in effect until it is terminated by a court.

While both guardianship and conservatorship can provide valuable relief to legal complications associated with serious mental illness, both processes can be avoided by taking steps to plan for a person's incapacity. As mentioned earlier, court processes are expensive, inconvenient and intrusive. Families who plan ahead won't find such proceedings necessary.

Civil commitment, or court-ordered treatment, discussed in the next section of this chapter represents the system's most extreme response to a person's lack of planning. In the absence of a mental health power of attorney or court-appointed guardian, the court may order an individual with a mental illness into treatment. While there are legal protections in place to assure that an individual's rights are protected, the process, nevertheless, remains difficult and demeaning and is worth avoiding.

The message cannot be overemphasized. Understanding the implications of mental illness requires understanding the laws impacting individuals with a mental illness. The illness and the laws are often linked.

Whether the legal system and the law are seen as more burdensome hurdles for advocates to overcome, or as aides to the advocate in managing mental illness, is up to the reader. It is within your power to take positive steps to avoid having to look to the courts for help.

Have your family member prepare powers of attorney. Let all of the individual's wishes be known about managing a mental health crisis. See to it that your family member writes them down and communicates them to others. Have your family member designate individuals to be his/her agents, and to be in charge of carrying out his/her wishes.

In this way, your family member and you can avoid becoming over-whelmed with the legal system stress that is often associated with mental health crises. The health care and financial tools are summarized in Table 1.

ESTATE PLANNING

Many individuals with mental illnesses ultimately become recipients of government entitlement programs. If your family member is a recipient of an entitlement program, one important goal of estate planning is to see that the money, property, and possessions you want to provide for your loved one go to him/her. You probably do not want those resources to go to cover costs that the government (SSI, Medicaid, Social Security) would otherwise pay. Whether or not your family member is eligible for entitlements, a second aspect of estate planning is that assets you want to go to the well-being of your family member are not squandered or in some other way mishandled. These two issues are near and dear to many families. There are a variety of approaches to providing assets to your loved one, but the best one and the one you should definitely consider is a special needs trust (sometimes referred to as a discretionary trust). This type of trust holds assets designated for a person with a disability and is managed by someone other than the individual for whom the assets are meant to benefit.

The great advantage of such a trust is that it can be structured such that the assets are designed to supplement —*not replace* — any public assistance or entitlement program. When structured correctly, the assets do not count as resources, which might otherwise disqualify the individual from receiving government benefits. As long as the beneficiary does not have direct access to the trust, the trust will not be considered an asset in determining the individual's eligibility for public assistance. Obviously, choosing a trustee is critical. You must choose someone you know will look after your relative properly. Someone you trust to have your loved one's best interests at heart.

In setting up a trust it is important that you work with an attorney who is knowledgeable and understands any concern you might have about the resources you want to provide for your loved one.

WHAT IF YOU CAN'T AFFORD AN ATTORNEY?

Most states have a *Protection and Advocacy* agency that can provide assistance with completing Advance Directives. The Bazelon Center for Mental Health Law Web site (http://www.bazelon.org/) is also an excellent source of information and contains both Advance Directive forms and instructions, and links to state protection and advocacy agencies.

The Arizona Center for Disability Law is the protection and advocacy Center in Arizona and is a good resource for helping with a variety of legal issues, including advance directives. The center can be reached at (800) 927-2260 or (800) 922-1447. The Web site address is www.acdl.com.

The State Bar of Arizona Young Lawyers Division runs a *Modest Means Program* that provides low-cost legal assistance. One of the areas where they provide assistance is in the preparation of advance directives. To be eligible, an individual must earn less than 200 percent of the Federal Poverty Guidelines. For more information, call the Arizona Modest Means Project at (602) 266-2322.

Table 1   Summary of Legal Tools for Health Care and Finances

Issue	Legal Tools for Health Care and Mental Health Care		Legal Tools for Finances	
Approach (Tool)	Health Care Power of Attorney	Guardianship	Financial Power of Attorney	Conservatorship
How it is implemented	A proactive decision made by an individual at a time when the person has the capacity to understand what the act accomplishes. It is prepared proactively by an attorney in collaboration with the individual and family.	There must be a petitioning of the court by an interested party and then a court proceeding. A judge will, if the petition is successful, appoint a guardian.	A proactive decision made by an individual at a time when the person has the capacity to understand what the act accomplishes. It is prepared proactively by an attorney in collaboration with the individual and family.	There must be a petitioning of the court by an interested party and then a court proceeding. A judge will, if the petition is successful, appoint a conservator.
What it does	Voluntary transfer of authority to make health care decisions from the individual with a mental illness to a trusted individual. It can be prepared to go into effect immediately or at some later time, if and when the individual becomes incapacitated.	Court-imposed transfer of authority to make health care and other well-being decisions from the individual with a mental illness to another individual.	Voluntary transfer of authority to handle the financial affairs from the individual with a mental illness to a trusted individual. It can be prepared to go into effect immediately or at some later time, if and when the individual becomes incapacitated.	Court-imposed transfer of authority to handle financial affairs from an individual who is incapacitated to a trusted individual.

Chapter 12 Section 2

Involuntary Treatment/ Civil Commitment

Suzanne Hodges, J.D.

There can be times when an individual with a mental illness is not compliant with treatment and as a consequence the person's symptoms become more and more severe. As the symptoms become more severe, families obviously worry about the safety of the individual, and in some cases are concerned about their own safety or the safety of others. The family might try to talk to their loved one and try to convince the individual to take his/her medication.

The difficult question for families is what to do if, after many attempts at trying to convince their family member to comply with treatment, the individual still does not comply. One of the most difficult decisions a family member will ever have to make is when, or even whether, to seek involuntary commitment of a loved one. Involving the legal system (complete with law enforcement, service of petitions, attorneys, hearings, testimony, and judges, etc.) in treatment decisions can be traumatic. It can also have long lasting effects on family relationships. Those who seek involuntary commitment of a loved one are almost always seen by that family member in an "enemy" role for at least awhile. There are few situations that elicit as negative a response from persons with mental disorders, which is understandable. From the perspective of the individual with the illness, it is horrible to be detained in a hospital against your will, to undergo evaluations that you find useless and biased, and to have people you love testify "against" you in front of a judge. And as ill as you might be, you are aware that the judge can make you take medications that you honestly believe are unnecessary and detrimental.

To avoid these horrors, family members should always try to plan ahead with a mental health power of attorney or guardianship, as was discussed in the previous section. However, when these alternatives are unavailable, impossible or impractical to obtain, the civil commitment process may be the only way to obtain needed treatment for loved ones whose illnesses make it impossible for them to understand the need for treatment or to accept it voluntarily.

All states have laws providing for involuntary treatment/civil commitment. While the processes vary from state to state, they have several features in common. First, Involuntary Commitment is a "civil" not a "criminal" process. Unlike a criminal order for incarceration, probation or parole meant to impose punishment for illegal actions, the purpose of civil commitment is to obtain a court order requiring a person to comply with treatment needed to alleviate the symptoms of a mental illness. As traumatic as it might seem, family members should have some comfort in recognizing that a civil commitment process may be the only way to obtain help for a loved one whose illness interferes with the ability to recognize the need for help. There are no criminal consequences, no findings of guilt, and no orders for incarceration. The sole purpose of a civil commitment is to obtain treatment that will improve a loved one's quality of life. Always keep in mind that the civil commitment process is designed to do what is best for loved ones at those times when they are not capable of making good decisions about what is in their best interest.

Family members should also be aware that civil commitment is not synonymous with being "locked up." Few civil commitment procedures today result in long-term confinement in inpatient facilities. Many states allow courts to enter commitment orders that combine inpatient and outpatient treatment and require judges to order the least restrictive treatment alternatives available. These combined orders usually result in short, stabilizing inpatient stays followed by outpatient treatment under court-ordered plans that can be revoked if a person fails to comply with the terms of the court order. Revocation most often results in a return to inpatient care for further stabilization until the person is again ready for discharge to outpatient treatment under a plan prescribed by the court.

States derive their power to involuntarily commit persons with mental illness from two sources, police power (laws that protect society from danger) and *parens patriae* power (laws that allow society to act on behalf of those who are incapable of acting on their own behalf). The specific involuntary commitment standards for each state can be found on the Treatment Advocacy Center Web site (http://www.psychlaws.org/).

POLICE POWER

Laws permitting the civil commitment of persons with mental illnesses whose behavior makes them dangerous to themselves or to others are authorized under the states' police power. Police power is used in two areas:

- Danger to Self. To be a danger to oneself, a person must exhibit behaviors that suggest that he or she is in danger of actually inflicting serious physical harm upon him/herself. The danger must go beyond mere threat. There must be evidence that the individual will actually carry out the self-harm. Dangerous behaviors could include walking into traffic, prolonged refusal to eat, or failure to attend to necessary medical care if the person's health is imminently jeopardized. Recent incidents of serious physical injury that might be related to dangerous personal relationships and exposure to the elements could also be considered evidence for likely self-harm.

- Danger to Others. A person is a danger to others when his or her mental disorder so impairs judgement that he or she can be reasonably expected to cause serious physical harm to another. If a mental illness results in careless and reckless driving, a person who continues to get behind the wheel could be seen as a danger to others. Threats of harm to others are sufficient to consider the person dangerous if the individual has the means of carrying out the threat. This is especially true if the person has a history of violence.

PARENS PATRIAE POWER

States can and do act on behalf of individuals who are considered incapable of acting in their own best interest. Literally translated from Latin as "Father of the Country," the concept of *parens patriae* originated in Roman law, was incorporated into English law and then passed on to the American colonies. Upon independence, the colonies gave the power to the state legislatures where it still resides. Under the power of *parens patriae*, the state has both the right and the duty to protect individuals who are unable to care for themselves because of a mental illness. States have long used their *parens patriae* power to provide involuntary treatment to persons whose mental illness makes it impossible for them to care for themselves or provide for their basic needs, thereby endangering their health and safety. Over the past twenty years a number of states have expanded the use of their *parens patriae* authority to permit civil commitment of persons whose mental illness, if not treated, has a substantial probability of causing them to suffer harm. The two areas where parens patriae power is used are:

• Grave Disability. Until recently, grave disability was the primary basis for using *parens patriae* power to civilly commit a person whose mental illness makes it impossible for the individual to provide for his or her own basic needs. Traditionally, however, this has been a difficult standard to meet, as courts have required evidence that the person is currently suffering harm as a result of an inability for self-care. Families, who provide shelter, support and care for a loved one, might need to stop providing assistance and allow the person to suffer harm to meet the requirements for grave disability. Obviously, this is not an acceptable option for caring families.

• Persistently or Acutely Disabled (PAD). In order to address the seemingly inhumane dilemma with grave disability, a number of states have adopted a "fourth standard" for civil commitment. In order for the court to consider a person as persistently or acutely disabled, he or she must suffer from a severe mental disorder, which if not treated has a good likelihood of causing the individual to suffer severe mental or physical harm. In other words, while grave disability requires actual harm, PAD requires only the likelihood of harm. In most states, there is also a requirement that the individual has a reasonable prospect of being treatable. In enacting PAD criteria, some states have determined that they have the authority under their *parens patriae* power to intervene prior to a mentally ill person's condition reaching crisis proportions. The standard has endured challenges claiming that it is unconstitutionally over-broad since it does not require a showing of dangerous behavior and permits involuntary commitment of persons simply because they are mentally ill and in need of treatment. In upholding the PAD standard, state courts have found that a person is sufficiently dangerous when his or her mental status poses a substantial probability that he or she will suffer harm and prevents him or her from recognizing the benefits that he or she could derive from treatment. Involuntary treatment orders based on the PAD standard have increased steadily over the years as states have come to terms with their responsibility to help an individual who is a danger to self precisely because the nature of his/her illness prevents him/her from seeking and accepting treatment.

The specific standards for each state can be found on the Web site www.psychlaws.org. Once on the site, go to "Legal Resources."

DUE PROCESS PROTECTIONS

Since the 1960s it has been well established that decisions to detain a person involuntarily or to require involuntary administration of psychiatric medications are judicial decisions. As such, and because civil commitment involves a significant deprivation of liberty, courts have consistently concluded that states must afford due process protections. So what does "due process" require? While there might be some differences from state to state, due process generally requires that:

- A person is given notice and receives a fair hearing. A fair hearing includes being provided legal counsel, having the right to be present at the hearing, being able to confront witnesses and call witnesses on one's own behalf.
- There is testimony of mental health professionals.
- There is testimony of witnesses as to specific behaviors.

The facts proving the need for court-ordered treatment must be established by "clear and convincing evidence." This standard of proof is higher, and therefore more difficult to satisfy, than the normal standard of proof in civil actions, which is a "preponderance of the evidence." It is less stringent, however, than the standard used in criminal cases, which is "beyond a reasonable doubt."

BEHAVIORS MUST BE RELATED TO A MENTAL ILLNESS AND THE PERSON MUST BE UNWILLING TO ACCEPT TREATMENT

A very important point to remember is that the civil commitment process, whether based on police power standards or parens patriae, is based on two important assumptions:

• The individual's behaviors are the result of a mental illness (as opposed to substance abuse, mental retardation or an anti-social personality disorder.)
• And the person is unable or unwilling to accept treatment voluntarily.

I mention these requirements because they can prove tricky to establish and it is often family members who provide the essential information through their testimony. For example, mental illness and substance abuse coexist on such a prevalent basis (see Chapter 9) that it is sometimes difficult to establish which causes a person's behavior. There is always the old "chicken or the egg" dilemma (i.e., does she drink because she's depressed or is she depressed because she drinks?). If the person's behavior is for reasons other than a mental illness, regardless of how dangerous or disabling, the courts will not commit the individual.

Whether a person will comply voluntarily with treatment can also be a sticky issue. Confronted with the prospect of being ordered to undergo treatment, it is not unusual for a person to tell an evaluating physician that he/she will comply voluntarily. Family members may know differently from past experience. It is important to let the evaluators know if a person has a history of not following through with treatment. An expressed willingness to agree to treatment will not be the determining factor if there is testimony documenting failures to follow through with treatment agreements.

THE INVOLUNTARY CIVIL COMMITMENT PROCESS

Each state has its own specific civil commitment statutes. In all states there will be multiple levels of review to ensure that your family member's rights are protected, and that he or she is carefully evaluated to determine his or her need for treatment. To find out more about the process for civil commitment in your community you should contact the local county attorney's office.

The Specifics of the Arizona Civil Commitment process are addressed in Chapter 13

Chapter 12 Section 3

Criminal Justice Issues

Michael Shafer, Ph.D.

*Most were arrested for sitting in the parking lot of a convenience store...
and the situations escalated from there.*

All too often, individuals with a mental illness will find themselves entangled with the criminal justice system. Indeed, in many communities, law enforcement personnel and criminal justice systems are finding themselves the de facto front door into the publicly funded mental health system. Although the numbers might vary slightly, depending on which research study you read, approximately three quarters of a million individuals with a mental illness are placed in U.S. jails every year. At any one time, nearly 300,000 individuals with a mental illness are residing in jails and prisons. The number residing in jail and prison is extraordinary, especially when you consider that it is approximately four times higher than the number of individuals who are residing in state and county psychiatric hospitals. What makes the problem even more disturbing is that many individuals with a mental illness who are incarcerated committed minor offenses such as disturbing the peace, vagrancy and trespassing. Not only are the offenses often minor, they are often crimes of survival, a natural consequence of an individual's mental illness and related social problems. For example, in one study nearly a third of newly arrested individuals, who were identified as having a mental illness, were homeless at the time of their arrest. Homelessness and poverty are not illegal, but vagrancy is a misdemeanor. Individuals who are delusional or in some other way psychotic can be arrested for disturbing the peace when the symptoms of their illness frighten others in a convenience store.

The consequences of being arrested and placed in the criminal justice system can be enormous and have a snowballing effect. For example, when individuals have been arrested and jailed there is the increased likelihood that they can loose their SSI/SSDI benefits. The loss of those benefits can make getting treatment more difficult, and result in a greater chance of the individuals falling further down the ladder of stability.

The problem for individuals with a mental illness becoming ensnarled in the legal system is not just a problem in a few communities. It is a problem in many communities. For example:

- Sixteen percent of the inmates in the Los Angeles County jail system require mental health services on a daily basis. Based on sheer volume, it is the largest psychiatric facility in the country.
- The county jail in Austin, Texas, houses 300 inmates. The state hospital in Austin, located only a few miles away has a census of about 340.
- Sixteen percent of state prison inmates, seven percent of federal inmates, 16 percent of people in local jails, and 16 percent of probationers have a diagnosed mental illness.

Given the significant number of individuals with a mental illness in the criminal justice system, it is important for families to be aware of the reasons underlying the problem. More importantly, families need to be aware of the things that they can do to prevent their family member's involvement in the criminal justice system, and what to do if their loved one is arrested.

There are a number of excellent publications that address various issues relating to mental illness and jail. At the end of this chapter we provide a listing of some of the more important books and articles.

REASONS FOR THE PROBLEM

Based on the work of Dr. Richard Lamb, there appear to be four reasons why individuals with a mental illness have such a high involvement in the jail and prison system:

- Deinstitutionalization
- Strict criteria for civil commitment
- Attitudes of the police and society towards deviant behavior
- A shortage of programs and facilities for persons with a serious mental illness

Deinstitutionalization

Prior to the late 1960s and early 1970s, it was not uncommon for an individual with a serious mental illness to spend time in a local county hospital, if not a state hospital far from home. During the 1960s, as more effective medications were readily available and as the country was going through tremendous social change, there was a shift in policy concerning the hospitalization of individuals with mental illnesses. The *Community Mental Health Center Act* of 1963 set the philosophy that long-term hospitalization was appropriate only for the most treatment-resistant individuals. Others were to be discharged from hospitals and treated in a federally funded community mental health center. Younger, newly diagnosed individuals would not have to ever experience long-term hospitalization.

As it turned out, the part of the equation that dealt with getting individuals out of hospitals was much easier to accomplish than ensuring that those same individuals received adequate treatment in the community.

Tens of thousands of individuals who had been living in state and county hospitals were released to the community. In 1950, nearly 600,000 individuals resided in state and county hospitals. By 1996, that number was about 60,000. Unfortunately, the system of care that would have been required to care for those individuals was not in place. As a consequence of inadequate treatment and rehabilitation resources, and lack of opportunity, many of the individuals became involved in the legal system through the commission of a minor offense.

The irony is that through deinstitualization many individuals were released from confining hospitals and a short time later found themselves in even more confining jails and prisons. A common term for what has happened is the *criminalization of the mentally ill.*

Strict Criteria for Civil Commitment

A generation ago, it was much easier to force an individual into inpatient treatment than it is today. In most ways, the stricter criteria have been a very good thing. It can be easily argued that historically many individuals with a mental illness had their civil rights violated through the civil commitment process.

As medications have become more effective, and individuals can more readily be treated on an outpatient basis, there has been a reduced use of the civil commitment process. Many families, however, believe that the pendulum has swung too far and now it is an uphill battle to have a loved one with a mental illness hospitalized at those times that he or she is extraordinarily symptomatic but refuses voluntary treatment.

Attitudes of the Police and Society Towards Deviant Behavior

The criminal justice system is responsible for protecting society. One of the methods of protection is to arrest individuals who are accused of committing crimes and place them in jail. Law enforcement agencies and the courts are often reluctant to release individuals into the custody of a mental health system, where security might be compromised.

A Shortage of Programs and Facilities

Many communities lack resources to serve the large number of individuals with a severe mental illness. Lack of resources is in both the number of qualified staff (ranging from case managers to psychiatrists) and the number of programs, particularly housing programs. As a consequence, many of the most challenging individuals "fall through the cracks" of the mental health system and find themselves in the criminal justice system.

RECOMMENDATIONS FOR PREVENTION

Over the past 10 years, a great deal has been learned about how to keep an individual with a mental illness from being involved with the criminal justice system. The four most important factors are:

• Diversion programs
• Increased availability of programs and services
• Assertive case management
• Active family involvement

Diversion Programs

Many communities have established special cooperative programs between mental health systems, law enforcement and criminal justice systems to assist in the identification and diversion of persons with mental illness from criminal prosecution and incarceration. By diversion, we are referring to specialized programs that identify, screen, and link persons that have committed (or have been arrested for committing) a criminal offense with mental health services. Jail diversion programs have developed in many communities because our court systems and jails are not effectively set up to meet the special needs of persons with mental illness, and there's a general recognition that a person with mental illness who has committed a crime does not represent a criminal. Simply put, law enforcement and criminal justice systems by and large are not interested in prosecuting and incarcerating persons with mental illness when other alternatives are available. As such, prosecutors, judges and jailers are increasingly looking at programs that deflect or divert persons with mental illness away from criminal prosecution and to effective mental health treatment.

The mechanisms that are being developed in many communities to address these issues are diverse. The two most common mechanisms by which persons with mental illness are being diverted from prosecution and incarceration are front-end and back-end diversion programs.

By front-end diversion programs, we mean specialized systems of crisis intervention and police response systems that avoid the arrest and prosecution of persons with mental illness who have committed a crime. Perhaps the most noted example of front-end diversion has been developed in Memphis, Tennessee, which has a program referred to as Crisis Intervention Training (CIT). In this type of program, police officers have received specialized training in how to identify individuals who are mentally ill and have learned specialized techniques to handle people in crisis or who are symptomatic. Once trained, these officers become recognized as CIT officers and wear special pins identifiable in the community. These officers are then dispatched to scenes where other, untrained officers have encountered an individual who is behaving irrationally, or whom they believe to be mentally ill. The CIT officer will then assume control of the situation, stabilize the individual, and then transport the individual to a specialized crisis stabilization and assessment unit, usually operated by a hospital or a residential treatment agency. Once there, the individual is assessed for mental health symptoms, and if need be, referred to a mental health treatment facility. In this type of specialized program, the police do not typically file any charges against the individual and subsequent prosecution and incarceration is avoided all together.

Other communities have implemented differing forms of front-end diversion alternatives, often times referred to as "MAC teams." MAC teams refer to Mobile Acute Crisis teams, usually a two-person team of mental health professionals who work in tandem with local law enforcement. The MAC team often assists police in de-escalating crisis situations and transporting individuals to crisis stabilization facilities where the individual can be safely and reliably assessed. Regardless of the specific form of front-end diversion that may be in place in a community, there are important features that should be adhered to:

- A close, trusting relationship between law enforcement personnel and local community mental health providers. This in itself is not an easy feat, given the vast differences in organizational cultures and values that permeate mental health treatment systems and law enforcement/criminal justice systems.
- Alternatives places to take individuals who are in crisis where they can be safely and securely assessed, treated, and if need be, referred (and transferred) to ongoing mental health treatment. Repeatedly, law enforcement personnel have expressed frustration at the lack of alternatives to jail where they can take individuals who are in mental health crisis. As such, providing safe and secure settings, where MAC teams and law enforcement personnel can transport and drop off individuals who are in crisis, is a critical aspect of effective front-end diversion programs.
- Criminal prosecution is almost always avoided in front-end diversion programs, eliminating the need for costly court proceedings and incarceration.

The second form of jail diversion alternatives that have developed in many communities are back-end diversion programs. By back-end diversion, we are referring to specialized arrangements that allow for the dropping of criminal charges and subsequent incarceration of individuals *after* they have been arrested and charged by local law enforcement personnel. In these forms of programs, individuals who are mentally ill and in crisis and have committed an offense are arrested and booked into jail by local law enforcement personnel. Once booked, however, individuals are screened for mental illness, and if it is determined to be present, considered for diversion. In these types of situations, special arrangements are made between the prosecutor, the public defender, and the courts, whereby the individual is released from custody and pending criminal charges in exchange for an agreement to receive mental health treatment. In some communities, the original criminal charges are dropped entirely; in other communities, the charges are suspended, pending continuing participation in court-mandated mental health services, generally 90 days to six months in duration. A more recent development is specialized mental health courts to process these back-end diversion cases. In mental health courts, a team including a lawyer from the prosecutor's office, the public defender's office, and staff from the court and typically the local mental health system work together to review and process the cases of individuals who are known to be mentally ill and have charges pending against them. These mental health courts have been shown to be more efficient since a dedicated team, representing all facets of the criminal justice system work together, and are better informed about mental illness and the community resources that are available to help persons with mental illness.

Increased Availability of Programs and Services

There are some individuals who at times in their life require a highly supervised, structured environment. Although the criminal justice system is a rigidly structured environment, it should not be used as a substitute for the mental health system. Mental health systems need to have the kinds of programs that can help keep people out of the criminal justice system. This would include intensive, structured activity and housing programs. It also means the availability of services beyond the traditional 8 a.m. to 5 p.m., Monday through Friday.

Assertive Case Management

Assertive case management can serve two functions. First, it can provide the amount of monitoring necessary to help prevent an arrest in the first place. Second, many individuals with a mental illness are arrested for minor crimes. Knowing that the individual is involved in assertive case management can play a role in helping the criminal justice system feel more comfortable in releasing the person to a mental health diversion program.

Active Family Involvement

Family involvement is important for two reasons:

- You will be in a better position to help ensure that your loved one is receiving the necessary intensity of treatment and case management. This is especially true at those times when your family member might have the potential for involvement with the police.

- The criminal justice system might be more likely to allow for quicker release if there is strong family involvement.

Caught Between Two Systems

A few years ago a television newsmagazine produced a story about a young man who was caught between the mental health and criminal justice systems.

The young man was diagnosed with schizophrenia when he was 19. But even prior to his diagnosis he was a troubled youngster. He never did well in school and never interacted well with others. He was picked on quite a bit in high school and was targeted as the "odd schoolmate." So when he became very ill in his senior year, we were not terribly surprised. He has never responded well to medication, even when he would take it, which was not often or regular. He has always been resistant to getting treatment. His parents did everything that they could to try to get him services. They would even take him to his appointments. Most of the time he would refuse to go, and the mental health center said there was nothing they could do to force him to accept treatment if he didn't want treatment. They said that if he wasn't dangerous he couldn't be treated against his will.

For years his parents pleaded to get him into treatment, but the mental health system said that unless he voluntarily came in there was nothing they could do. They begged for their son to be forced into treatment. The professionals shrugged. They indicated that their hands were tied. Then, after five years of pleading, the young man stole two of his father's guns.

His reason was related to his delusion of vampires and the need to protect himself. It was this act that finally got him some attention. Unfortunately, it was not the attention of the mental health system. It was the attention of the police. A neighbor complained about the young man walking around in the back yard yelling profanities at the trees and waving the gun back and forth. Not only did he wave the gun around, he actually discharged two rounds. When the police arrived, they were not concerned with his mental illness. They were more concerned with the safety of the community and the individual himself. They were wearing bulletproof vests and helmets. At one particular moment they came from all directions. He was knocked to the ground and the rifle knocked away from him. Fortunately, no one was hurt. But that was just the beginning of a long, drawn-out criminal proceeding.

Submitted by J.U.

Would a Mental Health/Law Enforcement Team Have Made a Difference?

A man with a mental illness was killed by police. The man's sister said her brother may not have understood officers when they yelled at him to drop a large butcher knife. "I'm not sure if he understood when other people would speak to him," Mary said Tuesday afternoon.

Ray, 52, was killed Monday at the group home where he lived. Four officers fired at him after they said he lunged toward them with the knife. "I think they acted a bit too quickly," Mary said. "I believe they should have sent someone more trained for that situation."

The police said they used great restraint, telling Ray several times to drop the knife. Ray, who was threatening the group home's caretaker, steadfastly refused, police said.

Mary remembers her brother as a gentle, playful soul who needed 24-hour supervision.

When Ray came to the front door of the house with the knife in his hand, a police officer shot him four times with non-lethal beanbag rounds. "But this had little effect on Raymond," said a police department spokesperson. "At that point, they're faced with a life-threatening situation."

After being struck four times with the beanbag rounds, Ray walked back into the house, leaving the front door open and allowing four police officers inside. Once inside, they said Ray lunged at them holding the large butcher knife over his head. That was when officers fired ten rounds.

Mary said her brother relied on medication to keep him stable, but even with medication he often heard voices in his head. She said he believed the voices were stealing from him and he would argue with them. "He would get mad at the voices," she said. But she said he wasn't violent and didn't believe the voices told him to act violently.

Based on a story in The Arizona Republic, June 27, 2001

CHAPTER 13

The Arizona System of Care:
Things Families Need to Know

"God gives every bird its food, but he does not throw it into the nest."
—Josiah Holland

Rhonda Baldwin, MSW, CISW
Suzanne Baldwin Hodges, J.D. (Civil Commitment Section)

Have you ever tried assembling a child's swing set? The colorful, fully assembled picture on the front of the carton belies the fact that you are about to begin a task that is next to impossible. If you have ever attempted such a project, you probably know the frustration of trying to make sense of instructions that make very little sense. The diagram instructions are printed in a font so small and light that they are hard to read without a magnifying glass. And for some reason the parts that are listed don't always match the parts that you have in your little cellophane packet. The instructions never tell you that the assembly will take much longer than you anticipated or that the "simple" process of connecting the parts requires a team of individuals with backgrounds ranging from mechanical engineering to carpentry. You won't find anywhere in the instructions the fact that there will be screws, bolts and other assorted parts left over, and that you will spend the night wondering what you did wrong. You will wonder how long it is going to be before the swing set falls over or in some other way falls apart. You pray that if it does collapse, it won't do so while your child or a friend of your child is swinging as high as they can.

One interesting thing about assembling something like a child's swing set is that it is only *after you have been through the process* that you begin to understand the instructions.

This can also be said of trying to understand and make the best use of local mental health systems. At first, the process can appear to be unwieldy, complex, bureaucratic, and user-unfriendly. This is particularly true since the first experience of most families with the mental health system is during a time of crisis or escalation of symptoms — not necessarily the best time to try to understand the intricacies of how to obtain care. It is only after having been involved with the mental health system for some time that families begin to understand how it operates and how to make sure that their family member gets the most out of the system.

In Arizona, the mental health system is structured around a combination of federal and state funding, and implemented on a regional basis. (While there can be some county funding, it is not a major part of the system of care.) As with any government program, there are a number of rules and regulations that are passed down with the funding. These rules and regulations determine many of the operations of the programs that your loved one might be using. As the money to fund the system filters down from one layer of government to the next, each adds its own rules and regulations. At times, these rules not only seem confusing and cumbersome, but also they actually appear to be in conflict with each other. However, if you understand these rules (the instructions to the system if you will), they can assist you and your family in receiving care.

The purpose of this chapter is to provide you with an understanding of the "instructions" for operating the public mental system in Arizona.

As with other chapters, the goal is for you to be able to take the information and use it to the benefit of your loved one. The aspects of the system that are important for you to understand are:

- The Mental Health System in Arizona Is a "Carve Out" and There Are Implications for You and Your Family Member
- How the System of Care Is Funded and Managed
- Where to Go to Get Services in Your Community
- Getting Enrolled in Services
- Treatment Planning and Services
- What to So If You Have a Concern or Complaint
- Arnold v. Sarn: The Lawsuit That Made a Difference
- The Civil Commitment Process
- The Network of Family Support
- Information Used to Determine a Serious Mental Illness

Before addressing the topics just listed, I want to discuss the phrases *behavioral health system* and *mental health system*. In Arizona, the agency responsible for the delivery of services to individuals with various mental illnesses and substance abuse is the *Division of Behavioral Health Services*. In other states, the equivalent governmental entity might be referred to as the Department of Mental Health. In still other states it is the Department of Mental Hygiene. In Arizona, because the responsible agency has the phrase *Behavioral Health* in its name, the services are often referred to as *behavioral health services*. Many families do not like this term, however, because it implies that the individuals served have behavioral as opposed to biological problems. I bring this up not so much to discuss the merits of the words, but rather to explain why I will use the phrase *mental health system* in this chapter rather than behavioral health system. It is after all a mental illness, not a behavioral illness.

THE MENTAL HEALTH SYSTEM IN ARIZONA IS A "CARVE OUT" AND THERE ARE IMPLICATIONS FOR YOU AND YOUR FAMILY MEMBER

The first thing you need to know about the public mental health system in Arizona is that it is what is referred to as a "carve out." In health care terminology, a "carve out" (one of those managed-care terms that didn't even exist 20 years ago) is an array of services that is provided somewhat separately and distinctly from other aspects of health care.

For most other health care problems, people go to their family doctor. If your doctor believes that a specialist is needed, an appropriate referral is made. Your family doctor will likely refer you to a specialist with whom he or she is familiar. Even illnesses that require long-term specialty care are likely part of a larger system that is affiliated with your family doctor. This is not the case, however, for public mental health services. In Arizona, public mental health services are provided in a system that is somewhat separate from the rest of health care.

HOW THE SYSTEM OF CARE IS FUNDED AND MANAGED

Funding of the System

Funding for the public mental health system in Arizona comes primarily from two sources, the federal and state governments. (As mentioned, some counties in Arizona also provide some funding. The county funding, if it does exist, is often quite restricted in its use.)

The federal and state money passes through, and is coordinated by, the Arizona Department of Health Services/Division of Behavioral Health Services (ADHS/DBHS).

• Federal Dollars: The Center for Medicare/Medicaid Services (CMMS), (formerly known as The Health Care Finance Administration) provides the federal share of Medicaid funding to the Arizona Health Care Cost Containment System (AHCCCS). AHCCCS in turn, has a contract with the (ADHS/DBHS) to provide mental health services for people who are eligible for the Medicaid program. Thus, ADHS/DBHS is the mental health "carve out" described above. To be eligible for Medicaid, an individual must meet certain financial criteria.

In 2000, prior to the passage of Proposition 204, eligibility for Medicaid in Arizona was set at approximately 34 percent of Federal Poverty Level (FPL). The result was that many individuals and families who were in fact very needy could not quality for Medicaid. For example, at the 34 percent FPL, *a family of four that made $5,200 in 2000 would not be eligible* for Medicaid. *And, a single person making more than $2,500 would not be eligible.* Proposition 204 increased the eligibility to 100% of the FPL. Thus, in 2001 a family of four can make over $17,000 and still be eligible and a single individual can make approximately $8,500. As with other Medicaid programs, AHCCCS coverage can include payment of Medicare premiums, coinsurance and deductibles for individuals who are QMB eligible (see Chapter 11). In Arizona as elsewhere, legislation is continually changing and hence it is important to keep up to date.

In addition to CMMS, there are two other federal agencies that provide funding. The Center for Mental Health Services provides funding through what are called Mental Health Block Grants. And the Center for Substance Abuse Prevention and Treatment, through Substance Abuse Block Grants, also provides funding to ADHS/DBHS.

• State Dollars: The Arizona State Legislature allocates money to ADHS/DBHS to provide services for individuals with mental illnesses and substance abuse problems who are not eligible for the Medicaid program. The state dollars are also used to fund non-Medicaid allowable services for individuals who are Medicaid eligible. The state funding (referred to as subvention funding) that is used to provide services to adults is separated into three categories. There is funding for:

  - General Mental Health
  - Serious Mental Illness
  - Substance Abuse

The fact that the funding is separated into three populations or categories has significance to families because:

  - The dollars cannot be moved from one population to another.
  - The amount of money available differs across the populations.
  - There are restrictions that govern who may or may not benefit from the funds as well as what types of services can be provided.

ADHS/DBHS takes the federal and state funds it receives, pools the funding, and contracts with private organizations to manage and implement local programs. These organizations, called Regional Behavioral Health Authorities (RBHAs), are directly answerable to ADHS/DBHS for making sure that mental health and substance abuse services are available and accessible in the geographic regions of the state for which they are responsible[1]. While the RBHAs are private organizations, they must comply with the rules and regulations that are laid out by the funding sources.

The funding picture is illustrated in Figure 1. A map identifying the RBHAs and geographic regions of the state for which they are responsible can be seen in the map in Figure 2.

There are also Tribal RBHAs. For information concerning the Tribal RBHA system, including geographic responsibilities, you should contact ADHS/DBHS.

Figure 1

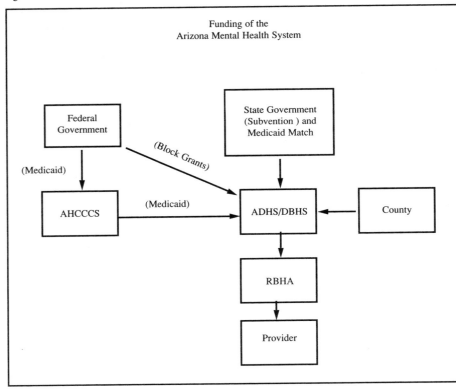

Funding of the
Arizona Mental Health System

Management of the System

The way in which services are funded and managed has changed over time. In the 1970s and into the 1980s, services were funded under what were referred to as Grant-In-Aid programs. Under such funding, someone who showed up at a Community Mental Health Center (CMHC) would be admitted into one of the programs that was provided by the CMHC. This worked fairly well as long as the programs offered by the CMHC matched what the individual wanted and needed. If there were no programs that matched the needs of a particular individual, however, it is quite likely that the individual's needs would not be met.

Programs were in place and the needs of the people had to meet the program as opposed to the program meeting the needs of the people.

There was also very little linkage and coordination between programs. Individuals were often treated as though they were "hot potatoes." It was not uncommon during Grant-In-Aid funding for individuals to be referred back and forth between programs, with no one agency taking responsibility to make sure that the individual's needs were being met.

During this same period, as advances were being made in the biological and psychosocial treatment of mental illness, the costs for health care were increasing. As a way to help meet the needs of individuals, and also to reduce costs, many private and public health care programs began implementing "managed care." The intent of managed care was to fit treatment to the individual's specific needs. It was believed that an individual would be able to maintain a higher level of wellness if one agency was assigned responsibility for managing his or her care. An underlying assumption of managed care is that treatment/rehabilitation services need to match the specific and unique needs of individuals. The criticism of managed care is that while individuals may need specific types of services, they are often not available. Additionally, because of the cost cutting nature in which some managed care programs have been implemented, some families have maintained that service availability has actually been reduced.

Managed care, like any other approach to health care delivery, has both good and bad points, and it is likely that the debate over managed care will continue for some time.

Figure 2

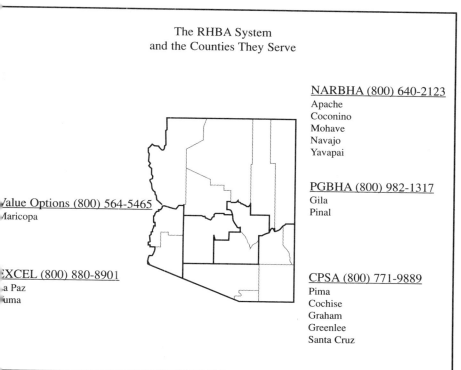

The RHBA System
and the Counties They Serve

NARBHA (800) 640-2123
Apache
Coconino
Mohave
Navajo
Yavapai

PGBHA (800) 982-1317
Gila
Pinal

Value Options (800) 564-5465
Maricopa

CPSA (800) 771-9889
Pima
Cochise
Graham
Greenlee
Santa Cruz

EXCEL (800) 880-8901
La Paz
Yuma

As mentioned above, RBHA's manage mental health services regionally. A RBHA's primary role is to monitor the quality of care and make sure that people are receiving the services they need.

A RBHA:

- Can be a not-for-profit or for-profit organization.
- Can be responsible for one or more of the six regions of the state.
- Has three- to five-year contracts that are awarded by ADHS/DBHS through a competitive bidding process, which means that the RBHAs may change over time.
- Can provide services directly or contract with local agencies and individual practitioners to provide services.

As you can see, there can be many layers between the initial funding and your family member's actual service provider.

WHERE TO GO TO GET SERVICES
IN YOUR COMMUNITY

The RBHA's, as of summer 2001, are listed in the following table along with the counties that they are responsible for, their phone numbers and Web sites.

County	RBHA	Telephone Number and Internet Web site
Yuma La Paz	EXCEL Group	(800) 880-8901 www.excelgroup.org
Pinal Gila	Pinal-Gila Behavioral Health Association (PGBHA)	(800) 982-1317 www.hs.state.az.us/bhs/pgbha.htm
Pima	Community Partnership of Southern Arizona (CPSA)	(520) 325-4268 (800) 959-1063 www.cspa-rbha.org
Cochise Graham Greenlee Santa Cruz	Community Partnership of Southern Arizona (CPSA)	(520) 325-4268 (800) 959-1063 www.cspa-rbha.org
Apache Coconino Mohave Navajo Yavapai	Northern Arizona Regional Behavioral Health Association (NARBHA)	(800) 640-2123 www.narbha.com
Maricopa	Value Options (VO)	(800) 564-5465 www.hs.state.az.us/bhs/voptions.htm

If, for whatever reason, you cannot reach your local RBHA, you can call ADHS/DBHS at (800) 867-5808 or (602) 381-8999 for information and assistance. They can direct you to the appropriate resource. ADHS/DBHS also has a Web site (www.hs.state.az.us/bhs) that might be helpful.

As mentioned above, there are categories of funding within the mental health system referred to as categorical. Specific "pots" of money are used to support treatment of a specific category of disability (such as substance abuse or mental illness) or a category of people (such as children, Medicaid recipients, pregnant substance abusers or persons with serious mental illness). The issue of how services are funded is important to families for two reasons:

• Resources are limited.
• The group that your family member falls into (both funding and category) can determine when *and even if* treatment will be provided.

For instance, CMMS provides significant funding and it *mandates* that programs that receive its funding make services available for individuals who are eligible for Medicaid. As Medicaid money passes from HCFA to AHCCCS to ADHS/DBHS to the RBHAs, the mandate remains. If your family member is not Medicaid eligible, then the funding for services comes from the Federal Block Grants and state subvention resources. If an individual is not Medicaid eligible, there are no mandates from HCFA, and the non-eligible individual may have a harder time gaining access to care.

The good news is the passage of Proposition 204 in November 2000. Prior to Proposition 204 to be eligible for Medicaid in Arizona an individual could make no more than 34 percent of the FPL. Thus, if the FPL were $8,500 for a single individual, *someone making $3,000 in Arizona would not have been eligible for Medicaid services.* Proposition 204 raised the poverty level in Arizona to 100 percent of the FPL. The implication for families is that individuals who previously were not eligible for Medicaid and its benefits are now eligible.

GETTING ENROLLED IN SERVICES

In order to receive publicly funded mental health services in Arizona, the first step an individual must take is to make an intake appointment with the RBHA or an agency that has a contract with the RBHA. Each RBHA has a slightly different process for scheduling an intake, and processes at the RBHA and ADHS/DBHS level can change over time, so it is important to contact the RBHA and find out the specifics of their process.

• Within a few days after someone calls to request services, he or she should receive an evaluation. One of the purposes of the evaluation is to determine whether or not the individual has a serious mental illness. As mentioned earlier, this determination has significant implications. Individuals who receive the determination of having a serious mental illness are more likely to receive intensive services not generally available to individuals who are designated as not having a serious mental illness.

• At the evaluation, information about current symptoms, history of past treatment, past diagnoses, medications that may have been prescribed, and a family history will need to be presented. The intake worker will also want information and documentation concerning income, eligibility for entitlement programs and any existing insurance coverage. If possible, it would be good for your family member to have a copy of past medical records.

• The individual who conducts the evaluation may or may not be a psychiatrist or psychologist. The person will, however, be qualified to evaluate your family member's mental health problems. A psychiatrist or psychologist will review the evaluation and your family member's past history and make a decision as to whether or not your family member has a serious mental illness. The decision will be based on a process known as the *SMI Determination Process*. The process is based on a number of criteria, such as diagnosis and functioning level. The specific criteria are included at the end of this chapter.

• Within one to two weeks after the request for services, your family member will receive a call informing him/her of the decision.

• Once it is has been determined that an individual meets the criteria for a serious mental illness, the person will be enrolled in services and assigned a clinician or a case manager who will be responsible for coordinating the individual's care.

  - An appointment with a case manager should occur within approximately a week of enrollment in the SMI system of care.

  - An appointment to see a psychiatrist should be scheduled within a month. An appointment with a psychiatrist will be scheduled sooner if there is a need.

  - Upon enrollment, your family member should be provided with a statement of an individual's rights, along with information on how to file complaints. Your family member should also receive a handbook that describes available services. It is important to keep this information for reference.

It should be noted that even though the system of care in Arizona receives federal and state funding, the providers of services have "co-payment" schedules. This means that while anyone who meets criteria might be eligible for services, those services are not necessarily free. Individuals with no resources will likely not pay anything. However, the more income or resources available to the individual, the more the provider agency might charge for services.

If it is determined that your family member does not to have a serious mental illness, he/she will be referred to general mental health services. Each RBHA has its own approach to providing general mental health services. You will need to contact the RBHA to learn about its approach. If you disagree with the determination that your family member does not have a serious mental illness, you can file an appeal. (See the Appeals and Grievances section later in this chapter.)

TREATMENT PLANNING AND SERVICES

One of the first things that should happen once your family member becomes enrolled in services is the development of a treatment plan (often referred to as an Individual Service Plan or ISP). Treatment planning is an extremely important activity and consists of two parts. One part is the goals (both short- and long-term) that your family member sets. The other aspect of the treatment plan is the identification of services that will need to be provided for your family member to achieve his/her goals. Treatment planning is very important because it becomes a blueprint for the types of services your family member will receive.

Depending on the individual's needs and the goals that have been set, the recommended services may vary from outpatient counseling to hospitalization. Psychiatric services, psychotropic medication, counseling, some types of housing services, residential programs and hospital services are all available, depending on the person's needs. Each RBHA's Member Handbook identifies the particular services that are available.

I can't emphasize enough the importance of the treatment plan. It is, essentially, a contract between your family member and the provider. And the treatment plan is important, not just at enrollment, but as long as your family member is enrolled in services. It should be updated regularly and serve as a roadmap for where your family is going and how they are going to get there.

WHAT TO DO IF YOU HAVE
A CONCERN OR COMPLAINT

In the best of all worlds, your interactions with the mental health system will be positive and your family member will receive all of the services that you and he/she believe are appropriate and necessary. Unfortunately, receiving what you believe is appropriate and necessary is not always the case for people trying to get care for a loved one with a mental illness. It is not uncommon for families and individuals receiving services to disagree with the treatment provided or the way it is provided. If you are having difficulty obtaining care for your family member, or if you disagree with his/her treatment plan, there are number of options available to you. The system has mechanisms to assist people in getting the care they need. The mechanism does not always work fast but it does work.

Staff members employed in the mental health system are likely working there because they want to help people. By and large, they are caring individuals. Families can find, however, that it sometimes seems like there are barriers to care. One of your jobs as an advocate is to make sure staff find a way to say "yes" to providing services that your family member needs. If you are not experienced as an advocate when the treatment/rehabilitation process starts, *you will become skilled* as the process moves along. It has been mentioned many times in this book that one way to become a skilled advocate for your family member is to get involved in NAMI and to learn from other families. Some specifics that are important in your advocacy are:

• Get a Signed Release: Your family member should sign a release that will allow you to be involved in their rehabilitation. The release will give the treatment team the authorization to share information with you.

• Get Organized: When advocating for your family member, you will need to be organized. A three-ring binder is a great organizational tool. Keep copies of important documents, such as psychiatric evaluations, treatment plans, copies of letters, notices of meetings, other important medical records, an insurance card, and benefits information. You will likely be asked for copies of these documents more than once so you might want to keep them together. You can also use the notebook as a place to document phone calls you might have with the people who are providing services. When you receive or place a phone call, you should make a note of the day and time, the name, title and phone number of the person you spoke with, and what was discussed.

- Keep a Telephone Directory: You might also want to have a section of the three-ring binder listing phone numbers to call in case you want more support and assistance. Some important phone numbers include Member Services at your RBHA; ADHS/DBHS Grievance and Appeals office; and support groups in your area, such as NAMI or the Mental Health Association.

- Get Support: Think about whether making a complaint is a process that you feel comfortable doing alone. Dealing with mental health professionals can be intimidating. At times, families can feel as though they will be "targeted" if they complain. You may find yourself in a room with a psychiatrist, case manager, social worker, nurse or others who may try to persuade you and your family member to accept things that you really do not believe will be in your family member's best interest. It can be helpful to have a friend or another family member with you to offer support for your point of view. It is best if your family member agrees to have you participate with them in making sure they get the services they need.

- Remember! You're the Expert: Families are experts when it comes to the needs of their family members. They have known and loved them during good times and bad. They know their symptoms. Families are also the ones who often have to deal with the consequences of inadequate treatment. When you are asking for help, you are doing it because you, more than anyone else, know the consequences of not receiving help. The mental health system in Arizona has family involvement as one of its core values. You need to make it a reality for your family member. With your family member's permission, inform the staff that you want to be part of any treatment planning efforts, you want to be listed as a primary contact, and you will be calling for periodic updates about the treatment efforts.

In every way you can, convey to the staff that you want to be a member of the treatment team in the care of your family member. If you can, try to put your ideas in writing. It does not need to be lengthy. For example, after any meetings that discuss a plan for treatment, drop a note to the lead staff person and keep a copy for your notebook. The note can read something like the following:

"Thank you for our meeting yesterday about the care my son needs to receive. We got a lot accomplished. You will be contacting my son by Friday to work out his new therapy schedule and you will have set up an appointment for him to look at housing alternatives by the end of the month. We did not resolve the problems he is having with his current medication, but you will set up an appointment with his psychiatrist on the 10th for a review of his current status. If there is any change in what we discussed, please call."

This type of note does a couple of things. First, the person you wrote to will know that you are appreciative. This might seem like a small thing, but staff members rarely get thanked for the good that they do. Even if you are disagreeing with them, you can do it in an agreeable way. It will help keep the lines of communication open.

The note can also serve as a written record of who is responsible for certain tasks. This can be an invaluable document if you end up in a formal appeal process and must produce documents that tell your story. If you do not have time for a written note, then you can accomplish the same thing by placing a telephone call. Just make sure that you document your call. Remember also to always convey that you see yourself as an active participant in your family member's treatment.

There may be budgetary or other agency issues that make provision of services difficult. If the case manager is having a difficult time finding resources for your family member, the manager may try to get you to empathize with his/her dilemma. The reality is that the manager probably does not have sufficient resources to provide everything needed by every person on his/her caseload. Managers have large caseloads and there are enormous needs. They might hope that if you feel empathetic toward their problems, you will lessen the pressure on them and accept something less than what you believe is right. *You should be empathetic about their problems, but systemic problems are issues for another forum and they cannot be your primary concern today.* Make them your concern tomorrow. You can be respectful of the case manager without giving up your own concern. For example, you might say the following:

"It must be extremely difficult to be in your position and see so many people with so many needs. I am glad that my only goal right now is to make sure that my daughter has the things we agreed to in her treatment plan. How are we going to get that accomplished?"

You will possibly find that over time you are becoming more knowledgeable about community resources and programs than your loved one's case manager. There is high turn over and many staff members are new to the community. As a matter of fact, one of the major complaints of families is the number of times their family member's case manager changes. Feel free to make suggestions and come up with different ideas about how to serve your family member. You should be part of the team that is finding creative solutions to the problems that are faced by your family member. Your creativity might help some of the staff think about other creative solutions.

Appeals and Grievances

If your family member continues to have problems in obtaining the services you believe are appropriate and necessary, or if you believe that your family member's rights were violated, an appeal or grievance can be filed. It is important to be aware, however, that *only the person, their guardian, or a designated representative may file an appeal*. RBHAs will likely deny appeals filed by family members who are not designated representatives. (See Chapter 12 and make sure to talk to your family member about this important topic.)

As indicated above, before filing an appeal or grievance it is important to first try to resolve the problem with the case manager, clinician, psychiatrist, supervisor or anyone else in a position of authority.

• The Appeal Process: An appeal is a *formal* disagreement. An appeal can be filed over either a decision with which you disagree, or a complaint about services that your family member is receiving. The two primary situations leading to appeals are:

  - Your family member was denied eligibility for SMI service and you believe that they have a serious mental illness and should be eligible. In that case, you would file an appeal to present additional evidence to show that your family member is suffering from a mental illness that is covered by the ADHS checklist.

  - You have complaints about any of the services that your family member is receiving or not receiving, or concerns about something that is going to happen in the future (e.g., a reduction of services that is scheduled for next month).

Each RBHA can provide you with the specifics of their particular procedures. ADHS/DBHS mandates that all RBHA appeal processes follow state guidelines. If you file an appeal, you need to make sure that you follow the procedures and timelines identified in the RBHA's Member Handbook. Failure to do so could jeopardize your right to file an appeal.

Once you have filed an appeal, you should get a response from the RBHA within five working days. The initial response will invite you to attend an "informal conference" to discuss the problem. If at that conference the problem is not resolved, the appeal will move to the next level. Eventually, you could have a hearing before an Administrative Law Judge. The final resolution could even end up in court. Most appeals, however, are resolved at the informal conference. There is every incentive for the RBHA to resolve issues before they get to the higher levels of state government. If you have any questions or concerns about the process and the RBHA has been unable to answer your questions, you can call the ADHS/DBHS Office of Grievances and Appeals ((602) 381-8999). The Arizona Center for Disability Law (800) 927-2260 can also provide assistance with filing appeals.

• The Grievance Process: You use the grievance process if you believe that your family member's rights have been violated, or that they have been abused or mistreated by staff of the RBHA or contractors of the RBHA. For example, if your family member is in a group home and was denied visitors or mail, his/her rights might have been violated. If your family member has been hit or sexually abused, you would obviously have a grievance. The grievance process applies only to people who have a serious mental illness.

The process for filing a grievance is similar to that of filing an appeal, and is described in the RBHA Member Handbook. If you believe that your family member has been mistreated, it is important for you to use the grievance process to let others know that these abuses have occurred. It is everyone's responsibility to make sure that treatment programs are safe, therapeutic places for people to receive care.

If you are unsure about whether your concern involves an appeal or grievance, you can call your RBHA or ADHS/DBHS to find out the answer. It is important to file something, even if you are not sure whether your complaint is an appeal or grievance. Someone will review your complaint and decide if it is an appeal or grievance.

ARNOLD VS. SARN: THE LAWSUIT THAT MADE A DIFFERENCE

People with serious mental illness, even those who are not Medicaid eligible, have a high priority for services based on the outcome of an Arizona Supreme Court decision in the Arnold vs. ADHS lawsuit (generally referred to as Arnold vs. Sarn). The decision made it clear that a continuum of care must be available for persons with a serious mental illness, irrespective of cost.

It has been argued for years, however, by providers that the state does not provide the funding to pay for all the services necessary. Consequently, there is always a tension between the people who need the services and the organizations that are responsible to pay for them. In the year 2001, over 15 years after the original suit, the issues of Arnold vs. Sarn are still being worked out.

THE CIVIL COMMITMENT PROCESS

In Chapter 12, civil commitment was addressed. One of the major points made was that all states derive their power to involuntarily commit persons with mental illnesses from two sources: *police power* and the *parens patriae power*. Laws permitting the civil commitment of a person with a mental illness whose behavior makes him dangerous to self and others is authorized under the state's police power. Laws permitting the civil commitment of persons whose mental illness makes it impossible to care for their health and safety is authorized under *parens patriae* power.

This next section addresses the specifics of the civil commitment process in Arizona. That is, what does a family do if they have a family member with a mental illness who is not complying with treatment and that individual is either unable to care for her health or safety, or is potentially dangerous to herself or others?

In Arizona, Civil Commitment laws can be found in the Arizona Revised Statue. You might also hear civil commitment laws referred to as Title 36.

The Civil Commitment Process: How Does it Start?

In Arizona, the commitment process can be started in two ways: through an application for emergency admission to an inpatient facility or through an application for court-ordered evaluation. An application for emergency admission is made when a person is imminently dangerous to self or others and is likely to suffer serious physical harm or illness, or inflict serious physical harm on another person without immediate hospitalization. Such an application is made in writing to an inpatient evaluation agency by a person with knowledge of the facts requiring admission and based on personal observations of the applicant. A family member's call to 911 may precipitate an emergency admission to an inpatient facility and an application for emergency evaluation if the loved one is unwilling or unable to accept emergency admission. A family member who has witnessed dangerous behavior or heard serious threats should be prepared to serve as the applicant for an emergency evaluation and to testify at the commitment hearing.

Any responsible individual may apply for a court-ordered evaluation of a person with mental illness who exhibits behaviors demonstrating that she is a danger to herself or to others, gravely disabled, or persistently or acutely disabled. This process should not be used if the person's behaviors are imminently dangerous since the pre-petition screening process may take up to 48 hours, excluding weekends and holidays, to complete. The application is made to a licensed evaluation/screening agency on a prescribed form that must be signed by the applicant and notarized. In filling out the application for evaluation, a family member needs to provide basic demographic information about the person to be evaluated and the behaviors and situations demonstrating that the person meets one of the four categories for court-ordered treatment. The evaluation/screening agency will answer questions and assist in properly filling out the form.

Evaluation and Screening

Within 48 hours (excluding weekends and holidays), the evaluation/screening agency will conduct a pre-petition screening to determine whether reasonable cause exists to believe that the person's behaviors meet the requirements of one of the commitment standards and whether she is willing to accept treatment or evaluation voluntarily. The pre-petition screener will interview the applicant and, if possible, the person alleged to be in need of treatment.

Petitions

If the evaluation/screening agency determines that there is reasonable cause to believe that the person meets the criteria for civil commitment, but is unwilling to undergo voluntary evaluation, the agency prepares a report of opinions and conclusions. The agency then files, either directly or through the county attorney's office, a *Petition for Court Ordered Evaluation*. The petition recommends whether the evaluation should take place on an outpatient or inpatient basis. If the court determines that there is reasonable cause to believe that the person meets the criteria for commitment and is likely a danger to self or others or might further deteriorate prior to a hearing for court-ordered treatment, it will order that the person be taken into custody and evaluated at an inpatient evaluation agency. If the court determines that an evaluation is warranted but that the person is not likely to be dangerous or further deteriorate prior to a hearing, it will order the person to appear at an outpatient evaluation agency for scheduled evaluation appointments. If the person fails to appear at the appointments, the court may order that the person be taken into custody by a police officer and delivered to the evaluation agency.

If the evaluation/screening agency determines that there is reasonable cause to believe that the person meets the criteria for civil commitment but is willing to undergo an evaluation voluntarily and is unlikely to present a danger prior to evaluation, no petition for evaluation is filed. In such a case, a voluntary evaluation on either an inpatient or outpatient basis must occur within five days at an evaluation agency selected by the person. The person undergoing voluntary evaluation must sign a form acknowledging her understanding that information gathered during the evaluation may be used in a hearing and may result in a court order for involuntary treatment.

Arizona law defines the evaluation conducted for purposes of determining whether court-ordered treatment is warranted as "a professional multidisciplinary analysis." The evaluation consists of examinations by two licensed physicians, preferably psychiatrists or at least experienced in psychiatric matters, and two other individuals, psychologists or social workers, familiar with mental health and social services available as placement alternatives. The examination includes an exploration of the person's past psychiatric history and of the circumstances leading up to the current presentation, a psychiatric exploration of the person's present mental condition, and a physical examination.

An inpatient evaluation must be completed within 72 hours of admission. An outpatient evaluation is due not later than the fourth day after the first appointment. Both time frames exclude weekends and holidays.

Due Process

A person undergoing involuntary evaluation must be served with the petition for court-ordered treatment, copies of the evaluating physicians' affidavits, and notice of the time and place of the hearing. A fair hearing requires that a person be represented by counsel, have the right to be present at the hearing, be able to confront witnesses, call witnesses on her own behalf, have the *Arizona Rules of Evidence and Civil Procedure* followed, and have the facts proving the need for court-ordered treatment established by "clear and convincing evidence." This standard of proof is higher, and therefore more difficult to satisfy, than the normal standard of proof in civil actions, which is a "preponderance of the evidence," but less stringent than the "beyond a reasonable doubt" standard used in criminal cases.

A fair hearing must include the testimony of two licensed physicians, preferably psychiatrists or at least experienced in psychiatric matters, who have conducted independent evaluations of the proposed patient, including personal examinations. There must also be testimony from two other individuals who are acquainted with the proposed patient. All four witnesses will be cross-examined by legal counsel for the proposed patient who may also call additional witnesses including a third, independent psychiatric evaluator chosen by the proposed patient.

In most cases, an attorney connected with the County Attorney's Office provides representation for those seeking the commitment order. Family members quite often are called upon to serve as witnesses to provide firsthand information about the behaviors that warrant civil commitment. Since the County Attorney's Office may not be aware of all persons with pertinent information, family members should be sure to contact the County Attorney's Office to discuss the need for testimony and provide background information that may be important in the hearing.

If the evaluation convinces the evaluators that the person meets the criteria for court-ordered treatment, the evaluation agency files a *Petition for Court-Ordered Treatment*. If the court grants the petition, it sets the hearing, part of the due process procedures discussed above, to be held within six days of the filing of the petition. If the court finds that the hearing has established by clear and convincing evidence that the person meets the criteria for involuntary treatment, an order for court-ordered treatment is entered.

In Arizona, courts have the authority to enter up to 365 days of combined inpatient/outpatient treatment, with the maximum number of inpatient days available determined by the standard under which the person is committed (90 days for danger to self, 180 days for Danger to Others and Persistently or Acutely Disabled (PAD), and 365 days for Gravely Disabled). Typically, a person remains in an inpatient facility for a short period of time following the commitment hearing in order to stabilize and allow the responsible outpatient supervising agency to develop an outpatient treatment plan. In most cases, the outpatient treatment plan must be approved by the court prior to the person's release from the inpatient facility. The plan details where the person must live, requirements for supervision and medication and other requirements specified as conditions for continued outpatient treatment. If the person fails to comply with the terms of her outpatient treatment plans, the supervising agency may obtain an order from the court authorizing law enforcement to return her to an inpatient facility.

The outpatient supervising agency will work with the person to encourage compliance with the treatment plan and will periodically review the person's progress in treatment and the continued need for the court order. The outpatient treatment plan can be amended as treatment needs change and the supervising agency physician may request that the person be released from court-ordered treatment if it is determined that the person no longer meets the criteria for any commitment standard. Additionally, every 60 days the supervising agency must advise the person receiving court-ordered treatment of her right to request a judicial review of the continued need for the order. If the person requests the judicial review, the supervising agency will submit a report to the court detailing the person's condition. The court has discretion in whether or not to hold a hearing to consider the request for judicial review. In most cases, the review is based on the written report submitted by the supervising agency and no additional hearing is held.

IF YOU NEED AN ATTORNEY AND CAN'T AFFORD ONE

The State Bar of Arizona Young Lawyers Division runs a *Modest Means Program* that provides low-cost legal assistance. One of the areas where they provide assistance is Family Law, including guardianship and wills. To be eligible an individual must earn less than 200 percent of the Federal Poverty Guidelines. For more information call *Arizona Modest Means Project* at (602) 266-2322 or contact the State Bar.

THE FAMILY SUPPORT SYSTEM

In this chapter, we focused on the formal, funded system of care in Arizona. I also urge you to become familiar with the family support system that is available. While there are a variety of places to turn to for support, one of the first places you should consider is an affiliate NAMI. There are currently 11 NAMI affiliates in Arizona. The knowledge, support, and friendship that you can gain from becoming involved with NAMI is enormous. NAMI members and staff are informed and experienced. More often than not, any problem you are having with the mental health system has been faced by another NAMI family. You can learn what they tried, what was successful, and what was less successful.

The phone numbers and Internet Web site addresses for the National office, the Arizona office and the Arizona affiliates are listed in the table below. (The Web sites all have mutual links, so you if connect with one, you can easily navigate to the others.)[2]

---

[2] Phone numbers and website addresses can change, but this is the most current information as of the publication of this book.

Affiliates	Phone Number	Web Address
National NAMI	(800) 950-6264	www.nami.org
NAMI Arizona	(602) 244-8166 (800) 626-5022	az.nami.org
NAMI East Valley Mesa, Chandler, Tempe, Gilbert, Awatukee, Apache Junction, Queen Creek	(480) 641-3629	az.nami.org/affiliates/nami_east_valley
NAMI North Valley N.Phoenix, Scottsdale, Paradise Valley Fountain Hills, Carefree, Cave Creek	(480) 945-8003	az.nami.org/affiliates/nami_north_valley
NAMI Family Maricopa County Central Phoenix, South Phoenix	(480) 948-5826	az.nami.org/affiliates/nami_family_maricopa_county
NAMI Phoenix Central Phoenix	(602) 369-9136	az.nami.org/affiliates/nami_phoenix
NAMI Yavapai County Prescott, Dewey, Mayer, Prescott Valley, Chino Valley, Humboldt	(520) 541-7554	az.nami.org/affiliates/nami_yavapai_county
NAMI Sedona Sedona, Verde Valley, Flagstaff, Cottonwood	(520) 282-1931	az.nami.org/affiliates/nami_sedona
NAMI SEA Cochise County and Southeastern Arizona	(520) 378-4266	az.nami.org/affiliates/nami_sea
NAMI Sun Cities / West Valley Sun Cities, West Phoenix, Peoria, Glendale Litchfield Park, Goodyear, Avondale, Tolleson, Buckeye, New River, Wickenburg	(623) 584-7655	az.nami.org/affiliates/nami_sun_cities_west_valley
NAMISA Tucson, Pima County	(520) 622-5582	www.namisa.org
NAMI Yuma Yuma and La Paz Counties	(520) 317-0556	az.nami.org/affiliates/nami_yuma

In addition to NAMI, the Mental Health Association of Arizona can be very helpful to families in their quest to access services for their loved one. The Mental Health Association can be contacted at (480) 994-4407 or (800) 642-9277. The Web site address is www.mhaaz.com

In Chapter 15, we provide a number of useful Internet sites that provide families with tremendous amounts of information. In addition to those national Web sites, and the NAMI affiliates listed above, there are a number of other Web sites relevant to Arizona families.

rizona State Legislature	www.azleg.state.az.us/
- Arizona House of Representatives	www.azhousetv.org/
- Arizona Senate	www.arizonasenate.org/
rizona Department of Health Services (ADHS)	www.hs.state.az.us/
rizona Department of Health Services/Division ' Behavioral Health (ADHS/DBHS)	www.hs.state.az.us/bhs
rizona State Hospital (ASH)	www.hs.state.az.us/bhs/ash
rizona State Health Care Cost Containment System (AHCCCS)	www.ahcccs.state.az.us/
epartment of Economic Security	www.de.state.az.us/
ental Health Dissemination Network of Arizona	www.azmentalhealth.org
rizona Center for Disability Law	www.acdl.com

Shake It Off and Step Up

A story is told of a farmer who owned an old mule. The mule fell into the farmer's well. The farmer heard the mule braying — or whatever mules do when they fall into wells. After carefully assessing the situation, the farmer sympathized with the mule, but decided that neither the mule nor the well was worth the trouble of saving. Instead, he called his neighbors together and told them what had happened and enlisted them to help haul dirt to bury the old mule in the well and put him out of his misery.

Initially, the old mule was hysterical! But as the farmer and his neighbors continued shoveling and the dirt hit his back, a thought struck him. It suddenly dawned on him that every time a shovel load of dirt landed on his back, he should shake it off and step up! This he did, blow after blow.

"Shake it off and step up... shake it off and step up... shake it off and step up!" he repeated to encourage himself. No matter how painful the blows or distressing the situation, the old mule fought panic and just kept right on shaking it off and stepping up! You're right! It wasn't long before the old mule, battered and exhausted, stepped triumphantly over the wall of that well! What seemed like it would bury him actually blessed him. All because of the manner in which he handled his adversity.

Reprinted with permission of Afterhours Inspirational Stories

INFORMATION USED IN THE
SMI DETERMINATION PROCESS

There are three components to the determination process.

- Qualifying Diagnoses
- Functional Criteria
- Risk of Deterioration

In order to be eligible for SMI services, an individual must:

- Have a qualifying diagnosis and meet functional criteria;
  or
- Have a qualifying diagnosis and be of risk of deterioration to meet the functional criteria if they do not receive treatment.

Qualifying Diagnoses

- Psychotic Disorders
- Bipolar disorder
- Obsessive-compulsive disorder
- Major Depression
- Other Mood Disorders
- Anxiety disorders
- A Personality Disorder other than Antisocial

Functional Criteria

As a result of a qualifying diagnosis, the individual has exhibited any of the three problems identified below for most of the past 12 months or for most of the past 6 months with an expected continued duration of at least six months.

- Dysfunction in Role Performance – Lacks the capacity to perform present major role function in society (i.e. school, work, parenting etc.)
- Inability to live in an independent or family setting without supervision.
- A risk of serious harm to self or others– They are unable to maintain conduct within the limits prescribed by law, and social expectations.

Risk of Deterioration

If the individual does not meet the functional criteria but may be expected to deteriorate without treatment they are also eligible.

She Changed a System of Care

Earlier in this book, we told the story of Dr. Patricia Deegan, an individual with schizophrenia who became quite successful. Families also survive and can even thrive in spite of the mental illness of a family member. As a matter of fact, some individuals and families thrive *because* of the mental illness of one of their children. They are enriched and actually achieve things in life that might not have occurred if it were not for the mental illness of a family member.

Eleanor is such a person. She is a family member who has had a positive and significant impact not only on the care of her daughter, but on the care of hundreds of other sons and daughters across Arizona. In many ways she (and her family) are the model for what I would like this book to accomplish. Eleanor's daughter was diagnosed with schizoaffective disorder before there was a strong, active family movement. There were no local NAMI (National Alliance for the Mentally Ill) affiliates in southern Arizona, and families were generally not welcomed as part of the treatment team.

Because they could afford it, Eleanor's daughter was treated in some of the finest and most expensive treatment facilities in the country. In each case, someone from the treatment facility would eventually call to tell Eleanor and her family that the facility was not equipped to deal with someone as difficult as her daughter and she was being discharged.

Eventually, Eleanor began working with a young, uncommonly gifted psychiatrist at the local county hospital. Through their joint effort, the first group home in the community for individuals with a serious mental illness was opened. The two also played a key role in bringing families together to establish a NAMI affiliate. Eleanor made it clear to the system of care that she was not going to sit on the sidelines; she was going to be an active participant in her daughter's rehabilitation. Twenty-something years later, it is easy to sit back and think that it's not important that a family member stood up and changed a system of care. But such thinking is somewhat like believing that it was not a big deal for the first African Americans to say that they were no longer going to sit at the back of the bus.

The system of care is quite a bit different than it was when Eleanor first got involved. And while other factors played a role, one of the more important factors in changing the system was the involvement of Eleanor and her family. As Eleanor mandated top-quality services for her daughter, services were improved for other sons and daughters. Eleanor and her family mandated that they be involved in treatment planning. Their insistence, resisted at first by some in the mental health system, set the stage for the changing of attitudes in our community.

Eleanor was later elected to the Arizona House of Representatives and served two terms. While in the house she was a dynamic leader for a number of social service causes.

—*Mike Berren*

CHAPTER 14

Recovery: The Vision

"No one can really pull you up very high when you lose your grip on the rope, but on your own two feet you can climb mountains."
—Louis Braneris

*About the only thing on the menu that looks good to me is **Recovery**.*

A decade ago, *recovery* was not even listed as an "option on the menu" for individuals with serious mental illnesses. Now, not only is recovery on the menu, but the waiting lines are out the door and down the street. It is what everyone is talking about. Personal stories about recovery abound in journal articles, newsletters and keynote addresses at conferences and workshops. People are talking about their own recovery, their family member's recovery and the recovery of others in the community. There are Web sites that focus on recovery and wellness. There are also Internet "chat rooms" that provide avenue for people to discuss their recovery experiences and to share the multiple coping and wellness strategies that have proven to be effective in supporting their individual recovery process.

The 1990s have been referred to as the *decade of recovery*, and recovery has become the vision of a number of state mental health authorities. In 1999, the Surgeon General addressed recovery in the first ever Surgeon General's Report on Mental Illness. In the report, recovery is variously called *a process, an outlook, a vision*, and a *guiding principle*. Regardless of what it is called, the important message is that hope and restoration of a meaningful life are possible, despite a serious mental illness. The Surgeon General's Report makes it clear that rather than just focusing on symptom relief, recovery focuses on the restoration of self-esteem and attaining a meaningful role in society.

Over half of the people diagnosed with major mental illnesses have the potential to achieve a significant and or even a full recovery. This is in dramatic contrast to historical beliefs and expectations. Historically, individuals with a serious mental illness, especially those diagnosed with schizophrenia, were seen as having a poor prognosis, with the illnesses having a uniformly downward spiraling course.

THE ORIGINS OF RECOVERY

Several important events paved the way for us to begin to embrace the concept of recovery. Looking back, the five most significant are:

• The Consumer Movement
• The Writings of Mental Health Consumers
• Research Findings
• The Family Movement
• More Effective Medication and Approaches to Rehabilitation

For the first time in history, individuals from different stakeholder groups, have come together to support the common vision of recovering from mental illness. These groups include mental health consumers, family members, mental health providers, primary healthcare providers, educators, researchers, policy-makers, and community members at large.

The train is rolling and the momentum is such that we are in the midst of experiencing a major shift in attitudes about mental illness and recovery.

The Consumer Movement

One of the most important factors has been the consumer movement. This movement began as a civil rights, advocacy and self-help movement that began in the 1970s. The movement incorporated consumers and former patients and emphasized personal, social, and civil empowerment as three factors that allowed a person to benefit from a focus on recovery. A statement in a newsletter articulated the focus of the consumer movement:

> Ultimately, patient empowerment is a matter of self-determination; it occurs when a patient freely chooses his or her own path to recovery and well-being. It is the job of mental health services to provide an environment of personal respect, material support and social justice that encourages the individual patient in this process.
> – *Sally Clay*

As a cornerstone of the movement, consumers expressed themselves by demanding to have a voice and choice in the kind of services delivered by systems of care. They expected direct involvement in planning, implementing, and evaluating services and treatments. The slogan "Nothing About Us Without Us" was stenciled on T-shirts that were worn at The *Alternatives Conference*, the first national consumer-run and consumer-focused conference. The *Alternatives Conference* continues to be held annually and is sponsored each year by a consumer-run and operated organization.

The Writings of Mental Health Consumers

An equally important factor in paving the way for the recovery movement are the writings of mental health consumers describing their own recovery experiences. William Anthony, a psychologist and a leader in the area of rehabilitation, drew his definition of recovery from themes identified by reading this consumer literature. Dr. Anthony suggests:

> Recovery is a deeply personal, unique process of changing one's attitudes, values, feelings, goals, skills and/or roles. It is a way of living a satisfying, hopeful and contributing life. Recovery involves the development of new meaning and purpose in one's life as one grows beyond the catastrophic effects of mental illness.

Research Findings

A third contributor to the acceptance of recovery as a realistic vision are research findings. A review of the research by Dr. Courtenay Harding clearly indicates that a deteriorating course for severe mental illness *is not the norm*. Her review showed shows that even among individuals with schizophrenia, recovery actually occurs. In one study it was found that individuals with schizophrenia have the potential for full or partial recovery, even in the second and third decades of illness. Overall, the research suggests that over 50 percent of individuals with schizophrenia have the potential to recover.

The Family Movement

Families banded together in the 1970s and demanded a voice in the treatment of their loved ones. In doing so, they influenced the design of mental health service delivery at the local, state and national levels. The family movement brought together small groups of grassroots advocates from across the nation, and resulted in a national organization, the National Alliance for the Mentally Ill (now referred to simply as NAMI).

If you get nothing else out of this book, hopefully you will find out what NAMI and its local affiliates can do to improve the quality of life of for your loved one who has a mental illness and for the rest of your family.

Families of persons with a mental illness also began to demand that practitioners, educators and systems of care quit blaming families for causing the mental illness of their family member. Psychological theories identifying families, especially mothers, as the cause of mental illness, were criticized as hurtful, unproductive and inaccurate. Families argued that the inaccurate beliefs held by mental health professionals created additional pain and suffering for families who were already experiencing a devastating situation. It was argued further that not only were the beliefs inaccurate and painful, but they also created barriers to family involvement in treatment.

At a NAMI conference in the mid 1980s, I heard family members demand that a national educational campaign be instituted to dispel the myth that families cause mental illness. They demanded that the burden on families as caregivers be recognized. They demanded further the creation of systems of care that were accessible, responsive and included families. Beginning to recognize their own influence, families demanded that systems of care offer an array of services to meet the needs of their loved ones who were living on the streets as the result of deinstitutionalization and inadequate community resources.

More Effective Medications and Approaches to Rehabilitation

Coinciding with the consumer and family movements, we have witnessed the introduction of new medications and improvement in approaches to psychosocial rehabilitation. These new biological and psychosocial treatments have contributed to the recognition that recovery is definitely an achievable goal.

WHAT WE KNOW ABOUT RECOVERY

Now that we have identified the origins, let's discuss the six aspects of recovery.

- Recovery Is Unique for Each Individual
- Recovery Is a Common Human Experience
- The Importance of Hope and Vision
- The Role of Choice, Empowerment and Self-Determination
- Language That Supports Recovery Is Important
- Recovery Should Focus on an Individual's Strengths and Abilities

Recovery Is Unique for Each Individual

Recovery is a process and a journey of self-discovery and renewal that is unique to each individual. This is not surprising given the fact that even individuals with the *same* diagnosis have more differences than they do similarities. Individuals with schizophrenia come from rural areas and urban areas, from families of wealth and families who live in poverty.

They are white, black and Hispanic. Some come from large families, some from small. Some have supportive families and others grew up in families that were not supportive.

It is also important to remember that recovery is not a straight line. Recovery can occur without complete symptom relief. Recovery can occur while an individual is actively experiencing psychiatric symptoms.

Recovery involves growth and setbacks, periods of rapid change and periods of little change.

Not everyone experiences recovery the same way. Some people go through stages of growth. Others do not go through specific stages or if they do, they experience the stages in less depth. Still others go back and forth between the stages as a part of the recovery process.

Recovery Is a Common Human Experience

It is helpful in understanding the concept of recovery to remind ourselves that while every individual's process of recovery is unique, recovery is also a common human experience. Before you continue with this chapter, engage in the following exercise:

> Think of a catastrophe in your own life that you have recovered from or are in the process of recovering from (for example, the death of a loved one, facing a serious disease, surviving a serious physical injury, a divorce, etc.). Now, think of how you felt at the time you were involved in the catastrophe. Do not focus on the situation itself, but rather on how you felt. Then stop and take a few minutes to remember what helped you to recover or get through the catastrophe and move on with your life.

Successful recovery from a catastrophe does not mean that the event did not occur. The effects might still be present. Your life might have been changed forever. However, you successfully recovered. You likely had periods where you experienced set backs, doubts and wondered if you would get through the experience. Looking back, you know that you are changed as a result of the experience and that the effects of the experience are possibly no longer the primary focus of your life. We go on with our life; perhaps we are even enriched by these difficult experiences. It is not uncommon that in any given decade of our life, we or someone very close to us experiences a major loss or catastrophe. The experience of learning that we survived and went on allows us to face the next experience with more confidence and assurance. Even though we know we will feel the pain, we know that we will move through the situation with a greater sense of ease.

The Importance of Hope and Vision

Hope and vision are crucial factors in the recovery process. It is important for your family member, the treatment team and you to know and believe that people can recover. When providers, family members and others talk about the possibility of recovery with the individual who has a mental illness, hope is restored. Being able to say to each other that over half of the people with a major mental illness recover and lead meaningful lives is important.

Having a positive vision for a better life and knowing that mental illness does not always lead to a never-ending downward spiral can provide the hope that can be the turning point in an individual's life.

> "...we rebuild ourselves on the three cornerstones of recovery: hope, willingness, and responsible action."
> —*Pat Deegan*
>
> "Recovery is the journey from resignation to hope and realistic optimism, and it is sometimes necessary for someone else to believe in better outcomes for an individual, even when the individual does not believe her/himself."
> —*Bill Anthony*

The Role of Choice, Empowerment and Self-Determination

There was a time when we believed that others should make decisions for individuals with a mental illness. Now we know that denying individuals with a mental illness the opportunity to make choices results in *learned helplessness*, a set of behaviors and feelings marked by depression, apathy, indifference, cognitive deterioration as well as loss of self-identity and self-esteem. In many ways, learned helplessness can be more disabling than the mental illness itself. Choice is very important in the empowerment process. We all learn through trial and error. People learn about themselves when they exercise choice, regardless of the outcome. Choice is critical to human development and growth. As much as we want to protect those that we care about from failure, we know that failure is as much a part of life as is success.

Choice should be reflected in the individual's treatment plan, which forms the map or guide for his or her recovery. Motivation is closely associated with actively choosing goals. When individuals set their own goals, they have a sense of ownership and a drive to achieve. However, far too often, people other than the individual with the mental illness complete the treatment plan *for* the individual. This often results in the person not working toward his goals and in turn being labeled as *noncompliant*. So, encourage your family member to let everyone know that she wants to be involved (and take the lead) in creating a treatment plan. Support her desire to set goals, even if you disagree with the goals.

Language That Supports Recovery

The individual who has a mental illness is *always a person first*. While this seems obvious, it has become a common bad habit to refer to a person, or to a whole group of people by a diagnosis. For example, we often hear people referred to as schizophrenics, borderlines and SMIs. This use of language has the effect of reducing people to a diagnosis or illness.

The consequence is the potential loss of treating every person as unique and acknowledging the individuality of every person's recovery process.

Family members rarely refer to their loved one by their diagnosis or by other labels, and therefore are in a unique position to educate their loved one about how important it is to not identify with their diagnosis. Family members are also in a position to advocate for a shift in the misuse of language by caregivers.

Strengths and Abilities Focus

Focusing on building on an individual's strengths is another important approach that supports the recovery vision. Defining people by their abilities rather than disabilities and validating an individual's strengths has been shown to have a powerful effect on engaging the individual in treatment. While this makes common sense, the mental health culture has historically for decades focused on symptoms, problems and pathology for decades. So, once again, it will take time, practice, and patience to change these habits. One of your roles as a family member is to be vigilant and make sure that your family member's strengths are an important part of the treatment planning.

RECOVERY: THE NEW ROLES

Recovery calls for a shift in the traditional roles of everyone involved in the mental health system. The individual with a mental illness is being encouraged and supported to take responsible action as the expert in guiding their recovery process. Providers are being asked to engage mental health consumers in relationships that involve respect. Leaders and policymakers are being asked to create systems of care and support staff to act in ways that support recovery and empowerment. Family members are being asked to talk to their loved ones and to others about the fact that restoration of a meaningful life is possible.

Two important points to remember about recovery to remember are:

> • *Instead of focusing on only symptom relief, recovery focuses on restoration of self-esteem and on attaining meaningful roles in society.*
>
> • *Recovery does not mean cured. It means <u>taking control and leading a satisfying life in the community</u>. People can be recovering while experiencing symptoms and setbacks.*

Weakness or Strength?

Sometimes your biggest weakness can become your biggest strength. Take, for example, the story of one 10-year-old boy who decided to study judo despite the fact that he had lost his left arm in a devastating car accident. The boy began lessons with an old Japanese judo master. The boy was doing well, so he couldn't understand why the master had taught him only one move after three months of training.

"Sensei," the boy finally said, "shouldn't I be learning more moves?" "This is the only move you know, but this is the only move you'll ever need to know," the sensei replied. Not quite understanding, but believing in his teacher, the boy kept training.

Several months later, the sensei took the boy to his first tournament. Surprising himself, the boy easily won his first two matches. The third match proved to be more difficult, but after some time, his opponent became impatient and charged; the boy deftly used his one move to win the match. Still amazed by his success, the boy was now in the finals. This time, his opponent was bigger, stronger and more experienced. For a while, the boy appeared to be overmatched. Concerned that the boy might get hurt, the referee called a time-out. He was about to stop the match when the sensei intervened.

"No," the sensei insisted, "let him continue." Soon after the match resumed, his opponent made a critical mistake: he dropped his guard.

Instantly, the boy used his move to pin him. The boy had won the match and the tournament. He was the champion. On the way home, the boy and the sensei reviewed every move in each and every match. Then the boy summoned the courage to ask what was really on his mind. "Sensei, how did I win the tournament with only one move?"

"You won for two reasons," the sensei answered. "First, you've almost mastered one of the most difficult throws in all of judo. And second, the only known defense for that move is for your opponent to grasp your left arm."

The boy's biggest weakness had become his biggest strength.

Reprinted with permission of Afterhours Inspirational Stories

Flaws

A water bearer in India had two large pots, each hung on one end of a pole which he carried across his neck. One of the pots had a crack in it, and while the other pot was perfect and always delivered a full portion of water at the end of the long walk from the stream to the master's house, the cracked pot arrived only half full. For a full two years this went on daily, with the bearer delivering only one and a half pots full of water to his master's house.

Of course, the perfect pot was proud of its accomplishments, perfect to the end for which it was made. But the poor cracked pot was ashamed of its own imperfection, and miserable that it was able to accomplish only half of what it had been made to do. After two years of what it perceived to be a bitter failure, it spoke to the water bearer one day by the stream. "I am ashamed of myself, and I want to apologize to you." "Why?" asked the bearer. "What are you ashamed of?" "I have been able, for these past two years, to deliver only half my load because this crack in my side causes water to leak out all the way back to your master's house. Because of my flaws, you have to do all of this work, and you don't get full value from your efforts."

The water bearer felt sorry for the old cracked pot, and in his compassion he said, "As we return to the master's house, I want you to notice the beautiful flowers along the path." Indeed, as they went up the hill, the old cracked pot took notice of the sun warming the beautiful wildflowers on the side of the path, and this cheered it some. But at the end of the trail, it still felt bad because it had leaked out half its load, and so again the pot apologized to the bearer for its failure.

The bearer said to the pot, "Did you notice that there were flowers only on your side of your path, but not on the other pot's side? That's because I have always known about your flaw, and I took advantage of it. I planted flower seeds on your side of the path, and every day while we walk back from the stream, you've watered them. For two years, I have been able to pick these beautiful flowers to decorate my master's table. Without you being just the way you are, he would not have this beauty to grace his house."

Each of us has our own unique flaws. We're all pots that have a flaw. Don't be afraid of your flaws. Acknowledge them, and you too can be the cause of beauty. Know that in our weakness we often find our strength.

Reprinted with permission of Afterhours Inspirational Stories

I Am Living Proof

I have an illness called paranoid schizophrenia. I also suffer from severe depression. What happened to me could happen to anyone. My father died in 1991. I entered college that same year. In addition to going to school I worked a full-time job. Less than a year later my mental illness "hit" and I was out of work, out of school and homeless. While I was homeless, I never begged for food, money or anything else (with the exception of cigarettes). I pretty much stayed to myself and never harmed anyone.

I had not had much contact with my brother for a few years, but he and a friend had heard about my condition and the part of town where I was hanging out. They spent days looking for me and eventually found me. They took me to the hospital. I was obviously very sick and needed help. My hospitalization lasted for three months, during which I was scared most of the time. I was, however, a model patient. I spent a lot of time with students studying to become doctors. They liked interviewing me because I was not as angry or frightening as some of the other patients. It was during my stay in the hospital that I became zealous about my recovery.

I was released to an apartment program and began attending day treatment regularly. Once I was able, I returned to college part time. The first return was not, however, very successful. The stress was too much and I had to drop out a short time later. I also worked as a volunteer advocate, and as a staff person in the social work department. I handled the collection of donated clothing. During this same time period, I moved on to supported housing. While continuing to work half-time in the social work department, I began taking classes to become a peer specialist. I graduated from the program and began working part-time at a hospital internship program.

Following the internship I was employed as a professional, helping others. I worked in various settings including shelters, residences, intensive supportive, as well as supported housing. Eventually I was hired to work full time, providing counseling and advocacy.

After a year working to help others in the mental health system, I resigned to handle a personal matter in my family. That was January of 1998. By the fall of that year, I was back in school part-time as a legal studies major. In the spring of 1999, I became engaged. (I finally bought the ring.)

I believe that I have made a great deal of progress on the road to recovery. I thank my wonderful brother Michael and his fiancée, my lovely and always supportive fiancée, the programs and schools I have attended, my medication, my peers, my country, myself and my Higher Power for bringing me to this point. Recovery is possible. I hope that others know that people can recover from mental illness. I know they can because I am living proof.

Reprinted with permission of New York City Voices

CHAPTER 15

Using the Internet for Information and Support

"Only dead fish swim with the stream."
—Anonymous

Michael R. Berren, Ph.D.

In preparing this book, we knew that it was important to maintain a balance between valuable information and readability. For some chapters it meant distilling hundreds of pages of government documents down to fewer than 20.

Because we summarized information and are aware that some families would like more details, we have provided a listing of recommended readings. The list includes the primary sources used by the authors as well as additional readings that contain useful information.

We are sensitive, however, to the fact that obtaining the recommended readings can be a significant cost both financially and in terms of time.

Books can be expensive and professional literature can be difficult to access, particularly if you do not live near a university library. For that reason, we recommend another wonderful way to obtain more information—the Internet. An individual can sit at a computer and, through the Internet, retrieve information that was unobtainable only a few years ago.

And not having a computer or Internet access at home is no reason to not have access to this wealth of information. Nearly every public library in the country has computers with Internet access.

There are Web sites on the Internet that address a wide variety of mental health, entitlement and legal information. Not only can the Web sites save you a great deal of time and energy, more importantly they can provide solid, up-to-date information. There are also Web sites that can provide support. Some sites, for example, have "bulletin boards," where families can share experiences and get feedback from other families. In the tables that follow (and in the Primary Source Table included in Chapter 11), we have listed a number of sites that we believe are among the best. While many of the sites provide information across a number of areas, we have separated the Web sites into six categories:

- Information About Mental Illness and Medication
- Legal Advocacy
- Family and Consumer Organizations, and Support
- Health and Wellness
- Federal Agencies, Entitlement Programs and Entitlement Information
- Professional Organizations

I recognize (and rather relish the fact) that the technology continues to improve and the number of Internet sites continues to grow. So please use this list as a starting place.

Information About Mental Illness

Site Name	Address
Schizophrenia.com (Good for medication information)	www.schizophrenia.com
Mental Health InfoSource	www.mhsource.com
Mental Health Resources	www.mentalhealth.about.com/health/mentalhealth
Expert Consensus Guideline Series	www.psychguides.com
Link to Departments of Mental Health (for all 50 states)	www.state.sc.us/dmh/usa_map
Medscape	www.medscape.com
Internet Mental Health (Good for medication information)	www.mentalhealth.com
McMahonMed.com (Good for medication information)	www.central-nervous-system.com/wworks/CHARTS/psycho
National Institute Mental Health	www.nimh.nih.gov
National Institute of Drug Abuse	www.nida.nih.gov
National Institute on Alcohol and Alcohol Abuse	www.niaaa.nih.gov
Substance Abuse and Mental Health Administration	www.samhsa.gov
Center for Substance Abuse Treatment	www.samhsa.gov/centers/csat/csat
Center for Mental Health Services	www.samhsa.gov/centers/cmhs/cmhs
Center for Substance Abuse Prevention	www.samhsa.gov/centers/csap/csap
Center for Mental Health Services	www.mentalhealth.org
National Clearinghouse for Alcohol and Drug Information	www.health.org
1999 Report of the Surgeon General	www.surgeongeneral.gov/library/mentalhealth
Mental Illness in US Jails: Diverting the nonviolent, low-level offender November 1996	www.soros.org/crime

Legal Advocacy

Site Name	Address
Bazelon Center for Mental Health Law	www.bazelon.org
National Association of Protection and Advocacy	www.protectionandadvocacy.com
Treatment Advocacy Center	www.psychlaws.org

Family and Consumer Organizations and Support

Site Name	Address
NAMI	www.nami.org
Mental Health Association	www.nmha.org
Foundation For Depressive Illness	www.depression.org
Bipolar Significant Others	www.bpso.org
Mental Wellness	www.mentalwellness.com
Schizophrenia Anonymous	www.sanonymous.org
The Experience of Schizophrenia	www.chovil.com
Manic Depression Association	www.ndmda.org
Mental Health Self-Help Clearinghouse	www.mhselfhelp.org
Center for Medicare Advocacy	www.medicareadvocacy.org

Health and Wellness

Site Name	Address
WebMD	www.webmd.com
Health A to Z	www.healthatoz.com
Healthweb	www.healthweb.org
Healthier You	www.healthieryou.com
Intelihealth	www.intelihealth.com
Nutrition.gov	www.nutrition.gov
Mayo Clinic	www.mayohealth.org
Fitnessonline	www.fitnessonline.com

Federal Agencies, Entitlement Programs and Entitlement Information

Site Name	Address
Housing and Urban Development	www.hud.gov
Social Security Administration (SSA)	www.ssa.gov
- SSA Benefit Publications	www.ssa.gov/pubs
- SSA Office of Disability	www.ssa.gov/odhome
- SSA Employment Support	www.ssa.gov/work
Dept. of Agriculture (Food Stamps)	www.fns.usda.gov/fns

Professional Organizations

Site Name	Address
American Psychological Association	www.apa.org
American Psychiatric Association	www.psych.org
National Association of Social Workers	www.naswdc.org
National Association of State Mental Health Directors	www.nasmhpd.org
American Society of Addiction Medicine	www.asam.org

References

Primary Sources and Recommended Reading

Books

Adamec, C., and D. J. Jaffe. 1996. How to live with a mentally ill person: A handbook of day-to-day strategies. New York: John Wiley & Sons, Inc.

Amador, X. 2000. I am not sick, I don't need help! New York: Vida Press.

Andreasen, N. C. 1984. The broken brain: The biological revolution in psychiatry. New York: Harper and Row.

Anthony, W., M. Cohen, and M. Farkas. 1992. Psychiatric rehabilitation. Boston: Center for Psychiatric Rehabilitation at Boston University.

American Psychiatric Association. 1994. Diagnostic and statistical manual of mental disorders: DSM-IV. Washington, D.C.: American Psychiatric Association.

Backlar, P. 1994. The family face of schizophrenia. New York: Putnam.

Bolton, R. 1979. People skills. New Jersey: Prentice-Hall.

Carter, R. 1998. Helping someone with a mental illness. New York: Times Books.

Copeland, M. E. 2000. Wellness recovery action plan. USA: Peach Press.

Diamond, R. J. 1998. Instant psychopharmacology: A guide for the nonmedical mental health professional. New York: Norton.

Duke, P., and G. Hochman. 1992. A brilliant madness: Living with manic depressive illness. New York: Bantam Books.

Esser, A. H., and S. D. Lacey. 1989. Mental illness: A homecare guide. New York: John Wiley & Sons, Inc.

Evans, K., and J. M. Sullivan. 1990. Dual diagnosis: Counseling the mentally ill substance abuser. New York: Guilford Press.

Grob, G. N. 1994. The mad among us: A history of the care of America's mentally ill. New York: Free Press.

Harding, C. M., and J. H. Zahniser. 1994. Empirical correction of seven myths about schizophrenia with implications for treatment. in psychological and social aspects of psychiatric disability. Boston: Center for Psychiatric Rehabilitation at Boston University.

Hatfield, A. B. 1990. Family education in mental illness. New York: Guilford Press.

Hatfield, A. B. 1999. Family education in mental illness. New York: Guilford Press.

Hatfield, A. B., and H. P. Lefley (eds.). 1993. Surviving mental illness: stress, coping, and adaptation. New York: Guilford Press.

Heinssen, R. K. Jr., and C. R. Glass. 1990. Social skills, social anxiety, and cognitive factors in schizophrenia. In Handbook of social and evaluation anxiety, edited by H. Leitenberg. New York: Plenum Press.

Hemley, R. 1998. Nola: A memoir of faith, art & madness. St. Paul: Graywolf Press.

Holley, T. E., and J. Holley. 1997. My mother's keeper: A daughter's memoir of growing up in the shadow of schizophrenia. New York: Morrow.

Issac, R. J., and V. C. Armat. 1990. Madness in the streets: How psychiatry and the law abandoned the mentally ill. New York: Free Press.

Jamison, K. R. 1995. An unquiet mind: A memoir of moods and madness. New York: Vintage Books.

Jeffries, J. J., E. Plummer, M. V. Seeman, et al. 1990. Living and working with schizophrenia. Toronto: University of Toronto Press.

Kreisman, J. J., and H. Straus. 1991. I hate you—don't leave me: Understanding the borderline personality. New York: Avon.

Kubler-Ross, E. 1969. On death and dying. New York: Simon & Schuster.

Lachenmeyer, N. 2000. The outsider: A journey into my father's struggle with madness. New York: Broadway Books.

Lafand, V. 1994. Grieving mental illness: A guide for patients and their caregivers. Toronto: University of Toronto Press.

Lefley, H. P. 1996. Family caregiving in mental illness. Thousand Oaks, Calif.: Sage Publications.

Lehman, A.F., and L. B. Dixon (eds.). 1995. Double jeopardy: Chronic mental illness and substance abuse. Langhorne, Pa.: Harwood Academic Publishers.

Lieberman, J., and R. Murray (eds.). 2000. Comprehensive care of schizophrenia. London: Martin Dunitz.

Linehan, M. M. 1993. Cognitive-behavioral treatment of borderline personality disorder. New York: Guilford Press.

Marsh, D.T. 1998. Serious mental illness and the family: The practitioner's guide. New York: John Wiley & Sons, Inc.

Mason, P.T., and R. Kreger. 1998. Stop walking on eggshells. Oakland, Calif.: New Harbinger Publications.

Minkoff, K., and R. E. Drake (eds.). 1991. Dual diagnosis of major mental illness and substance abuse. New Directions for Mental Health Services. San Francisco: Jossey-Bass.

Mondimore, F. M. 1999. Bipolar disorder: A guide for patients and families. Baltimore: John Hopkins University Press.

Moorman, M. 1992. My sister's keeper. New York: Norton.

Mueser, K. T., and S. Gingerich. 1994. Coping with schizophrenia: A guide for families. Oakland, Calif.: New Harbinger Publications.

Preston, J. D., J. H. O'Neal, and M. C. Talaga. 2000. Consumer's guide to psychiatric drugs. Oakland, Calif.: New Harbinger Publications.

Seligman, M. P. 1975. Helplessness: On depression, development, and death. San Francisco: Freeman.
Sowers, C., C. D. Peabody, S. W. Ryan, et al. 2000. Solutions for wellness: Nutrition, wellness, and living a health lifestyle. Indianapolis: Eli Lilly and Company.

Spaniol, L. R., M. Koehler, and D. Hutchinson. 2000. The leader's guide recovery workbook: Practical coping and empowerment strategies for people with psychiatric disability. Boston: Center for Psychiatric Rehabilitation at Boston University.

Thorton, J. F., and M. V. Seeman (eds.). 1995. Schizophrenia simplified: A field guide to schizophrenia .for frontline workers, families, and professionals. Ashland, Ohio: Hogrefe and Huber Publishers.

Torrey, E. F. 1997. Out of the shadows: Confronting America's mental illness crisis. New York: John Wiley & Sons, Inc.

Torrey, E. F. 2001. Surviving schizophrenia: A manual for families, consumers, and providers. 4th edition. New York: Quill.

Torrey, E. F. 1988. Nowhere to go: The tragic odyssey of the homeless mentally ill. New York: Harper & Row.

Walsh, M. 1985. Schizophrenia: Straight talk for families and friends. New York: William Morrow.

Weiden, P.J., P. L. Scheifler, R. J. Diamond, et al. 1999. Breakthroughs in antipsychotic medications: A guide for consumers, families, and clinicians. New York: W. W. Norton.

Woolis, R. 1992. When someone you love has a mental illness. New York: Putnam.

Journal Articles

Abram, K.M., and L. A. Teplin. 1991. Co-occurring disorders among mentally ill jail detainees: Implications for public policy. American Psychologist. 46:1036–1045.

Andreasen, N. C. 1982. Negative symptoms in schizophrenia. Archives of General Psychiatry. 39:784–788.

Andreasen, N. C., M. Flaum, V. W. Swayze, et al. 1990. Positive and negative symptoms in schizophrenia. Archives of General Psychiatry. 47:615–621.

Andreasen, N. C., and W. T. Carpenter Jr. 1993. Diagnosis and classification of schizophrenia. Schizophrenia Bulletin. 19:199–214.

Anthony, W. A. 2000. A recovery-oriented service system: Setting some system level standards. Psychiatric Rehabilitation Journal. 24:159–167.

Anthony, W. A. 1993. Recovery from mental illness: The guiding vision of the mental health service system in the 1990s. Psychosocial Rehabilitation Journal. 16:11–24.

Baronet, A. M. 1999. Factors associated with caregiver burden in mental illness: A critical review of the research literature. Clinical Psychological Review. 19:819–841.

Bellack, A. S., and K. T. Mueser. 1993. Psychosocial treatment for schizophrenia. Schizophrenia Bulletin. 19:317–336.

Bond, G.R., R. E. Drake, K. T. Musser, et al. 1997. An update on supported employment for people with severe mental illness. Psychiatric Services. 48:335–346.

Carling, P. J. 1993. Housing and supports for persons with mental illness: Emerging approaches to research and practice. Hospital and Community Psychiatry. 44:439–448.

Caton, C. L., M. F. Cournos, and B. Dominguez. 1999. Parenting and adjustment in schizophrenia. Psychiatric Services. 50:239–243.

Chamberlin, J. 1995. Rehabilitating ourselves: The psychiatric survivor movement. International Journal of Mental Health. 24:39–46.

Chamberlain, J. 1984. Speaking for ourselves: An overview of the ex–psychiatric inmates' movement. Psychosocial Rehabilitation Journal. 8:56–64.

Corrigan, P.W., and D. L. Penn. 1999. Lessons from social psychology on discrediting psychiatric stigma. American Psychologist. 54:765–776.

Cramer, P., J. Bowen, and M. O'Neill. 1992. Schizophrenics and social judgement: Why do schizophrenics get it wrong? British Journal of Psychiatry. 160:481–487.

Curtis, L., and N. Jacobson. 2000. Recovery as policy in mental health services: Strategies emerging from the states. Psychiatric Rehabilitation Journal. 23:333–339.

Cutting, J., and F. Dunne. 1989. Subjective experience of schizophrenia. Schizophrenia Bulletin. 15:217–231.

Davidson, L., and J. S. Strauss. 1992. Sense of self in recovery from severe mental illness. British Journal of Medical Psychology. 65:131–145.

Deegan, P. E. 1988. Recovery: The lived experience of rehabilitation. Psychosocial Rehabilitation Journal. 11:11–19.

Deegan, P. E. 1997. Recovery and empowerment for people with psychiatric disabilities. Journal of Social Work and Health Care. 25:11–24.

Dickerson, F. B., N. Ringel, and F. Parente. 1999. Predictors of residential independence among outpatients with schizophrenia. Psychiatric Services. 50:515–519.

Dietzen, L. L., and G. R. Bond. 1993. Relationship between case manager contact and outcome for frequently hospitalized psychiatric clients. Hospital and Community Psychiatry. 44:839–843.

Drake, R. E., C. Mercer-McFadden, K. T. Mueser et al. 1998. Review of integrated mental health and substance abuse treatment for patients with dual disorders. Schizophrenia Bulletin. 24:589–608.

Drake, R. E., S. M. Essock, A. Shaner, et al. 2001. Implementing dual diagnosis services for clients with severe mental illness. Psychiatric Services. 52:469–476.

Drake, R. E., S. J. Bartels, G. B. Teague, et al. 1993. Treatment of substance abuse in severely mentally ill patients. Journal of Nervous and Mental Disease. 181:606–611.

Drake, R. E. 2000. Introduction to a special services series on recovery. Community Mental Health Journal. 36:207–208.

Frese, F. J., and W. W. Davis. 1997. The consumer-survivor movement, recovery, and consumer professionals. Professional Psychology: Research and Practice. 28:243–245.

Geller, J. L., J. M. Brown, W. H. Fisher, Grudzinskas, et al. 1998. A national survey of "consumer empowerment" at the state level. Psychiatric Services. 49:498–503.

Goldman, H. H. 1998. Deinstitutionalization and community care: Social welfare policy as mental health policy. Harvard Review of Psychiatry. 6:219–222.

Goldman, H. H., and J. P. Morrissey. 1985. The alchemy of mental health policy: Homelessness and the fourth cycle of reform. American Journal of Public Health. 75:727–731.

Green, M. F. 1996. What are the functional consequences of neurocognitive deficits in schizophrenia? American Journal of Psychiatry. 153: 321–330.

Harding, C. M., G. W. Brooks, T. Ashikaga, et al. 1987. The Vermont longitudinal study of persons with severe mental illness: I. Methodology, study sample, and overall status 32 years later. American Journal of Psychiatry. 144: 718–726.

Harding, C. M., G. W. Brooks, T. Ashikaga, et al. 1987. The Vermont longitudinal study of persons with severe mental illness: II. Long-term outcome of subjects who retrospectively met DSM-III criteria for schizophrenia. American Journal of Psychiatry. 144:727–735.

Harding, C. M. 1997. Some things we've learned about vocational rehabilitation of the seriously and persistently mentally ill. WICHE West Link. 18.

Kane, J. M. 1985. Compliance issues in outpatient treatment. Journal of Clinical Psychopharmacology. 5:22–27.

Kanter, J. 1989. Clinical case management: Definition, principles, components. Hospital and Community Psychiatry. 40:361–368.

Kessler, R. C., C. B. Nelson, K. A. McGonagle, et al. 1996. The epidemiology of co-occurring addictive and mental disorders: Implications for prevention and service utilization. American Journal of Orthopsychiatry. 66:17–31.

Lamb, H. R. and L. E. Weinberger. 1998. Persons with severe mental illness in jails and prisons: A review. Psychiatric Services. 49:483–492.
Lehman, A.F. 1996. Measures of quality of life among persons with severe and persistent mental disorders. Social Psychiatry and Psychiatric Epidemiology. 31:78–88.

Lehman, A. F. 1995. Vocational rehabilitation in schizophrenia. Schizophrenia Bulletin. 21:645–656.

Liberman, R. P., C. J. Wallace, G. Blackwell, et al. 1998. Skills training versus psychosocial occupational therapy for persons with persistent schizophrenia. American Journal of Psychiatry. 155:1087–1091.

Liberman, R. P., K. T. Mueser, and C. J. Wallace. 1986. Social skills training for schizophrenics at risk for relapse. American Journal of Psychiatry. 143:523–526.

Lovejoy, M. 1984. Recovery from schizophrenia: A personal odyssey. Hospital and Community Psychiatry. 35:809–812.

Lovejoy, M. 1982. Expectations and the recovery process. Schizophrenia Bulletin. 8:605–609.

Lyon, E. R. 1999. A review of the effects of nicotine on schizophrenia and antipsychotic medications. Psychiatric Services. 50:1346–1350.

Malmberg, A., G. Lewis, A. David, et al. 1998. Premorbid adjustment and personality in people with schizophrenia. British Journal of Psychiatry. 172:308–313.

Malla, A. K., and R. G. Norman. 1994. Prodromal symptoms in schizophrenia. British Journal of Psychiatry. 164:487–493.

Mannion, E. 1996. Resilience and burden in spouses of people with mental illness. Psychiatric Rehabilitation Journal. 20 13–23.

Marder, S. R., W.C. Wirshing, J. Mintez et al. 1996. Two-year outcome of social skills training and group psychotherapy for outpatients with schizophrenia. American Journal of Psychiatry. 153:1585–1592.

Miller, F., J. Dworkin, M. Ward, et al. 1990. A preliminary study of unresolved grief in families of seriously mentally ill patients. Hospital and Community Psychiatry. 41:1321–1325.

Minkoff, K. 2001. Developing standards of care for individuals with a co-occurring psychiatric and substance use disorder. Psychiatric Services. 52:597–599.

Mueser, K. T., A. S. Bellack, and J. J. Blanchard. 1992. Co-morbidity of schizophrenia and substance abuse: Implications for treatment. Journal of Consulting and Clinical Psychology. 60:845–856.

Peyser, H. 2001. What is recovery? A commentary. Psychiatric Services. 52:486–487.

Rice, D.P. 1999. The economic impact of schizophrenia. Journal of Clinical Psychiatry. 60: 4–6.

Solomon, P. 1992. The efficacy of case management services for severely mentally disabled clients. Community Mental Health Journal. 28:163–180.

Steadman, H. J., S. M. Morris, and D. L. Dennis. 1995. The diversion of mentally ill persons from jails to community-based services: A profile of programs. American Journal of Public Health. 85:1634.

Swanson, J.W., M. S. Swartz, R. Borum, et al. 2000. Involuntary out-patient commitment and reduction of violent behavior in persons with severe mental illness. British Journal of Psychiatry. 176:224–31.

Swartz, M.S., J. W. Swanson, H. R. Wagner et al. 1999. Can involuntary outpatient commitment reduce hospital recidivism? Findings from a randomized trial with severely mentally ill individuals. American Journal of Psychiatry. 156:1968–1975.

Torrey, E. F. and R. H. Yolken. 2000. Familial and genetic mechanisms in schizophrenia. Brain Research Review. 31:113–117.

Torrey, E .F. 1995. Editorial: Jails and prisons—America's new mental hospitals. American Journal of Public Health. 85:1612.

Weiden, P. J. 1995. Using atypical antipsychotics. Journal of Practical Psychiatry and Behavioral Health. 1:115–119.

Young, S. L., and D. S. Ensing. 1999. Exploring recovery from the perspective of people with psychiatric disabilities. Psychiatric Rehabilitation Journal. 22: 219–232.

Newsletters and Internet Publications

Clay, S. 1990. Patient empowerment. Newsletter to empower and organize the psychiatrically labeled. Available from Mid Hudson Peer Advocates, P.O. Box 5010, Poughkeepsie, NY, 12602.

Schizophrenia: A Handbook For Families. 1991. http://www.mentalhealth.com/book/p40-sc01.html

Mental Health: A Report of the Surgeon General. 1999. http://www.surgeongeneral.gov/library/mentalhealth/home.html

Recovery Model: A Work in Process. 1999. http://www.mhsip.org/recovery/

World Health Organization Press Release. 2001. http://www.who.int/world-heathday/messages.en.html.